The Early Film
Criticism of
François Truffaut

The Early Film Criticism of François Truffaut

by WHEELER WINSTON DIXON

with translations by
Ruth Cassel Hoffman, Sonja Kropp,
and Brigitte Formentin-Humbert

INDIANA UNIVERSITY PRESS
Bloomington and Indianapolis

The paper used in this publication meets the minimum requirements of American National Standard for Information Sciences—Permanence of Paper for Printed Library Materials, ANSI Z39.48–1984.

Manufactured in the United States of America

Library of Congress Cataloging-in-Publication Data

Truffaut, François.
    The early film criticism of François Truffaut / by Wheeler Winston Dixon ; with translations by Ruth Cassel Hoffman, Sonja Kropp, and Brigitte Formentin-Humbert.
        p.   cm.
    Includes bibliographical references (p.   ) and index.
    ISBN 0–253–31807–6 (cloth : alk. paper). — ISBN 0–253–20771–1 (pbk. : alk. paper)
    1. Motion pictures. 2. Motion pictures—Reviews. I. Dixon, Wheeler W., date . II. Title.
PN1994.T717 1993
791.43'75—dc20   92-19375
1 2 3 4 5 97 96 95 94 93

For Gwendolyn, my muse in so many things

Contents

ACKNOWLEDGMENTS   ix

1. The Boundaries of Canon   1
2. A Private Pantheon   41
3. A Passion for the Cinema   78
4. The Egalitarian Spirit   111

NOTES   157
ARTICLES BY FRANÇOIS TRUFFAUT IN THIS
   VOLUME   167
BIBLIOGRAPHY   169
INDEX   172

Acknowledgments

My first debt is to François Truffaut.

Gwen Foster-Dixon suggested I write this book; Eugene P. Walz showed the way; Roma Rector typed and proofed the manuscript.

Truffaut's reviews from *Cahiers du Cinéma* and *Arts* appear through the courtesy of Truffaut's production company, Les Films du Carrosse. I particularly wish to thank Truffaut's widow, Madeleine Morgenstern, and Laura, Eva, and Joséphine Truffaut, Truffaut's children, for their help in making these materials available. Claudine Paquot of Les Editions de l'Etoile was also of great help in securing permission to reprint Truffaut's reviews from *Cahiers du Cinéma*. My thanks to all for their help in making this book possible.

The first third of this manuscript originally appeared in *New Orleans Review*; John Mosier generously gave permission to reprint this material here. Many thanks to Jean-Marc Poisson, who assisted with necessary correspondence during the production of this volume. This work was partially supported by a grant from the Research Council of the University of Nebraska, Lincoln, and many members of the Department of English at UNL read and commented on various drafts of the manuscript. My thanks to them, and to Dr. Stephen Hilliard, chair of the department, for his unfailing support of my work.

Three different translators worked on this volume: Ruth Cassel Hoffman, Sonja Kropp, and Brigitte Formentin-Humbert. Each translation is marked at its conclusion by the initials RCH, SK, or BFH, to signify the translator of each individual piece. Those few sentences or phrases deleted from a specific article (in all cases for reasons of clarity and compression) are indicated by ellipses or line spaces.

In the interest of clarity, I have silently corrected most spelling errors. Ruth Cassel Hoffman, along with other readers, reviewed the final manuscript for accuracy in the translations; my sincere thanks to her for excellent work under often difficult (and highly idiomatic) circumstances. Wherever possible, I have given both the French and English titles for each of the films reviewed by Truffaut.

The Early Film
Criticism of
François Truffaut

1 The Boundaries of Canon

Recent collections of articles from *Cahiers du Cinéma*,[1] one of the most important journals of cinema theory and practice ever published, do a great deal to shed light on the formative years of the *politique des auteurs*. However, these two collections, ably edited by Jim Hillier, which cover the decades of the 1950s and '60s at *Cahiers*, are curious in that they seemingly seek to substantiate the Sarrisinian directorial pantheon formulated by that critic in the spring of 1963.[2] All the selections chosen by Hillier deal with films that have become, through the years, "recognized classics" of the cinema. What Hillier omits is any criticism that deviates from the now-established canon. There are other selections, previously untranslated, that demonstrate that several of the principal *Cahiers* critics, including François Truffaut, were interested in a far greater variety of filmic expression than is generally believed.[3] *Cahiers* editor André Bazin urged his reviewers to see all kinds of films, and his editorial policy allowed Truffaut the greatest possible latitude.

Cahiers has been translated only fitfully into English; for a short time, *Cahiers du Cinéma in English* was published, but it never replicated the success of the French original. Thus, Truffaut's writings have only been sporadically translated into English, and while his seminal "Une Certaine Tendance du cinéma français,"[4] as well as a condensed interview with Jean Renoir (conducted with the assistance and collaboration of Jacques Rivette),[5] a short piece on the film *Dr. Cyclops*,[6] a review of Lang's *The Big Heat*,[7] and other occasional pieces, has been made available to the English-speaking public, a large number of untranslated articles remain. In Hillier's two volumes, only a few pieces by Truffaut are favored with translation. These articles are on "mainstream" films, such as Nicholas Ray's much canonized *Johnny Guitar*, or Jacques Becker's *Touchez pas au grisbi*. The selections (by other writers) in the two *Cahiers* anthologies discuss films such as *The Lusty Men, Rebel without a Cause, Beyond a Reasonable Doubt, Rear Window, Angel Face*: "A" films all. This revisionist strategy leaves many questions unanswered.

There is also the factor of Truffaut's own shifts in critical position with the passing of years, most noticeably in the case of John Ford. In a 1956 essay quoted later in this volume,[8] Truffaut condemns Ford's *The*

1

Searchers (1956) in the strongest possible terms, calling Ford "senile" and saying that Ford "bores us." Yet by 1973, Truffaut had changed his mind on the matter completely, as his brief memorial essay "About John Ford" demonstrates.[9] Is Truffaut's reevaluation of Ford the result of careful consideration, or is his final appreciation of the director's work a sentimental response to Ford's death? The highly charged and nonspecific language of Truffaut's "About John Ford" would seem to lend some credence to this interpretation, though Truffaut was always passionately involved with the subject matter of his critical essays. Truffaut wrote his attack on *The Searchers* before he became a director; did it take some time and additional practical knowledge for Truffaut to appreciate Ford's "invisible" (Truffaut's word from the 1973 piece) style? Or is it that as a member of the accepted canon himself, Truffaut, no longer the outsider with nothing to lose, must now support the system that values his own work so highly? Other questions also remain.

Truffaut's colleague Jean-Luc Godard dedicated his first film as director, *Breathless* (1959), to Monogram Pictures, the archetypal "B" studio.[10] How did Truffaut (who, after all, wrote the brief scenario for *Breathless*) feel about the potential worth and value of the "B" film? How did Truffaut approach a critical appraisal of the "B" film, or even the "A" melodrama, as he did in his piece on Henry Hathaway's *Niagara*, which will be discussed later in this text? How much did he reveal of *himself* in these hitherto unavailable writings? Can one see in Truffaut's early work some of the concerns that were mirrored in his later work as a director? Why was he attracted to the "B" film, the genre film, the serial, the crime film, and films of sexual obsession (certainly evident in Truffaut's lifelong love affair with the films, and themes, of Alfred Hitchcock)?

It seems to me that all of these questions may be profitably explored. However, the corpus of Truffaut criticism now available attacks these queries only tangentially, while, as will be seen in this book, Truffaut himself, particularly in his early critical writings, confronts his obsessions (theoretical, social, and sexual) head-on. Many of Truffaut's early reviews were collected by the filmmaker in his volume *The Films in My Life (Les Films de ma vie)* in 1975. However, these reviews concern themselves, for the most part, with "A" films, and Truffaut has excised most of his negative criticism. This still leaves a great deal of material to be explored, and this volume seeks to examine these previously untranslated critical writings.

Truffaut wrote extensively about "B" films, and, like his mentor Jean Renoir, he often prized the "B"s above the "A"s. In an interview Truffaut conducted with Jacques Rivette in the April 1954 issue of *Cahiers du Cinéma*, Renoir was quite emphatic on this particular point. Speaking of the production of his film *Woman on the Beach (La Femme sur la plage)* (RKO, 1947), Renoir spoke of the American "B" producer Val

Lewton, who produced an extraordinary series of gothic thrillers during the '40s and who served (informally) as Renoir's producer during the preproduction of *Woman on the Beach*.

I'll say a few words about Val Lewton, because he was an extremely interesting person; unfortunately he died, it's already been a few years. He was one of the first, maybe the first, who had the idea to make films that weren't expensive, with "B" picture budgets, but with certain ambitions, with quality screenplays, telling more refined stories than usual. Don't go thinking that I despise "B" pictures; in general I like them better than big, pretentious psychological films—they're much more fun. When I happen to go to the movies in America, I go see "B" pictures. First of all, they are an expression of the great technical quality of Hollywood. Because, to make a good western in a week, the way they do at Monogram, starting Monday and finishing Saturday, believe me, that requires extraordinary technical ability; and detective stories are done with the same speed. *I also think that "B" pictures are often better than important films because they are made so fast that the filmmaker obviously has total freedom; they don't have time to watch over him.* [my emphasis] (RCH)[11]

At this point in his career, Truffaut was only a critic and writer, some five years away from the creation of his first feature, *Les Quatre Cent Coups (The 400 Blows)* (1959). However, Truffaut certainly agreed with Renoir's thesis. In the following selections from Truffaut's early critical writings, one can see that the American genre film, in particular the American crime and action thriller, had a great influence on Truffaut's later work as a film director.

In researching this book, I was immeasurably aided by Eugene P. Walz's excellent *François Truffaut: A Guide to References and Resources* (Boston: G. K. Hall and Co., 1982), which, for the first time, offers an extensive bibliography of Truffaut's writings not only in *Cahiers du Cinéma* but in the now-defunct journal *Arts* and other small but influential critical magazines that flourished in France in the early 1950s. Using this resource as a guide, I located the texts for a number of critical articles that have not, until this time, been available in English. These texts appear here for the first time in translation since their original publication in French in the early 1950s.

As these writings made clear, Truffaut was extremely egalitarian in his appreciation of American filmmaking. If anything, he sided more with those artists who worked on the fringes of the cinema rather than with directors who had the double-edged "advantages" of major studio backing and/or distribution. Not that Truffaut was uncritical of the genre film. In his book *The Films in My Life*, Truffaut includes a short paragraph on William Beaudine's *The Feathered Serpent* (Monogram, 1948).[12] This brief, jocular piece effectively outlines the defects of the film: the inadequacy of Roland Winters in the principal role (detective Charlie Chan) and William Beaudine's indifferent direction.[13]

Certainly this Beaudine film deserves little more than a cursory dismissal. Yet, even when considering a director so obviously mired in the twilight world of the small American "program-picture" studios (Monogram, PRC, and other small companies), Truffaut is capable of treating each Beaudine film as an individual entity, rather than dismissing, as most critics have (and with some justification) Beaudine's work in its entirety. In his review of Beaudine's *Tuna Clipper* (Monogram, 1949) (released as *Le Pari fatal* in France), Truffaut praises Beaudine's mise-en-scène as "completely creditable" and singles out the actress Elena Verdugo as one of the film's principal attractions.

Tuna Clipper
American film by William Beaudine.

Here is a little film from "Monogram," that modest company that said "no" to the crisis and decided to double the number of its productions.[14] A scenario whose charm lies in its modesty and honesty: a captivating tuna-fishing expedition. William Beaudine's mise-en-scène is completely creditable, as we would have liked it to be for the same director's *Charlie Chan*. We are drawn by the one-and-only female actor with the promising bodice; no, generous; or rather, willing, I would say; that bodice is still well behaved, friendly also, and sort of hospitable, promised to the most deserving one, the nicest one. Let us recall together the name of this delicate personage: Elena Verdugo. [signed] R. L. (RCH)[15]

Several things here are worth noting. First, the article is signed not by Truffaut but rather by a mysterious "R. L." These initials stand for Robert Lachenay, Truffaut's best friend during his high school years, with whom he often played hooky from school. Later, Lachenay would work as an assistant on one of Truffaut's early short films, *Les Mistons* (*The Brats*) (1958), and Lachenay's name would pop up, assigned to various characters, in several later films by the director.[16] While we cannot be certain as to the reason for this pseudonym, there are probably two factors that dictated its use. First, Truffaut was remarkably prolific as a critic: Walz lists more than 500 articles in his complete bibliography,[17] exclusive of interviews. As one of the more prominent contributors to *Cahiers*, perhaps Truffaut (or editor Bazin) felt that he should be a little less conspicuous.

Second, many of Truffaut's articles are polemical, or at least highly idiosyncratic. This brief review is emblematic of Truffaut's highly personal style, one that seems as interested in the details of Verdugo's "bodice" as it is in Beaudine's mise-en-scène. Further, there is no mention of the nominal star of the film, Roddy McDowall, or any other of the cast members. In short, while Truffaut obviously is taken by the film (which was certainly a "B" film, shot in a mere twelve days),[18] his reasons for favoring the film seem nearly evanescent.

As a writer for *Cahiers*, Truffaut was being given an enormous amount of freedom in his work. Bazin's editorship of these pieces seems lenient in the extreme. Nevertheless, Truffaut applies the *auteur* theory here as equally as he applies it to all the other films he considers in his reviews. Beaudine is seen as the *author* of the film. Though smitten with the "hospitable" bodice of Verdugo, Truffaut sees *Tuna Clipper* principally as a work by Beaudine, which is worthy of slight, but real, consideration. It is interesting to note that this brief commentary on *Tuna Clipper* is the only non-trade review the film received.[19] Once again, *Cahiers* emerges as a conscientious, almost fanatical critical journal in its desire to cover every film it possibly can.

The last consideration here, it seems to me, is Truffaut's attitude toward women, which might most charitably be called "pre-feminist." A mitigating factor in the obvious sexism displayed in this piece might be Truffaut's forthrightness in declaring his fascination with Elena Verdugo's chest. Nevertheless, this insistence on viewing the female body as an object, a locus of male desire, can become quite disconcerting in other of his critical writings.

Nowhere is this tendency more pronounced than in Truffaut's long, elegiac celebration of Marilyn Monroe's anatomy as displayed in Henry Hathaway's steamy melodrama, *Niagara*. In this piece, Truffaut abandons a consideration of the film almost entirely to concentrate on the details of Monroe's wardrobe, her legs, and her undergarments. What emerges from the following paragraphs is a fetishistic obsession with the details of constructed sexuality. Truffaut's style, at times willfully lacking in conventional syntax (as seen in the piece on *Tuna Clipper*), here becomes a succession of stuttering pronouncements. It is as if Truffaut's sexual frustrations overwhelm his critical sensibilities to the point where one wonders, with justification, whether this "review" should properly be considered film criticism or inspired automatic writing.

Niagara's Underpinnings by Robert Lachenay.
   High heels were fighting with high skirts
   So that depending on the site and the wind
   Sometimes ankles shone, too often
   Intercepted—and we liked this fool's game.

                                                           —Paul Verlaine

The essential thing is not Niagara, nor Hathaway, nor yet the scenario, nor even the admirable Technicolor, as one might suspect. Let's not play for nothing this most useful of games. Once we have blamed the producer for his role in the scenario, admitted that the mise-en-scène is short on ideas, but "knock-knock"—that is, each blow meets its mark, but the blows are predictable; invention plays no part in it—let's approach "*her*," from the front or from the back, or even better in profile.

A prisoner in a too-narrow skirt, one knee escapes and moves forward, provocatively; lips that one feels are reddened but a moment ago, half open as if to promise heaven, already called to witness by the shoulder-shrug of two breasts whose entire mystery has been unveiled by the reprinting of the famous calendar.

No doubt here: Marilyn is definitely the girl she is said to be: plastically irreproachable and more, from her toes—on which the morning dew, reddened by the blood of her victims, reposes—to the very tip of her golden hair, displayed prominently enough to make you die.

It would be good if one day soon a conference on Erotomania were held in Paris, in order to reach an agreement about eroticism in the cinema. I would probably surprise Cécil Saint-Laurent—who, recently, in *Cinémonde,* compared (to his own advantage) the adaptations of *A Whim of Dear Caroline* and *Diary of a Country Priest*—if I declared that there is more eroticism (to my way of thinking) in the three minutes of the *Ladies of the Bois de Boulogne* when Elina Labourdette, all dressed up, seated in a chair, raises her bare legs one after the other in order to better slip over them those silky pre-nylon stockings, and her garment is then covered over with the ingenious raincoat—more eroticism, I say, than in all of *Caroline,* beloved, capricious, and dry as a desert.

What is more dangerous than the association of ideas? When Martine Carol—some do not hesitate to call her the French Marilyn—takes a milk bath, the milk overflows and I think of butter, good butter of course, then of the word "cheese," which becomes a catastrophe. . . . But there is no cheap plastic flesh on Marilyn, pink, she is beautiful and here and real, and censorship that has long been known to arouse talent—even genius—gives us those beautiful pictures where, naked beneath the sheets, Marilyn moves her legs in a skillful and promising way. What is round is fun; what is angular is less so. Marilyn is certainly not a pimp's girl. Comedy is soft and smoky, but tragedy is sharp-edged.

We agree willingly that she is not made to be a vamp, nor a *femme fatale,* any more than Maria Casarès is made to play the characters of Paulette Dubost. This is the main error of Marilyn's "bosses." There are others. When they ask Marilyn, "What do you put on when you go to bed, Miss Monroe?" and she answers, "Just my alarm for nine o'clock," I agree. To heck with these pajamas worn by girls whose purity I don't believe in, which just annoy me. But I get very angry about the publicity on the absence of underwear, not about the publicity, but the absence of underwear.

So, beneath those skimpy skirts—which save the supposed reverse shots from a likewise supposed immorality, since slipping in even the shadow of a hand would be absolutely impossible—well, beneath those skimpy skirts, those bosoms heaving with joy, there is said to be nothing, no underwear. But what is this Sunday eroticism that is ignorant of the subtle play by which the trained eye learns the appropriate angles to reveal the fabric, the color of the bra, and thereby the life itself of that bosom? A face may pretend, modesty be false, virtue simulated, but the bra doesn't lie. Sharp angles, sharply caught when an arm is raised to arrange a curl. Drawings on the diagonal, panty edges revealed by the walk: their humbleness or their pride are thus known by all. Because of a leg crossing or uncrossing, we are delighted by the pretty lace on a slip. And the complicated patchups, the idyllic intertwinings, the mysterious bonds that link all these little patterns of silk—what are they? Stupidly revealed by the hateful transparent blouse, as ridiculous as a man wearing sock garters, we would rather guess at them, as if by chance, mysteries long observed—knowledge acquired in the long run being the best reward.

We are a long way from Marilyn Monroe's hips, farther yet from Niagara Falls,* but luckily *Niagara* was not made from outtakes. What is important here is: "Please, Marilyn put on some underwear." (RCH)

This review is illustrated by a still from *Niagara*, which Truffaut has captioned: "Jeanne Peters (left) and Marilyn Monroe are not rivals in Henry Hathaway's *Niagara*, but they incarnate two completely different forms of feminine seduction. The discreet, distinguished charm of the former is the opposite of the loud, tacky 'sex-appeal' of the second. Something for everyone's taste. . . ."[20]

Whatever one might think of the foregoing, the quote from Verlaine that precedes Truffaut's commentary is appropriate. Verlaine, the *maudit*, was one of the early apostles of artificially induced "ecstasy," whether through sex, drink, drugs, or the "fool's game" this framing quote describes. It is a game that obviously intrigued Truffaut. One thinks of *The Man Who Loved Women*, Truffaut's dark 1977 film, in which Charles Denner obsessively chases every woman he meets, until he is struck down by an automobile while chasing a young woman through midtown traffic, and subsequently dies in the hospital.

Certainly this is a "fool's game," which in *The Man Who Loved Women* results in a fool's death. It is a death without meaning or resonance, a cap to a life filled only with momentary pleasures. What Truffaut here is "celebrating" is not Marilyn Monroe, nor her imagistic construct, but rather his own sexual voraciousness, which seems deeply rooted in

---

* Some colleagues—completely competent ones—assure me that I know nothing about film criticism and that I am cheating the reader out of the "review" that he has a right to expect. Therefore I will call attention to a completely new use of Technicolor, the weakness of the scenario, the technical competency of Hathaway, the use of numerous transparencies, but not too many, and the acting, most notably of Jeanne Peters, the shorts she wears under her skirt at the end of the film—let's stop here. (RCH)

childhood fears and fantasies. In her perceptive essay on Edgar Ulmer's "B" film *Detour*, Tania Modleski quotes Melanie Klein's *The Emotional Life of the Infant* in her discussion of *Detour*'s sexual dialectic:

> In *Detour* the heroine's early abandonment of the hero may be seen to correspond to the child's unwelcome discovery that his mother has a life independent of his own. Psychoanalysis documents the impotent rage engendered in the child by this knowledge. Melanie Klein, who extensively studied the psychoanalysis of small children, tells us that the frustration experienced by the child at this stage gives rise to the paranoid position in which the child, unable to cope with his or her ambivalent feelings, projects them onto the mother. As a result, she is split into two, and from the child's point of view there develops an antithesis between the "good breast" and the "bad breast." The frustrating (bad) object is felt to be a terrifying persecutor, the good breast tends to turn into the "ideal" breast which should fulfill the greed, desire for unlimited, immediate and everlasting gratification.[21]

These same comments might be profitably applied to both the *Tuna Clipper* review and the article on *Niagara*. It seems that Truffaut has not progressed beyond the infantile stage of "unlimited, immediate, and everlasting gratification," and while he is aware that his desire is impossible, he has yet to come to terms with this fact. Instead, he rattles the bars of his self-imposed sexual prison, reducing Monroe to a series of attitudes and poses and denying utterly her cinematic, or real, humanity. While it may be further argued that Monroe was a willing participant in her own objectification (and it seems that this must be true to some degree), nevertheless by playing into this artificially composed web of "attractions," Truffaut has consigned himself to the fool's game and does not seem likely to rise above it.

Tangentially, while *Niagara* is indisputably an "A" film in budget, I would argue that it is "B" in spirit, as well as in execution. Marilyn's performance in the film, ineluctably mediated by the interplay of light and shadow that Hathaway clearly delights in, is really a "rehearsal." Discovering that Monroe tended to become mechanically repetitious and artificial doing multiple "takes" of the same scene, Hathaway began filming the camera rehearsals for each scene without Monroe's knowledge and then doing one or two takes "for real" to cover up his deception.[22] This lends a documentary air to the film, while the narrative strains against any attempt at verisimilitude with a plot that is simultaneously outrageous and conventional. What has attracted Truffaut to this film is not Hathaway's skill as a designer of images but rather the image Hathaway constructs of Monroe. It is an image that both Hathaway and Truffaut conspire to create, working (within the confines of Truffaut's article) as unconscious collaborators. It is perhaps significant that Truffaut again assigned this "review" to the pseudonymous Lachenay.

Giving added credence to the fact that it was the image of Marilyn as created for the screen that fascinated Truffaut even more than any of the films the actress appeared in is his essay "The Presence of Marilyn," which is a combination of biography and appreciation of Monroe's cinematic persona. It makes reference to *Niagara* as Monroe's "first starring film" and traces the long path from bit-player obscurity to major stardom that Marilyn had to endure. This essay was written some time after the review of *Niagara*; Marilyn had just finished *The Seven Year Itch* and was about to embark upon *Bus Stop*, the film that would establish her in the eyes of many observers as an actress, rather than a "presence." Truffaut does not condescend to Monroe in this essay, but rather treats her desire for self-determination, and her wish to control her career rather than to continue to exist as an image controlled by others, as a valid and altogether reasonable ambition.

Truffaut, while drawn to male-centrist images of the "feminine" in films not only with Marilyn Monroe but with Brigitte Bardot and other directly sexual cinematic icons, refuses to treat these actresses as mere projections of their sexual identities. The fetishistic aspect of Truffaut's appreciation is, as I've remarked, pronounced, but it is mitigated by a genuine respect for the process of acting and the risks of bodily presentation that so uniquely belong to the cinema. Unlike the mise-en-scène of the stage, the requirements of the filmed narrative structure indicate that the master shot, the major component of cinematic syntax in narrative, must be broken down into close-ups, inserts, two-shots, and other variations on the point of view first taken by the camera and hence by the spectator. Inasmuch as the classical Hollywood cinema's imagistic structure is deeply wedded to the locus of the male spectatorial gaze, when women appear in patriarchal cinema, they are inevitably "divided" into body parts.

Marilyn's "presence" on the screen, particularly in the repressive, politically hysteric 1950s, is the result of a series of tightly confining close-ups, which systematically intrude upon the actress's presentational space. These close-ups, in conjunction with the tightly controlled pin-spot lighting employed in conventional "glamour" photography, can be seen as an extension of the tightly constricting gowns, dresses, and sweaters that Marilyn wore in her films. (Truffaut notes this in the *Niagara* review, commenting on Marilyn's image as "a prisoner in a too-narrow skirt.") This immediate objectification of the "feminine" thus serves as a barrier to the primacy of the narrative and to the actress's role as an interpreter of that narrative.

Woman as object *becomes* the narrative for much of *Niagara*, as well as *Gentlemen Prefer Blondes* and *The Girl Can't Help It* (Truffaut's comments to the contrary in *Présence* notwithstanding). Thus the style used by Hathaway, Hawks, and Tashlin in these films encourages us to denigrate the women who appear as their nominal "stars": the real star of these films is the male viewer, safely hidden in the darkness of the theater. Should we take Marilyn, or, for that matter, Bardot or Mansfield, seriously? Truffaut seems to think so, even as he falls prey to the "fool's game" of objectification practiced by these *auteurs*. It seems that at least he is aware of the process. Most members of the 1950s audience, of course, never gave the matter a passing thought, imbedded as they were in '50s culture, and particularly in view of the fact that Marilyn seemed such a willing participant in her own imagistic exploitation.

The Presence of Marilyn Monroe

Marilyn Monroe—her real name is Norma Jean Baker—was born in Los Angeles on June 1, 1928. Two years later, her father is killed in a car crash. This stroke of fate causes the sanity of her mother, Gladys Baker—already seriously stricken—to falter. Mrs. Baker entrusts a friend, Mrs. Grace Goddard, with her daughter and retires into a rest home.

Marilyn is ten years old and taking classes at Emerson Junior High School in Los Angeles, when Anna Lowrer, Mrs. Goddard's sister, decides to show her hospitality. A good-hearted woman, insofar as she can financially afford it, Mrs. Lowrer does everything she can to make life nicer for Marilyn, whom she considers as her own daughter.

Unfortunately, in 1941, Mrs. Lowrer is taken ill. Marilyn has to leave her benefactress. The Los Angeles orphanage places her with a family who lives in Van Nuys, where she can go on studying. In 1943, the people who put her up decided to go east and, unable to take her along, marry her to a young sailor, Tom [actually Jim; Truffaut is in error here] Dougherty. This marriage only lasts a few months and ends in a quiet divorce.

At sixteen, both her studies and her marriage over, Marilyn, to make a living, joins Radio Place Co. and launches into a job checking parachutes. To increase her income, she poses as a cover girl and, with luck, manages to appear on the front page of four magazines in the same month. Producer-aviator Howard Hughes, who is slowly getting over a terrible plane accident, notices her. But, before he has time to make a screen test with her, 20th Century-Fox has already hired her for a year. After a short appearance in a scene in *Scudda Hoo, Scudda Hay* [1948; Dir. F. Hugh Herbert], which is cut when the film is edited, she is forgotten.

However, the increasing success she experiences as a model prevents Marilyn from losing heart. She rents a room in the Studio Club, where numerous starlets live, limits her meals to the bare minimum, and takes drama lessons with Natacha Lytess, who has since become one of the drama instructors at 20th Century-Fox and still advises her.

One day, she hears that director David Miller, who is shooting *Love Happy* [1950], is looking for a sexy blonde to shoot a scene with Groucho Marx. She goes, is hired, and the shooting starts. The scene hardly lasts thirty seconds, but the result is sensational—to the point that Cowan, enthusiastic, persuades her to go and introduce the film in every big American city.

Marilyn Monroe manages wonderfully, and when she comes back, Lucille Ryman, talent scout of Metro Goldwyn Mayer, offers to put her up and takes her under her wing. She manages to get her a supporting part in *A Ticket to Tomahawk* [1950; Dir. Richard Sale], another one in *Asphalt Jungle* [1950; Dir. John Huston], a third one in Joseph Mankiewicz's *All About Eve* [1950]. Her "presence" in this last film induces Darryl F. Zanuck to sign a long-term contract between her and 20th Century-Fox.

In 1951 and 1952, she makes nine movies, among which it is advisable to remember only Fritz Lang's *Clash by Night* [1952] and Howard Hawks's *Monkey Business* [1952].

Niagara [1953] is her first starring film. Henry Hathaway, who directed this extraordinary Technicolor movie, mainly took care of the framing and Marilyn, very badly directed here, caricatured, is used based on a misunderstanding: Marilyn is not a "femme fatale" but a good girl. That is what Howard Hawks and Otto Preminger understood when they respectively made *Gentlemen Prefer Blondes* [1953] and *River of No Return* [1954].

It is shortly after the making of *The Seven Year Itch* [1955; Dir. Billy Wilder] that Marilyn took control of her career and refused to shoot just anything. She obtained permission from the studio to choose her director.

While waiting to film *The Brothers Karamazov,* a project she yearns to shoot, Marilyn has accepted an offer to be directed by Joshua Logan in *Bus Stop* [1956], which she personally considers will be her best movie.

Recently, the weeklong "Marilyn Monroe" retrospective in the movie theater Le Marbeuf allowed all those who had the sense to see it a chance to realize how much today's greatest star has improved from film to film. (BFH)[23]

While many of the "facts" in this biography are incorrect,[24] the picture Truffaut paints of Marilyn, alone and essentially without help, working her way to the top, is generally correct. Truffaut's comments concerning *Niagara* at the end of the article are of great interest. He considers the film "extraordinary," claiming that Marilyn is "very badly directed" in the film, while in his review of *Niagara,* he praises Hathaway's "technical competence." This does not seem at odds with his contention in *Présence* that Hathaway "mainly took care of the framing," but it fails to examine in sufficient detail just how important and all-encompassing this "framing" is to the film, as I've discussed. Further, Truffaut's contention that Marilyn's "use" in *Niagara* is "based on a misunderstanding: Marilyn is not a 'femme fatale' but a good girl" exposes the critic's generally conscious participation in the stereotypical role assignments women were subjected to in Hollywood during this period, and indeed are still subjected to today. Modleski and Klein's analysis of the male spectator, positioned outside the film yet always at the center of its construction, is supported by this telling piece of sexist categorizing. Both the "femme fatale" and the "good girl" are role positionings demanded by the male-centrist cinema; they bear no relation to equitable social commerce.

Aside from the fact that I would disagree with Truffaut's contention that Marilyn is "badly directed" in the film, the fact remains that within the confines of the narrative and the setups given to her by Hathaway, Marilyn is essentially directing *herself* in *Niagara*, offering her own interpretation of the role. Hathaway, ever conscious of the need to keep filming on schedule and within the budget, is, in many ways, the ideal collaborator. He does not force Marilyn to go through endless takes and endless rehearsals: he films a few rehearsal takes and lets the true Marilyn shine through. Billy Wilder, who would insist that he deserved "a purple heart" for directing Monroe in *The Seven Year Itch*, behaved in exactly the opposite manner, attempting to control the actress with Langian totality in every scene. The result is both uninspired and sniggering. Sir Laurence Olivier, when he co-starred with and directed Monroe in *The Prince and the Showgirl* (1957), also attempted to employ didactic, autocratic methods, with the same mechanistic results.[25]

In his review of *Sudden Fear*, Truffaut indulges in the same discursive style he brings to his observations on *Niagara*. While he skirts around the film itself, Truffaut here is more interested in explicating his critical platform (as he did in "Une Certaine Tendance du cinéma français") than in any obsessional iconic reveries. In his checklist of Truffaut's works, Eugene Walz notes: "Ostensibly a review of *Sudden Fear* by David Miller, this is more like a personal manifesto in which almost all of Truffaut's critical concerns are laid out."[26]

Extremes Meet (Me) (Le Masque arraché) by François Truffaut

SUDDEN FEAR, American film by David Miller. *Screenplay:* Fred Benson, adapted from the novel by Edna Sherry. *Photography:* Charles Lang, Jr. *Music:* Elmer Bernstein. *Set Design:* Edward G. Boyle. *Cast:* Joan Crawford, Gloria Grahame, Jack Palance, Bruce Bennett, Virginia Huston. *Production:* RKO, 1952.

Sometimes they make films in the streets of Paris. A few extras [are there], more gapers, but no stars.

Concerned that you are not mistaken for one of the Béotians [people from the rue de la Béotie] who are hoping for the arrival of Suzy Carrier or Philippe Lemaire, you spot an assistant. You explain to him that you are not who he thinks you are. You directed a public debate at the Ciné-Club de Chamalières in Puy-de-Dôme on *pure* cinema before at least eighty people, and there is nothing you don't know about the theme of failure in John Huston or about the misogyny of American cinema.

Supposing this first or second assistant hears you out, you ask him the ritual question, "What are you filming?" To which he replies-what *could* he reply?—"We're filming a linking shot."

For that's French cinema: three hundred linking shots end to end, one hundred ten times a year.

If Aurenche and Bost were adapting *Le Voyage au bout de la nuit (Journey to the End of the Night),* they would cut sentences, even words: what would remain? A few thousand suspension points; that is, rare angles, unusual lighting, cleverly centered. The notion of a shot in France has become concern for clothing, which means following fashion. Everything happens to the right and to the left, *off* the screen.

This preamble, in order to introduce a film that is completely different. An American film. David Miller is the director of *Sudden Fear.* He made *la Pêche au trésor* [*Love Happy* (1950)] and *Celle de nulle part* [*Our Very Own* (1950)]. Before that he assisted in [the World War II Allied propaganda series] *Why We Fight.*

While respectable, nothing in his recent career led us to suspect that David Miller would give us the most brilliant "Hitchcock style" known in Franco.

Outside of two very short but fairly unpleasing sequences (a dream and a planning sequence in pictures), there is not a shot in this film that isn't necessary to its dramatic progression. Not a shot, either, that isn't fascinating and doesn't make us think it is a masterpiece of filmmaking.

If the audience laughs when it isn't suitable to do so, I take that as a sign of daring, of finish. The public has lost the habit of intensity. Twenty years of adaptations that are guilty of excessive timidity have gotten the public accustomed to golden insignificance. Filming Balzac has become impossible. Put into pictures, Grandet's deathbed agony reaching for the crucifix would cause gales of laughter in the same people who swoon with admiration when a legless cripple hurtles down a street at fifty kilometers an hour.

The "in" public, the public of the Ciné-Clubs, is hardly any different. Although they may allow *Ladies of the Bois de Boulogne* [1945] (no doubt because of Diderot and Cocteau), they are ready to burst out laughing at all of Abel Gance's films. What Ciné-Club has shown Nicholas Ray's *They Live by Night* [1949] or Robert Wise's *Born to Kill* [1947]— the most "Bressonian" of the American films?

As for the films, films of psychological anguish, laughter is a form of revenge of the spectator on the *auteur* of the story, which he is ashamed to have believed in. Yes, twenty years of fake great subjects, twenty years of *Adorable Creatures, Return to Life, Don Camillo,* and others like *Minute of Truth* have created this blasé public, whose sensibilities and judgment alike are alienated by the base and despicable "fear of being duped," denounced by Radiguet.

No doubt it is this attitude of the public that has made Hitchcock pretend not to believe in the subjects he is dealing with by introducing into his films that element of humor—English, so they say—that is useless in my opinion, and that Hitchcock's detractors claim is the "tithe" through which the *auteur* of *Strangers on a Train* [1951] will be able to claim a right to the purgatory of bad filmmakers of good will.

A weekly paper that no one is obliged to take seriously affirms that Joan Crawford herself financed *Sudden Fear* with half of her personal fortune: half a million dollars. No matter.

The casting: it is permissible to have forgotten *Crossfire* [1947; Dir. Edward Dmytryk], but not a young blond woman who was better than an intelligent extra: as a prostitute, she danced in a courtyard. Even professional critics noticed the dancer; it was Gloria Grahame, whom we saw again in *L'as du cinéma* [*Merton of the Movies* (1947); Dir. Robert Alton] playing opposite Red Skelton.

Then Gloria Grahame became Mrs. Nicholas Ray and made *The Lusty Men* [1952], with Humphrey Bogart as costar, under the direction of Nicholas Ray himself.

Gloria is no longer Mrs. Ray, as far as we know, and is filming in Germany under the direction of Kazan. We will see her again even sooner in Cecil B. DeMille's *Greatest Show on Earth* [1952].

It seems that of all the American stars Gloria Grahame is the only one who is also a person. She keeps from one film to the next certain physical tics that are so many *acting inventions* and that can only be vainly expected from French actresses. Let's be serious (we are required to, since a production hangs in the cinematographic balance); Edwige Feuillère, Madeleine Robinson, Danielle Delorme, Michèle Morgan, and Dany Robin opposite the [production] that proposes among a hundred others Lauren Bacall, Joan Bennett, Susan Hayward, Jennifer Jones, and Gloria Grahame? It took all the genius of Renoir, Bresson, Leenhardt, and Cocteau to make Mila Parely, Maria Casarès, Renée Devillers, and Edwige Feuillère appear to have any genius. From one film to the next, on the other hand, Gene Tierney, Joan Bennett, and Susan Hayward equal themselves. That and the bill for American cinema, often perfect right down to "Series Z" films, upset the hierarchy that could not be the same in our country where the only things that count are ambitious screenplays and the producer's quote. In reality there are no directors of actors in France, except those four names whose praises can never be sung enough: Renoir, Bresson, Leenhardt, and Cocteau. Gloria Grahame's acting is all in correspondences between cheeks and looks. You can't analyze it, but you can observe it. Let us make ours the definition by Jean Georges Auriol: "cinema is the art of doing pretty things to pretty women," and let us wager that as he wrote that, he was thinking more of Jean Harlow than of Lisette Lanvin.

Jack Palance has been known to us since a good film of Elia Kazan's, *Panic in the Streets* [1950]. His character here is that of a young man with unusually fine physical qualities and who, by his exceptional charm, acquires the favors of women whose experience with men has made them less demanding and, at the same time, more so.

Joan Crawford? A question of taste. She takes her place in a category that I label rather crudely the "Raimu/Magnani tradition." But if it's really true that we owe the existence of this film to her. . . .

Each follows his own path. The one that Jack Palance and Gloria Grahame have chosen will lead them to death.

Joan Crawford's path is also the San Francisco street that seven years of American cinema from *The Lady from Shanghai* [1948; Dir. Orson Welles] to *They Live by Night* [1949; Dir. Nicholas Ray] have made familiar to us. An ingenious screenplay with a fine strictness, a set more than respectable, the face of Gloria Grahame and that street of Frisco whose slope is so steep, the prestige of a cinema that proves to us every week that it is the greatest in the world. (RCH)[27]

Certainly, it seems to me, one must agree with Walz's brief assessment of this piece, and one must also wonder why it has never been available in English before. Indeed, if "Une Certaine Tendance. . ." accurately notes the strictures and shortcomings that hobbled French cinema after World War II, this piece, with the strictest economy, shows us why Truffaut valued American filmmaking so highly.

When Truffaut considers *Born to Kill* "the most Bressonian of American films," the directness of this assertion, particularly in view of Truffaut's often elliptical syntax, makes his evaluation all the more credible. *Born to Kill* is rarely revived; *Sudden Fear* is remembered only because of Crawford. Yet, both are excellent films. Why have they been deleted from cinema history? This is more than a case of one film or filmmaker being elevated at the expense of another's work. It is an excision with little justification, one that has shaped the way we view film *and* the canon, or orthodoxy, that supports this perspective. In contrast to this didacticism, Truffaut finds Crawford "a question of taste," but he admits that "it's really true that we owe the existence of this film to her. . ." and then trails off, reluctant to assign too much credit to the actress. If Truffaut is rather hard on Maria Casarès, who delivers a brilliant performance in *Ladies of the Bois de Boulogne*, attributing her success entirely to Bresson and Cocteau (in his litany of the ten top box office actresses in France), perhaps this can be seen as a corrective measure, in a critical milieu that undervalued Gloria Grahame so shamefully.

Parenthetically, what of Roger Leenhardt, whom Truffaut mentions as one of "those four names whose praises can never be sung enough," and whom he links with Bresson, Renoir, and Cocteau? Given the date of this article, Truffaut must be referring to Leenhardt's work as a critic and maker of short films, who then had only one feature, *Les Dernières Vacances* (1948), to his credit. Going even further, what of Cocteau, whose star has been in decline in this country for quite some time now? Is it that Bresson is still alive, or that Renoir proved himself an artist beyond genre? Not that these two artists don't merit the acclaim they have garnered: both are deserving of only the highest admiration in their work. Nevertheless, I submit that both Cocteau and Leenhardt seem properly placed by Truffaut in this critical pantheon and that the undeniable qualities of Bresson and Renoir do nothing to detract from Cocteau and Leenhardt's *oeuvre*.

In his "manifesto," as Walz puts it, Truffaut clearly demonstrates that he holds the "B" film, even the "Series Z" film, in high regard and states that these so-called program pictures, which he feels are "often perfect" (an important point to remember), have "upset the hierarchy . . . in our country," which indeed they had, with *Cahiers*'s help. Again, there is the strongest sense in this article that Truffaut sees the American low-budget film as a liberating force against films based upon literature, films that are "adaptations," "guilty of excessive timidity," films that seem afraid of the kinetic power of the cinema. Because of these "excessive[ly] timid" productions, "filming Balzac has become impossible." The public no longer takes seriously these films, which announce their importance so aggressively, so ponderously, in every frame. "For that's the French cinema," Truffaut exclaims. "Three hundred linking shots end to end, one hundred ten times a year": an editorial structure which seeks to explicate the narrative.

Nowhere, however, is Truffaut's insistence on the reordering of existing priorities more evident than in his June 1953 essay in *Cahiers*, "From A to Z." Here, carefully and lovingly analyzing two American "B" films, Bruce Humberstone's 1950 film *South Sea Sinner (Le Bistro du Péché)*, and Richard Fleischer's 1952 film *The Narrow Margin (L'Enigme du Chicago Express)*, Truffaut presents his reasons for appreciating films that are made under obvious economic and temporal constraints. If a few of his facts are wrong (*South Sea Sinner* was produced in late 1949 and released in the United States in 1950; the date he gives is the French release), Truffaut effectively juxtaposes the stylistic and thematic concerns of Alfred Hitchcock and Orson Welles with Tay Garnett and Richard Fleischer, once again decrying the snobbism that has prevented these two "exquisite" "B" films from reaching a wider audience. Truffaut underlines the importance of remembering that one must not hold the commercial aspect of the cinema against itself and that there is no crime in work for profit. "We must not forget that Balzac wrote from lack of money," he admonishes the reader, and therefore that "it is incumbent upon us, then, as lovers of cinema, *to refute by ceaselessly reappraising it* a scale of values that belongs to business people," who judge a film by its stars and budget or, inversely, by the lack of these things (my emphasis).

From A to Z, by François Truffaut
  South Sea Sinner, American film by Bruce Humberstone.
  Screenplay: Joel Malone and Oscar Brodney. *Cast:* Luther Adler, Frank Lovejoy, Shelley Winters, MacDonald Carey, Helena Carter. *Production:* Universal, 1952. [Actually 1950.]
  The Narrow Margin, American film by Richard Fleischer. *Cast:* Charles McGraw, Marie Windsor, Jacqueline White. *Production:* Universal, 1952.
  A mystery that is certainly going to have to be opened up like a boil some day is the mystery of hierarchy or the sense of proportion.
  Not the least merit of the art we are concerned with here is that of making beauty bloom on branches that are almost always ugly.
  We must not forget that Balzac wrote from lack of money, for money.
  It is incumbent upon us, as lovers of cinema, to refute by ceaselessly reappraising it a scale of values that belongs to business people and that would seek to force us to admire *The Snows of Kilimanjaro*, *The Small World of Don Camillo*, or *The Wages of Fear* more than *Masks Off*, *Diary of a Love Affair*, or *Rue de l'Estrapade*.

  Insofar as the mental level of a film can be measured by the audience for which it is intended, it is very clear that the intellectual values of such and such a film can be appreciated more by the small number of spectators who will see it than by the roughness of that audience.
  The proof is that the great, or reputedly great, films are addressed to all (*Don Camillo, Gone with the Wind, The Wages of Fear*) while, if *Last Vacation, Devil in the Flesh, Les Dames du Bois de Boulogne* and *Born to Kill* had just one point in common, it would be that none has a dubbed version in any language and none, probably, has reached one million spectators.
  At a time when Bunuel and De Sica divide up the festivals and showings of *Los Olvidados* and *Miracle in Milan* bring out sparkling audiences dominated by mink, the films of Roger Leenhardt, Douglas Sirk, Robert Bresson, and Elmer Clifton enjoy the moral solitude of traitors and heroes.
  Nonetheless, it would be ludicrous to conclude that films about misery and poverty bring in the money while the more moral ones about riches and their vanity fail. So I won't say it.
  Instead, I'll sing about the *avant-garde* that seems to me to be wholly contained in the gentle *pastiche* humor of *South Sea Sinner* and in the virile allure of *The Narrow Margin*, which is charged with very moral

nitroglycerine but confers a grace that any sweaty driver of a heavy, slow-moving vehicle might envy.

South Sea Sinner is an exquisite little film, a very faithful remake of a film by Tay Garnett with Marlene Dietrich, *La Maison des sept péches* (American title: *Seven Sinners* [Universal, 1940]). It is proof that American cinema should pastiche itself rather sharply in order that Monsieur Paviot might not hurry and might learn to use a movie camera.

On the high seas, sailor Smitty has an attack of appendicitis; he refuses to allow an operation, so the ex-pharmacist bargain-basement doctor, Doc Mason, has to anesthetize him with his fists. Then they put the patient ashore on Oraca Island. How does the singer at the "Port of Good-Hope" bar (Shelley Winters) learn that Smitty is accused of spying and fall in love with him? How do they fall out of love? How, finally, will the couple fall together? My respect for this charming story commands me to keep that a secret.

Well, that's the sort of film we call "category Z."

South Sea Sinner has scarcely more than four sets, a love scene played on a beach of fifteen square meters, and, again for economy, the soundtrack music is exclusively classical music; for an hour and a half you can hear a dozen Chopin preludes, Beethoven's "Moonlight" Sonata, and large excerpts from Liszt's "Dreams of Love."

What makes this little film so rich is the "tone" in which it is handled. The *auteurs* tell us a serious story from the point of view of the humor of situations, and that is a very precious thing, for it seems that they've made us smile (and sometimes moved us) against all odds with a standard story in which parody—which would have been the easy solution—plays no role.

Will I be told that I'm blaspheming if I assure you that Shelley Winters here is so charming, funny, and moving that we forget to miss Marlene?

If by chance *South Sea Sinner* pops up in your pathway, go on in; they're drinking county fair foamy: it sparkles more than the Lido's.

I'm not aware that anyone knows the names of Charles McGraw, Marie Windsor, and Jacqueline White, the three actors in *The Narrow Margin,* for which Richard Fleischer, known in France for *Le Traquenard* [*Trapped* (1949)] and *Sacré Printemps* [*Follow Me Quietly* (1949)] is the *metteur-en-scène.*

As for the scriptwriters, they know their classics as well as Richard Fleischer. We find again in this film the pace of *The Lady Vanishes,* a variant on the theme of the exchanged murder from *Strangers on a Train,* the fat killer from *Journey into Fear,* and the phonograph in the same film.

Hitchcock and Welles are good people to refer to, and that's the case here, if you possess a sense for the "fascination" of the one and the "sentimental humor" of the other. The action takes place entirely on a train. A policeman is assigned to escort the widow of a gangster and to help her escape from a search undertaken by her husband's "colleagues," who have decided to kill her in order to prevent her from handing over to the court the list of "accounts settled." But the suspicious police replace the widow with a woman from the police, while the aforementioned widow travels on the same train without hiding. Those who reproach American cinema for its naively moralizing side will see here the Hollywood filmmakers taking liberties that we might envy them, since the police employee gets killed while the gangster's widow, safe and sound, pursues the perfect love affair with the policeman—and all to our greater joy, since the police lady was as vulgar as a gangster's woman and the criminal's widow is more distinguished than a lady cop could ever be.

The wanderings of the fat bodyguard in the train corridor are the delicious *leit-motif* of the film, for everyone must step aside to let him pass. The film ends with a charming line by this charming obese person: "A fat man is loved only by his tailor and his grocer." Let us note the cameraman's merits, since this film is full of special effects of all sorts, particularly photographic effects. So, a film to be included in the "Cinema of Special Effects."

The two films have no dubbed version; that says it all on the subject of their brief life. *South Sea Sinner* came out in a little theater on the place d'Anvers, and the exclusive showing lasted only a week. No critic saw fit to take the trouble.* *The Narrow Margin* has just come out at the Champs-Elysées, but I strongly doubt that it will do any better than that. If the expression "film maudit" (accursed film) ever meant anything, I think it would apply more to these two films than to some neorealist social pamphlet or some erotic delirium in which the symbol kills the filmmaker beneath its weight.

Finally, I express the wish that we not be too often duped by the modest appearance in which good works sometimes, with elegance, like to adorn themselves. (RCH)[28]

In this comparatively lengthy essay, Truffaut "open[s] up like a boil . . . the mystery of hierarchy" and finds that the reviews of the then-

---

*And yet, that's not true. Paule Sengissen, in *Radio Cinéma Télévision*, writes the following: "Poorly acted, poorly set, this film will interest only those cinephiles who find that bad cinema is cinema." Mlle. Sengissen seems not to know that Bruce Humberstone is also the *metteur-en-scène* for *If I Had a Million*; she doesn't know that *South Sea Sinner* is the remake of a film by Tay Garnett. Mise-en-scène must be Mlle. Sengissen's strong point, so I would ask her, if I had the chance to see her, to explain to me in what way *South Sea Sinner* is badly set. (RCH) established critics (such as Paule Sengissen) judge a film almost entirely on external physical characteristics while failing to explore at all the thematic core of the work in question. If Elmer Clifton, Sirk, Bresson, and Leenhardt "enjoy the moral solitude of traitors and heroes," it is because they work in a pre-damned cinema, a cinema as sure of critical and public neglect as "A" films are certain of general acclaim. If Truffaut clearly prefers South Sea Sinner or The Narrow Margin to Wages of Fear ("the virile allure of The Narrow Margin . . . confers a grace that any sweaty driver of a heavy, slow-moving vehicle might envy"), it is precisely because these small films lack the pomposity of those works that announce their importance with each new frame.

Truffaut sees nothing wrong in remakes and even suggests that, heretically enough, a modest "category Z" film may well top the original film it is based upon, and that one might find Shelley Winters "so charming, funny and moving that we forget to miss Marlene" (Dietrich, in the original). The film may have "scarcely more than four sets," a small strip of sand for a beach, and for "economy [have a] soundtrack . . . exclusively [of] classical music," but these budgetary restrictions have obviously, in Truffaut's view, been turned to a good account by the filmmaker. If a soundtrack of Chopin, Beethoven, and Liszt is cheaper to use than a big-scale Hollywood score, so much the better for the film.

Truffaut might well have added here that much of South Sea Sinner's music is played on a single piano, shown on the set, further increasing the economy of the production. (It should be noted parenthetically that the pianist is Liberace.) Truffaut notes that "what makes this little film so rich is the 'tone' in which it is handled" and adds that Humberstone has had the grace and dignity to avoid the easy solution to such inherently melodramatic material, which would be to burlesque it. "They've made us smile . . . against all odds with a standard story in which parody—which would have been the easy solution—plays no role." For incorporating all these virtues, Truffaut finds this "Z" film "wholly" avant-garde, and he prefers it to "some neorealist social pamphlet or some erotic delirium in which the symbol kills the filmmaker beneath its weight." "Finally," Truffaut says, "I express the wish that we not too often be duped by the modest appearance in which good works sometimes, with elegance, like to adorn themselves [my emphasis]." I agree with Truffaut on this.[29] The most superficial manner of judging a film is by its external characteristics, yet this is still precisely what most theorists continue to practice. Even Tania Modleski, in her essay on Detour mentioned earlier, states that "Detour . . . has achieved a certain cult status and is admired today even by practitioners and theorists of the avant-garde [my emphasis]."[30] There is no "even" about it: Detour rests squarely with the tradition of the avant-garde.

Considering Truffaut's perceptive view of the American "B" genre film, the concerns of the following short pieces should come as no surprise. It should be stressed, however, that even in such brief notices, Truffaut refuses to be bound by any canonical conventions as to directorial reputation, considering each film on a case-by-case basis. He remains an *auteurist*, certainly, advocating that one view these individual works within the context of an overall career. Yet he recognizes, as always, the existence of mitigating circumstances in any medium so inherently tied to commerce.

There is another factor that should be considered here: the ineluctable prejudgment accorded all genre films, precisely because they belong to certain generic groupings (westerns, musicals, horror films, science fiction films, etc.). As the following piece demonstrates, Truffaut was not entirely above such prejudgments himself. He obviously is no great fan of science fiction (his generally favorable remarks about *Dr. Cyclops* being a notable exception), and his summary dismissal of Jack Arnold's work in this genre seems without any discernable foundation. However, although he dislikes *It Came from Outer Space* (Universal, 1953), Truffaut still refuses to straitjacket Arnold as an *auteur* with the tag of "science fiction director." Here, Truffaut praises Arnold's work on the little-known *Girls in the Night* (Universal, 1953), which, he tells us, leaves him in "an intermediary state between surprise and delight."

Girls in the Night (Filles dans la Nuit)
American film by Jack Arnold.

Unless I am mistaken, Jack Arnold was unknown here before the appearance of *La Météore de la Nuit (It Came from Outer Space)*, which hardly incited one to wish to learn more about its author, and *Girls in the Night,* which belies that first unfavorable impression.

Let us leave aside the first film (science fiction in polaroid relief [3–D] and black and white, no less!) and get right to *Girls in the Night,* which leaves us in an intermediary state between surprise and delight.

It's a story of a few young boys and girls who live on New York's East Side and who hope to escape from that miserable neighborhood.

Through the author's tenderness for his youngsters (and without sentimentality), through the incredible violence of the fight scenes, through the dynamism of the whole, the beauty of the relationships among the characters, the tone of this film swings between Becker's *Rendez-vous de Juillet* [1949] and Nicholas Ray's *Ruelles du Malheur* (*Knock on Any Door* [Columbia, 1949]). Each scene, whether it is the first (the very lively election of Miss 43rd Avenue in a neighborhood movie theater), the last (a very carefully controlled chase), or yet a prodigious dance scene in a sleazy club, makes us think that it was the one that the author treated the most lovingly; the directing of the actors (all newcomers) is perfect. Jaclynne Greene and Don Gordon make such a convincing pair of rascals that when, after the word END that follows closely after their death, they get up to greet us with a smile, we don't fail to feel that a great weight has been lifted from our shoulders. (RCH)[31]

This slight piece of writing is nevertheless informed by a carefully rigorous critical impulse, which highlights the more successful scenes in the film and seeks to liberate Arnold from the generic prison he would soon, unfortunately, be left in. If Arnold's later films, particularly his films in *The Creature (from the Black Lagoon)* series (1954–1956) are indeed laughable hack work, Truffaut here is quite willing to ignore the shortcomings of Arnold's science fiction films to carefully examine *Girls in the Night*, which might well (along with *The Glass Web* [Universal, 1953]) have led the director to a different sort of career altogether.

In another brief commentary, Truffaut again appears as a prognosticator, accurately predicting the later prominence of Richard Brooks, who many years later would score a considerable commercial and critical triumph with his sharply cynical *Looking for Mr. Goodbar* (1977), not to mention such earlier successes as *The Blackboard Jungle* (1955), *In Cold Blood* (1967), and *Elmer Gantry* (1960).

Deadline (Bas les Masques)
American film by Richard Brooks.

Here is a film that succeeds by force of talent in proving to us—and in making us believe—that journalism is "the finest trade in the world."

Isn't the task of a work of art to solve the drama rather than expose it?

That's why I prefer this film to those films in which the baseness of journalism is painted with a . . . uh, *journalistic* objectivity inadmissible in art.

The screenplay of *Deadline* and the characters that it places on stage don't lack for real greatness, but the merit of Richard Brooks lies more in his knowing that cinematography is the art of petty details that do not strike one, and in his proving it through constant invention.

There will be more talk of Richard Brooks, who was also the screenwriter for *Crossfire* and for *Brute Force* and producer/writer for *Crisis* before he became the sole author of *Deadline*. (RCH)[32]

This short, prescient notice once again demonstrates that Truffaut was eager to seek out new talent, and that he had a firm grasp of cinema history, correctly giving Brooks's earlier credits as a basis for his (then) possible future frame. While the review fails to note that Brooks himself had considerable background as a journalist, principally as a sports reporter for the Philadelphia *Record*, Truffaut by implication isolates the near-documentary impulse of this work, which "succeeds by the force of talent in proving to us—and making us believe—that journalism is 'the finest trade in the world.' "

The Impact of Television

The early '50s marked the rise for the first time of television as a commercial and aesthetic force in commonplace existence, and audiences at the movie theaters began to dwindle as more people stayed home to watch the "free" entertainment on TV. Hollywood producers, understandably alarmed at this decline in revenues (and, by extension, cultural influence), sought ways to regain their hold upon the collective public consciousness. CinemaScope was one avenue actively pursued by the major producers, starting with 20th Century-Fox. CinemaScope was a panoramic/anamorphic recording/reproduction device that had first been theorized in 1860, patented in 1898, and successfully "developed and demonstrated"[33] by Henri Chrétien in the late 1920s. Public response to such early CinemaScope films as *The Robe* (1953) proved that, at least in the short run, the public was superficially impressed by the invention. Most filmmakers and aestheticians, however, were extremely displeased with the long, narrow, CinemaScope format (Fritz Lang once remarked it was fit only for "snakes and funerals"),[34] and such publications as *Sight and Sound* devoted several issues in 1954–55 to an examination of the practical implications of CinemaScope.[35] In the issue of *Sight and Sound* for spring 1955, in particular, the editors offered a public forum for directors to comment on the new process, and almost all of their comments were derogatory, Carl Th. Dreyer being a surprising exception to this.

In 1954, in an issue of *Arts*, Truffaut offered an introductory consideration of the CinemaScope format and of the other "new" formats that were proliferating in response to television. The "lexicon" of formats that Truffaut gives here is necessarily limited. Still, Truffaut accurately encompasses most of the various methods then being embraced by the cinema in the hope of luring customers to the box office.[36]

Small Lexicon of New Formats ("Petit lexique des formats nouveaux")

The common label "3-D" (three dimensions) groups all processes of cinema and of the big screen in relief. In eighteen months, approximately ten processes have made their appearance, and it is to be expected that the public experiences difficulties differentiating between them. For that reason I have put together this small guide for spectators.

CinemaScope

This process consists of three elements:
—Professor Chrétien's hypergonar [anamorphic lens, which squeezes the image onto a conventional 35mm frame]
—A large screen (proportions of 2.55 by 1 instead of 1.33 by 1)
—Stereophonic sound
The Hypergonar: when filming, a (hypergonar [in American and British usage, an anamorphic]) lens, literally compressing the picture, is placed on the face of the camera. When projecting, another lens decompresses the picture.
The stereophonic sound, also called sound relief, is produced by three

loudspeakers placed in the middle and on the sides of the screen. Stereophonic sound necessitates four soundtracks recorded on the film stock.

A few movies in CinemaScope: *The Robe, River of No Return, Written on the Wind.*

Cinepanoramic

Cinepanoramic constitutes the French reply to CinemaScope minus the stereophonic sound. (Only one movie is finished: *The Gold of the Pharaohs.*)

Cinerama

Cinerama is a spectacle that triumphed in America and in England. It requires a special camera equipped with three lenses for shooting. This way, three films are obtained, which then need to be simultaneously projected with three projectors on a concave screen. In the back of the theater, an engineer must continually supervise the synchronism of the three projectors. Cinerama is an extremely burdensome process. Feature films do not yet exist in Cinerama.[37]

Superscope

Superscope is a process that allows the projectionist to go from one film format to any other film format, on condition that the theater is equipped with a panning-shot panoramic screen. A camera with a variable anamorphic lens is placed on the projection apparatus. Let's suppose we have a standard film format (1 × 1.33). With a simple push of his finger, the projectionist can literally enlarge the picture (without clipping it on top or at the bottom), first to proportions of 1 × 1.85, then—if he wants to—up to 1.3. Superscope, ideal to enlarge cartoons, deforms real characters considerably. (SK)[38]

This brief consideration of the various formats then available (which does not, surprisingly, consider such 3–D processes as Natural Vision, easily the best of the 3–D systems used in the early 1950s and employed to great effect on André de Toth's *House of Wax* [1953])[39] is meant only as a general overview and does not go into detail on the advantages and drawbacks of these new technologies, particularly CinemaScope, which rapidly became the most accepted and widely used "panoramic" process in the commercial cinema. (CinemaScope, however, was displaced in the 1960s by Panavision and briefly by the cost-effective Techniscope process, which photographed two CinemaScope ratio images for every frame of film stock, thus affording a 50 percent saving in raw stock and processing costs.) However, as Truffaut makes clear throughout his early criticism, he has "no interest whatsoever" (see below) in any "3–D" process, so perhaps this omission is not so surprising.

In an article in *Cahiers du Cinéma* written roughly half a year before "Petit lexique des formats nouveaux," Truffaut seriously considered the first major CinemaScope release, Henry Koster's biblical spectacle, *The Robe*. The article not only examines the technical aspects of the new process but also discusses the numerous aesthetic and spatial problems caused by CinemaScope framing. We can see, more than thirty-five years later, that Truffaut was absolutely right in many of his assertions regarding the anamorphic system, and yet we can sense his enthusiasm for any new technical advance in the cinema. Truffaut is not willing to call CinemaScope a failure but rather feels that the jury is still out on the process. The article is entitled "En avoir plein la vue" ("On Being Dazzled").

Had he been among us that morning, our late friend Jean Georges Auriol would have been the most enthusiastic, he who always sat in the first row of the stalls saying, "at the movies, you really have to be dazzled."

This is a wonderful remark, totally vindicated by CinemaScope. The more people there are in movie theaters, the more we need to get closer to the screen, in order to make up for the odious critical objectivity of habit, which makes us blasé and consequently bad spectators.

So now, this closer relation—which some still denied themselves—comes to us on its own, annihilating the arbitrary boundaries of the screen and replacing them with the quasi-ideal ones of panoramic vision.

Journalists of the popular press made a serious error, and it is not necessary to look elsewhere for the causes of this deception, in focusing publicity for CinemaScope on an effect of "relief" [the so-called 3–D effect], nonexistent in reality, and of little interest. With the coming of the wide screen, cinema is reinventing the bas-relief of its own terms; an essential method in sculpture, it gives "depth" priority over "relief"; as we have experienced in recent films with polaroid glasses, it goes after farfetched objectives, which can only offer us a naively monstrous and totally unrealistic vision of the world. The thesis of André Bazin, according to which "the screen is a mask" (the same for J. P. Sartre: "To speak is to pass over words in silence")* still counts for CinemaScope; cinema remains a window opened to the world, but hasn't modern architecture done away with the vertical window in favor of the picture window, the oblong bay window (cf. skyscrapers; le Corbusier; *Rope,*

---

* This rather cryptic quotation from Sartre seems, in company with the Bazin quotation, to suggest an interplay of revealing/hiding in the visual aspects of the cinema. Just as we think we are seeing *better*, we realize that we are seeing *less*. (RCH)

etc. . . .)? We may be reminded here that cinema is an art of sight, that our natural vision is panoramic and that our two eyes are placed one next to the other and not one above the other; our eyes form a horizontal field together and are of no use to each other in vertical vision.

All the problems that come up when we think about CinemaScope—whether the close-up will survive and how effective camera movements can be—both vanish and are solved when we confront the *fait accompli.* The close-ups of Victor Mature in *The Robe* are absolutely convincing; the soft-focus on the faces reminds one of Hitchcock's *Notorious*; a long scene with Lauren Bacall assures us of the persistence of the American shot and of its heightened interest.

Every work is more or less the story of a man who is walking and there will be plenty of walking on CinemaScope screens.

It is pleasant to think about the films we like and to note that the elongated apartment of *Rope,* the cars of *Europa 51,* and the movements of *The Golden Coach* would gain in fascination.

It is certain, and the presented excerpts prove so, that the first films in CinemaScope will be very mediocre. How could the most brilliant directors of actors, and the most inventive directors of mise-en-scène, improvise the smallest original detail on a set where, having at their disposal all the money in Hollywood, you can't expose thirty feet of film without having twelve gentlemen in top hats each giving advice and refiguring the budget?

We will have to wait until shooting a film in CinemaScope becomes as natural as shooting an Academy-ratio film in black and white, and until directors enjoy equal freedom. It needs also to be admitted that, if CinemaScope is a commercial REVOLUTION, it is also an aesthetic EVOLUTION. If we agree that the achievement of perfection in the cinema depends on improved realism, then CinemaScope represents one step in that process, the most important one sincc talkies.

We are entering the era of wide vision. We will return to cinema, and we "will really be dazzled." (SK)[40]

In embracing the CinemaScope process while at the same time taking it to task for its inherent clumsiness, Truffaut shows once again that he is always open and receptive to new processes, even though the initial films made in that process may be "mediocre." Truffaut is quite correct in his assertion that it will be a long time before any really credible films are made in CinemaScope, and that this will happen only when the process has become a commonplace, as it had by the mid-1960s, when American International *Beach Party* films, Roger Corman *Poe* movies, and indifferent black-and-white war program pictures were shot in CinemaScope or its equivalent (and now more popular anamorphic process), Panavision. Particularly interesting here is the reference to human binocular vision and the fact that we all naturally see in a "panoramic process": CinemaScope, for Truffaut, naturally mirrors the work done by our own eyes.

I have entered into this brief digression on CinemaScope to frame Truffaut's July 1953 essay on the binocular 3–D films, and more specifically the Natural Vision process, which was the other method by which Hollywood hoped to recapture audiences. If Truffaut felt generally sanguine about the implications and impact of CinemaScope, he was considerably less impressed with Natural Vision. His review of *Man in the Dark* (Columbia, 1953) is really more interested in an analysis of that process's shortcomings than in explicating director Lew Landers's visual style, which he only tangentially examines. This piece indicates that even in mid-1953, when the Natural Vision process was relatively new to both critics and audiences, there had already been considerable debate on its merits and/or defects.

Man in the Dark (J'ai vécu deux fois) by François Truffaut
American film in binocular 3–D (Natural Vision process) by Lew Landers.

It has become a commonplace as well as a truth to note that 3–D films (Polaroid glasses) wind up with the opposite result from what was intended: these 3–D films give us a new sensation—of the flat—and, while aiming for a heightened realism, introduce us to a naively unaccustomed universe, a perfectly imaginary one.

It is perfectly clear that, in life, we don't see "in relief"; our sight adjusts to whatever is our concern at the moment, and seeing clearly both backgrounds and foregrounds, whatever their depth, is all the more disconcerting. This excessive clarity gives us the painful sensation of "cutting on the dotted line."

Paper cutout figures standing out against the decor: we will have to rediscover blurs, otherwise credulity wouldn't make sense.

It is amusing to note that the only effective scene from the point of view of subjectivity is the scenic railway, shot with an ordinary camera with the help of a transparency. (RCH)[41]

Landers was an American director with more than 100 feature films to his credit, both "A" and "B" films, including a number of entries in the Boston Blackie series, the Jungle Jim series, one film in the Whistler series, and the peculiar *Mask of Dijon* (PRC, 1946), starring Erich Von Stroheim.[42] It is perhaps, then, some indication of Hollywood's own estimation of the Natural Vision process that they would hire a journeyman director such as Landers, who was regarded as a reliable professional but little more by most critics, to direct *Man in the Dark*. Further, the accuracy of Truffaut's central assertion that "these 3–D films give us a new sensation—of the flat" is further proved by the fact that Warner

Brothers would hire André de Toth, who was blind in one eye, to oversee *House of Wax*.

As Truffaut notes, "It is perfectly clear that, in life, we don't see 'in relief,'" but perhaps Warner Brothers knew what they were doing. The exaggerated stylistic constructs Natural Vision requires may be better schematized by one who cannot normally see in depth. The aggressive compositions in *Man in the Dark, House of Wax,* and nearly all the 3–D films might be seen as attempts to compensate for this "flatness" inherent in cinematic representations. Truffaut here indicates that Natural Vision really doesn't work, and, by implication, that its days as an active cinematic agent are numbered. The correctness of this position is borne out by the fact that the Natural Vision process was dropped by Hollywood in late 1954 and has been revived only sporadically since, with dismal results.

Truffaut had little affection for 3–D, but he had even less respect for the Cinerama process. Indeed, Truffaut found it a series of cheap tricks and illusions that, for him, were directly opposed to all he held dear in cinema. The review of *Cinerama Holiday* (1956) that follows makes repeated allusions to the first Cinerama presentation, *This Is Cinerama* (1952), and for Truffaut, the second attempt at constructing a feature film in the multi-screen, multi-camera process is no better than the first. Truffaut is wrong when he states that Cinerama is "ineradicable"; in less than a decade, the process and the theaters constructed for projecting Cinerama films would both be gone. Yet Truffaut hits the mark directly with the comment that "Cinerama, for want of being able to hide its limits, is condemned to use itself as a subject forever." It is precisely this limitation that led to the eventual abandonment of the process. "Cinerama has nothing to say and says it badly," Truffaut asserts, effectively signaling that, for him, content will always be of more importance than any formal characteristics a work might possess. Truffaut's love for the more elegant aspects of cinematic syntax and shot-structure cannot diminish the primacy of the text, which must always be the dominant concern of an *auteur*. Truffaut finds what little "content" *Cinerama Holiday* contains objectionable because of its heavily "Americanized" ideological structure, coupled with a voice-over narration that habitually patronizes the viewer. Though Truffaut loves the Hollywood film, he despises the cultural complacency and self-satisfied smugness of *Cinerama Holiday*, as well as the inherent shallowness of the process in which it is made. If Cinerama has a certain immediacy, it conveys an impression that Truffaut finds quite disconcerting. "Cinerama—and this might be its only virtue—is precisely exactly the same as a trip to the U.S.A., since we leave the theater feeling fiercely anti-American. *Cinerama Holiday* can be one of the answers to Raymond Cartier's interesting question: 'Why are Americans hated?'" *Cinerama Holiday* is a two-hour commercial for the Cinerama process. Truffaut is quite correct in his assessment of the aesthetically bankrupt nature of the production. His review ends with the admonishment "if you like cinema, you must refrain from going to see *Cinerama*," and he recommends that the viewer see, instead, Abel Gance's *Magirama* (1956), one of Gance's later "Polyvision" (multiple-screen) works.

Cinerama Holiday ("Bad Circus and Low Propaganda")

Cinerama is ineradicable now, for it is not only a cinema show, but it also attracts tourists; the country cousin coming to Paris goes to the Empire after visiting the Folies-Bergères and Ingrid Bergman in *Thé et sympathie [Tea and Sympathy]*.

The first Cinerama film attempted to make a demonstration, rather unconvincingly, of the "possibilities" of this method: one could hope that the second program would show an improvement, but alas! We have to face our disappointment again this time. We now know that Cinerama has nothing to say and says it badly, in spite of Claude Dauphin's beautiful voice.

On the contrary to what has been asserted, *Cinerama Holiday* doesn't tell a story; the double honeymoon of a Swiss couple in America and an American couple in Europe is just an excuse to show, a bit less arbitrarily, the same things as in the first show. Everything is sacrificed to effect, by the very force of circumstances, since Cinerama is unable to show an "acted" sequence.

The camera men miss no opportunity to track in without cause, the camera being perched on a sleigh, a plane, a scooter, or wooden horses.

Sometimes, the people we see on the screen are preplanned "walk-ons," and we are shocked to witness a fabricated scene allegedly "taken from life." When, on the contrary, the camera moves among the crowd, it is unpleasant to meet the pedestrians' eye in the lens, all the more so because we see them abused by assistants, whom we imagine dealing out one dollar bills.

The mise-en-scène is pitiable, the editing unskillful, the picture often out of focus. The three screens are no better linked up than before, but the cameramen have been given instructions about this so that houses' angles and trees are casually superimposed on the edges of the central screen.

The most irritating in all this is the *tone* and the *content* [Truffaut's emphasis] of the show, the systematic flattery of the "dear audience," the extremist demagogy, the intensive publicity, and the propaganda.

Cinerama, for want of being able to hide its limits, is condemned to use itself as a subject forever; it is annoying to hear for two hours: "Dear audience, thanks to Cinerama, you're going to fly over this or that." Or else: "It's in Cinerama's company, dear friends, that you are going to go for a walk in Dache. . . ." And finally: "America not only sets the pace, but also . . . ," etc.

When we listen to friends coming back from a trip to the United States, we are shocked to hear their remarks, offensive to a country that we judge through good movies and good novels: Cinerama—and this might be its only virtue—is precisely the same as a trip to the U.S.A., since we leave the theater feeling fiercely anti-American. *Cinerama Holiday* can be one of the answers to Raymond Cartier's interesting question: "Why are Americans hated?"

The sequence about France is so extravagant that, during the projection reserved for the press, the organizers turned the sound off so that nobody could hear the sentences exchanged between the American couple and a French mother whose children are fighting in the war!

If you like cinema, you must refrain from going to see *Cinerama* and with the money you'll thus save, you can afford three or four beautiful Hollywood or other films. If you really want to "be dazzled," you can also go and see, more profitably, Abel Gance's *Magirama* in Studio 28. (SK)[43]

Truffaut rightly rejects Cinerama and Natural Vision as self-reflexive processes that add little to the narrative or emotional potential of the cinematographic image; he sees both techniques as gimmicks rather than potential advances. CinemaScope, for all its defects, has, for Truffaut, at least the potential of future application. With Cinerama, "everything is sacrificed to the effect." Rather than being the future of filmic representationalism, Truffaut recognizes Cinerama for the epic return to the past that it truly represents, when the cinema was little more than a novelty. With Cinerama, every other aspect of the production becomes subsidiary to the medium in which it is presented, resulting in a devaluation of both audience and *auteur*.

Working with "the Minimum"

Truffaut, while cautiously favoring anamorphic processes (but not at the expense of previous "flat" productions), is perfectly content with a small-screen, black-and-white image, if such an image is required by the filmmaker as the ideal medium for her or his work. Indeed, throughout all of Truffaut's writing, one gets the continual impression that with fewer resources, one may in fact accomplish more, as Bresson noted in *Notes on Cinematography*: "Someone who can work with the minimum can work with the most. One who can with the most, cannot, inevitably, with the minimum."[44] Perhaps this most eloquently expresses Truffaut's admiration for the small-scale American program picture; it works most effectively when it has the least in the way of physical production values, and it strips away the artifice that a grandiose presentation uses to disguise defects of the imagination. In all his early writings, Truffaut comes back again and again to those artists working on the edges of the cinema, precisely because those artists create out of faith, skill, and a transcendence of available materials.

Even with distinctly minor talents, such as the aforementioned André de Toth, Truffaut is generous, finding something to like even in the most modest of films. De Toth's *The City Is Dark* (also known as *Crime Wave* [Warner Brothers, 1954]) is primarily an entertainment, just as Truffaut says. Here, as in many of his other writings, the details of mise-en-scène continue to constitute for Truffaut the essence of the cinematic contract. This short paragraph manages to praise de Toth's "pleasant . . . nobility," while at the same time sardonically taking to task those censors who would force their views upon the public in the name of conventional morality.

The City Is Dark (La Chasse au gang) by R. L.
American film by André de Toth.

A one-eyed director, André de Toth of Hollywood would be king if Hollywood were blind. Nothing is farther from the truth, thank God, and de Toth doesn't keep his Cyclops eye in his pocket, but acts like the lynx. A pleasant man, de Toth makes nice movies that are not without nobility, since he is a man with a prefix ["de"]. *The City Is Dark* is one of those films that is very easy to watch and that which furthermore has the merit of showing us side by side, sleeping the same sleep, lying in the same bed, an American couple composed, as you know, of two individuals apparently of opposite sexes, belying in one fell swoop the terrible, backbiting, imported legend according to which there is supposed to be, on the other side of the Atlantic, some code of modesty that is supposed to stipulate that, for two movie spouses, twin beds, seventy centimeters, etc., etc. (RCH)[45]

Even with a film that he doesn't really like, Truffaut resists the urge to completely dismiss the work. His view of Christy Cabanne's *The Mummy's Hand* (Universal, 1940) is a perfect example of Truffaut's restraint in the face of a film that is resolutely a program assignment, and not a very competently handled one at that. Cabanne was a Hollywood old-timer at the end of his career when he made this film. As Truffaut mentions, Cabanne had started with Griffith, first as an actor in 1910, later as an assistant, and finally as a solo director in 1924, with *The Dishonored Medal* (Continental Films).[46] As Walz notes, Truffaut finds *The Mummy's Hand* "surrealist in spite of itself,"[47] and in his brief notice of the film, there is a genuine if grudging affection for both the *Mummy* series and for the straightforward absurdity of the plot and characterizations. Nevertheless, Truffaut draws the line at artificially elevating the film to the realm of true artistic endeavor: it is, he notes, "very boring." Once again, Truffaut seems more interested in the size of the "Egyptologist-American's bust" than in any of the detail of Cabanne's mise-en-scène.

The Mummy's Hand (La Main de la Momie)
American film by Christy Cabanne.

The mummy in question is no slouch. Having lived for 3,000 years under the influence of a fluid, Kharis—a mummy who is neither male nor female—jealously guards the tomb of Princess Ananka (17th dynasty of Pharoahs), which is precisely the thing the American Egyptologists would like to have a look at. Preoccupied as I was with the size of the female doctor-explorer-Egyptologist-American's bust, I completely forgot to pay attention to the story, but what does it matter? This lady marries her travel companion, who, in recompense, gets named "director of a large museum."

Let's not forget to say that this film, made by a pupil of Griffith—demi-angle of the "Triangle"—is very boring, and that only the Benayouns, the Kirous, and other Adonises will be able to monopolize it in order to puff up the very thin (in spite of itself) files of surrealist cinema. (RCH)[48]

Yet reviews in which Truffaut can find nothing to say are few and far between. Perhaps this is because he only chose to review those films he admired; perhaps it is because he reserved his real critical scorn for films which he felt were pretentious, the quality he despised most in the cinema. His paragraph on *Room for One More* (French release Title: *Cette sacreé famille*) (surely the French title is preferable) finds Truffaut praising as a "masterpiece" a film that he simultaneously excoriates as having "the most hypocritical scenario, the basest demagoguery" that he has ever witnessed in a Hollywood film. Even when he is being emotionally manipulated, and is fully aware of it, Truffaut is still moved by the film, so much so that his tears "punctuat[ed] the changing of the reels." "This rare enterprise is saved from infamy . . . [by] an astonishing mise-en-scène, made all the more astonishing by director Norman Taurog's usually faceless direction, which here rises to or surpasses the level of the hysteric script. Taurog had won an Academy Award for his direction of *Skippy* in 1931 (a film based on the popular comic strip character by Percy Crosby), but his later work lacks a distinctive visual signature. This makes him at once the perfect contract director, a frustrating example of what happens when a filmmaker emotionally removes himself from his work.

Perhaps Truffaut's reasons for liking *Room for One More* are cynically perverse. One wishes that he had been more specific in isolating exactly those aspects of the director's style that impressed him. Nevertheless, Truffaut's review here has at least one historical virtue: it is practically the only favorable review this film received, other than in the trade papers *Variety* and *The Hollywood Reporter*. Truffaut quotes Genet: "An action is only despicable if it is unfinished." Perhaps what Truffaut most appreciates about this film is that once having decided upon its true intent ("an apologia for adoption"), it never strays from pressing that point upon the audience.

Room for One More (Cette sacreé famille)
American film by Norman Taurog, 1952.

Should we keep silent or brave the ridicule that may be directed at us if we point out an admirable film and recommend it several months after its release? This is surely the most hypocritical scenario, the basest demagoguery, the most boyscoutish that has ever been written in Hollywood. An apologia for adoption, for generous care of others, for nice feelings; and yet our tears fall ten times, punctuating the changing of the reels. "An action is only despicable if it is unfinished," said Genet. Since it leads each scene to its ultimate development, each situation to its height, each gesture to its end, this rare enterprise is saved from infamy and astonishingly played with an astonishing mise-en-scène. Let's go again to weep over the comic-tragic adventures of Cary Grant and his wife Betsy Drake, and let us feel no remorse about it. Certainly form doesn't take precedence over content but justifies it and if necessary even rehabilitates it. All in all, a masterpiece. (RCH)[49]

In his short notice on George Cukor's *A Life of Her Own* (MGM, 1950), Truffaut is dealing with a director who has a considerably greater reputation than Cabanne, Miller, Taurog, or most of the other directors we have considered here. Nevertheless, this piece belongs with Truffaut's other work on genre films. For Truffaut, Cukor is a man "who makes, out of every five films, one masterpiece, three other very good ones, and the fifth still interesting." *A Life of Her Own* (French release title: *Ma vie à moi*) is surely a minor addition to the Cukor canon, but still Truffaut prefers it to David Lean's *Brief Encounter* (1946), because Cukor's film aims for less and so accomplishes more. For Truffaut, this is a film about beauty, "the beauty of Cukor's work," as he notes, but also the imagistic construct of Lana Turner's face, entering into the film "straight off from the very first image." This film seems more *maudit* than most Cukor projects: Ray Milland and Lana Turner make a very odd couple indeed. Yet Truffaut still places this film with *Vacation* (known as *Holiday* in America), *The Philadelphia Story*, and *Little Women*, by implication citing these films as some of Cukor's most accomplished work. Most critics would find the inclusion of *Little Women*, as well as *My Own Life*, in Cukor's "short list" as somewhat aberrational. Perhaps it isn't so peculiar at all, and this "admirable film" should be granted a second look within the context of Cukor's career.

A Life of Her Own (Ma vie à moi)
American film by George Cukor.

Lana Turner and Ray Milland are the heroes of this film, united and disunited by an impossible love. Whether or not their physical appearance is described, Madame de Morsauf, the Princess of Clèves, and Albertine are immediately beautiful. Fie on *Brief Encounter* [1945]. It took us a good hour and a half to admit that an ugly woman could be likeable. *Brief Encounter* ended at the very moment when we were about to agree to the ugliness postulate. Here beauty enters straight off from the very first image; the beauty of Lana Turner, the beauty of the story, and finally the beauty of Cukor's work, that extraordinary man who makes, out of every five films, one masterpiece, three other very good ones, and the fifth still interesting.

We must place this admirable film beside *Holiday* [1938], *Philadelphia Story,* [1940], and *Little Women* [1933]. (RCH)[50]

In the same series of brief reviews from this issue of *Cahiers*, Truffaut considers two films that he finds distinctly less "admirable": Robert Stevenson's 1952 *The Las Vegas Story (Scandale à Las Vegas)* and William Dieterle's 1952 *The Turning Point (Cran d'arrêt).* These two films get decidedly short shrift from Truffaut, who still praises William Holden for his work in the second film.

The Las Vegas Story (Scandale à Las Vegas)
American film by Robert Stevenson, produced by Howard Hugues [*sic*].

Everyone in Paris has already been talking about this car-helicopter chase. Is it necessary to make a special trip for this last quarter-hour, and for that quarter-hour, endure four more of equal dullness? I don't think so. Virtuosity isn't enough and its gratuity here is more than self-evident. After all, was *Banni* [American release title: *My Forbidden Past* (1952; Dir. Stevenson)] a good film? Nothing is less sure, and unfortunately we will never be able to decide about it since the film is withdrawn from distribution according to Mr. Hugues's [sic] express desires.

The Turning Point (Cran d'arrêt) by R. L.
American film by William Dieterle.

Dieterle is the sort of *metteur-en-scène* on whom one cannot count: capable of the best but also of the worst. *The Turning Point* seems to me far and away the best film of the unfortunate *auteur* of *Salome.* The presence of Horace MacCoy in the screen credits should count for a great deal in its success.

Holden, discovered in *Stalag 17,* is confirmed here as one of the three great American actors of tomorrow. (RCH)[51]

Those who may feel that Truffaut systematically sought out "B" films for critical adulation will find the following review of *Shoot First* (1953) instructive. *Shoot First,* also known as *Rough Shoot* (and really a British/American coproduction rather than being "shot in England" as Truffaut asserts), contains "not a single idea" as far as Truffaut is concerned. "Some of [American "B" films] are atrocious," he admits at the beginning of this piece, and he displays uncharacteristic enthusiasm for his task, as he viciously ridicules Parrish's film, which was produced by Stanley Kramer. Perhaps the movie deserves it: the "bluff, faked . . . effects" it traffics in are part and parcel of the Kramer style. While some may believe that this film "corresponds to the idea that half-witted critics have about Hitchcock, 'the master of suspense,' " for Truffaut the film is an unrelieved failure. It might also be noted that he is ahead of his time in observing that Kramer "sometimes has a rather bad influence" over the films he has a hand in either as producer or director. One gets the distinct impression that Truffaut felt that the "English soberness" this film displays is used to cover up a rather stiff approach to the material.

Shoot First (Coup de feu au matin) American film by Robert Parrish.
One should definitely not believe that we systematically defend and praise American "B" movies. Some of them are atrocious. Yesterday it was *Le Quatrième homme* [American release title: *Kansas City Confidential* (1952; Dir. Phil Karlson); see review following]; today it is *Shoot First* by Robert Parrish, whose rather flat *The Mob* [1951] we saw recently.
The film corresponds to the idea that half-witted critics have about Hitchcock, the "master of suspense." Here, all is bluff, faked, unseemly effects. Shot in England, this film breathes of English countryside, English soberness, English humor, English flatness, English nonexistence. Not one invention, not one detail, not a single idea. Evelyn Keyes's pretty face remains impassive and indifferent to Joel McCrea's supposed torment. Producer Stanley Kramer, whose every film is praised by the critics before they see it, sometimes has a rather bad influence. (RCH)[52]

That Truffaut was free of most vestiges of cult idolatry is indicated by his unfavorable review of *Le Quatrième homme*, alluded to in the previous notice. *Le Quatrième homme* is better known to American audiences as *Kansas City Confidential*. *Kansas City Confidential*, directed by Phil Karlson, an *auteur* much appreciated for such violent action/revenge dramas as *The Phenix City Story* (1955), *Walking Tall* (1973), and *Scandal Sheet* (1952), to name just a few, received critical approbation from nearly every other reviewer, yet Truffaut finds it a "schoolboy" exercise.

Kansas City Confidential (Le Quatrieme homme) [1952]
Kansas City Confidential[53] is hardly any better than its predecessor. I would even say that it's worse, since everything that Orson Welles takes part in is of some interest to us. In this film, cinema is unimportant. Everything happens to the right, the left, or below the screen, and al-

ways out of our line of vision. It is said that some critics have reproached the film for its "gratuitous sadism." Even gratuitously, sadism
wouldn't have bothered me, but how can they describe thus those
soundtrack tricks, those black eyes skillfully made up by clever makeup
artists, those pulled punches? All the fights are done by montage, just as
any schoolboy would have done.

The qualities of this film are outside the film itself:

1. Very anti-cop scenario;
2. Several censorship attacks;
3. The nicest advertising slogan: "The most unbelievable film of the
year";
4. A girl, not too pretty, is studying law, but her eyes are already
making a case for love—an exercise she seems to want very much to try
out, in order to fill up the long vacation evenings on this island, which
is not without references that evoke *Key Largo* [1948], which this film
plagiarizes here and there. *Kansas City Confidential,* or five fools on an
island? (RCH)[54]

It's also interesting to see that Truffaut's work as a critic is often at
variance with the generally accepted historical view of his aesthetic sensibility. Douglas Sirk is routinely lionized in the late 1980s as a stylist
on a par with Max Ophüls: Rainer Werner Fassbinder's well-known acknowledgment of the impact of Sirk's work on his own films has further
ensured Sirk's posthumous reputation. Truffaut places Sirk in a modest
critical position: below Hitchcock and Rossellini, yet still a director of
"sincerity and intelligence." As he notes, "others take Jean Dellanoy for
a mystical moralist," which Dellanoy certainly is not. While Truffaut
feels that Sirk's vision has distinct limitations, he is still impressed, almost in spite of himself, with Sirk's transcendent yet minor work in
Thunder on the Hill.

Thunder on the Hill (Tempête sur la colline)
American film by Douglas Sirk.

Sometimes, the police are fooled by the church. Sometimes the servants of God beat the cops at their own game, that of earthly truths.
Such situations delight the Christians that we are and come along at the
right moment to remind Sunday churchgoers that their worship of God
was born out of the violation of a law, amid the roars of the gladiators
in the arenas. This is perhaps the only common point between *Europe
51, I Confess,* and *Thunder on the Hill.* If Douglas Sirk doesn't have the
genius of Rossellini and Hitchcock, the sincerity and intelligence of his
directing make him worthy of it. Others take Jean Dellanoy for a mystical moralist. (RCH)[55]

Even more surprising is Truffaut's evaluation of William Nigh's *I Wouldn't Be in Your Shoes* (Monogram, 1948), which was first released in France in 1953 as *Le Condamné de la cellule 5*. The change in title is unfortunate. As Truffaut notes, the film concerns an innocent young newlywed, who "throws his shoes out the window [and] that's all it takes to get him accused of murder and condemned to death." The novel by Cornell George Hopley-Woolrich (aka William Irish) novel was adapted by Nigh into a tight little seventy-minute film. The best-known actor in the film was certainly Regis Toomey, always a "sidekick" figure in "A" productions. *I Wouldn't Be in Your Shoes* was Nigh's second-to-last film as a director, in a career that had started in 1911 and covered more than eighty films before his retirement in 1948 (Nigh died in 1955).[56] Most of Nigh's works are "B" films: many are perfunctory. Here, however, Truffaut finds Nigh's work of great interest and genuine quality, and he calls the film "one of the best . . . if not *the* best . . . of the detective films that can be seen at the moment in Paris."

I Wouldn't Be in Your Shoes (Le Condamné de la cellule 5)
American film by William Nigh.

A young man, a newlywed, throws his shoes out of the window and finds them, the next morning, with a nice fat wallet in one of them. That's all it takes to get him accused of murder and condemned to death.

It all gets sorted out in the last reel, the murderer being none other than the detective in charge of the investigation, who put on the shoes thrown out the window in order to commit his crime.

This quite unusual scenario is very intelligently adapted from an excellent novella by William Irish, unpublished in France.

I Wouldn't Be in Your Shoes is one of those films you go see while expecting the worst; it's the strength of American cinema to hold out a couple of nice surprises of this sort fairly regularly.

This one is a series C film, with no known actors, shot rather quickly with a tiny budget, and yet the work is more than respectable: we find no errors of taste; the directing of the actors, dialogues, mise-en-scène work together excellently to bestow maximum effectiveness on this good story.

So here is one of the best—if not *the* best—of the detective films that can be seen at the moment in Paris. (RCH)[57]

In an issue of *Arts*, Truffaut takes to task Victor Saville's *The Long Wait* (1954) (inexplicably titled *Nettoyage par le vide* [Throwing it all Out] in France; in view of Truffaut's opinion of the film, perhaps not a bad idea). Based on the novel by Mickey Spillane, the film is, for better or worse, a faithful reproduction of the novel, with all the routine violence predictably intact. Truffaut here really doesn't fault Saville's direction. What appalls him is the Spillane *mystique*, which for him consists of "multiplying by ten the things that make the *film noir* popular." He is right, of course: the Spillane strategy is overkill. Truffaut also demonstrates here that he can tell the difference between an ingeniously made low-budget detective thriller and an action film that is "abysmal, of course, but . . . not boring for a second."

The Long Wait (Nettoyage par le vide)
American film by Victor Saville.

Let's hope that the vogue for Mickey Spillane novels won't cross the Atlantic. There's nothing more hackneyed than this story of an amnesia victim whose only response to the police is, "I don't remember nothing." All the more so because what follows is predictable and expected: the amnesia victim is innocent and proves it.

The Spillane formula consists of multiplying by ten the things that make the *film noir* popular: so it is that a critic counted no fewer than thirty-four kisses in *The Long Wait*, every one of them passionate. One man, four women, a few killers. Punches and gunshots must number more than a hundred. The four ladies are pretty nice. One of them is named Vera, but which one? Not only can the hero of the film, suffering from amnesia, not figure out which one of his four women used to be his wife, but, what's more, she changed her face in the meantime under the scalpel of some Yankee quack.

All this, for better or worse, gets untangled at the end, after a quarter-hour of hair-raising and unintended avant-garde, intended no doubt to make up for the absence of money, sets, and means. Abysmal, of course, but, let's admit it, not boring for a second. (RCH)[58]

Truffaut was not really a "fan" of science fiction, and yet occasionally a film in that genre would pique his interest. Truffaut's review of Arch Oboler's *Five* (Columbia, 1951), which Oboler wrote, produced, and directed, recognizes the film for what it is, an *avant-garde* amateur film that reveals both the naivete and ambition of its author.

Five (Cinq Survivants) American film by Arch Oboler. *Scenario:* Arch Oboler. *Pictures:* Sid Lubow. *Music:* Henry Russell. *Cast:* William Phipps (Michael), Susan Douglas (Roseanne), James Anderson (Eric), Charles Lampkin (Charles), Earl Lee (Mr. Barnstraple). *Production:* Arch Oboler (1952). *Distribution:* Columbia.

Here, at last, a work among those that legitimize the *Cinéma d'Essai*.

There is no doubt, in fact, that *Five* would have found no one to distribute it, if *Cinéma d'Essai* had not put it on.

We must recall that *Five* is Arch Oboler's first film; the following one was the first 3–D with polaroid glasses: *Bwana Devil*. Arch Oboler, like Orson Welles in times gone by, is a radio man. Author of 400 [radio] plays, he has swept away all the radio awards.

Five is a very typical avant-garde film, if we accept such a label for a film conceived and made apart from all commercial considerations, with the means available to amateur films, based on a highly noncommercial subject and clumsily made, as is fitting.

No doubt, the "16mm spirit" that Cocteau praises so highly presided over the making of this film, whose technical conception is close to that of *After Sunset Comes the Night, Silence of the Sea,* and other American avant-garde films; but it doesn't have the crazy pretentiousness of some, the backward aestheticism of others—faults that a great generosity of spirit alone justifies.

A film of great honesty, of evenhanded sincerity and genuine naivete, *Five* imposes upon us the notion of getting along with people, which is very pleasant in our times when hating your mother is a proof of elegance, killing your father makes the biggest headlines, a time also whose moralists have no other conduct to recommend to us than to walk through life with a serpent in our fist.

Five takes as its subject the survival of five people on earth after the explosion of the atomic bomb. Three of them die and the history of the earth begins again with the couple.

Having lived in the atomic age is their original sin, and the film closes with the theme of Adam and Eve, or, if you prefer, that of Noah, survivor of the first flood and as such, purifier.

It is well known that this sort of story is the very archetype of the false "good" scenario. Beginning with the original idea, everything has to be invented and we must be able to resist the temptations that a universe free of all convention does not fail to offer.

Here, better than anywhere else, it is appropriate to recreate the world and to know "how far is too far" to go.

Arch Oboler has succeeded in constructing his scenario perfectly to the point of rendering it believable. The extreme fast pace of the scenes and their excessive soberness make them completely effective. Difficulties are never swept under the rug, and I remember nothing so terrifying as that scene when insanity grabs hold of the mountain climber when he sees on his chest the signs of deadly radiation poisoning: he shouts and goes off staggering among skeletons scattered here and there in the dead city and disappears in the "first street to the right."

We must call attention to the great beauty of the heroine whose joys and sorrows are written on her face, giving this film an air of news according to the atomic age. There, in any case, lies the miracle of this film; at no moment does one think it is a reconstruction; the film seems truly to have been made after the "explosion" with props and film miraculously saved.

Everything that characterizes amateur cinema is found in the mise-en-scène: blurry and grainy photography, pale faces (due to the use of floods instead of stage lights), shaky dolly shots, strange framing, odd angles, slow pace, "very 16mm" and rather limited acting almost devoid of invention.* Here are, indeed, the defects that keep us from taking seriously 16mm or 35mm experiments in which overstated commentary and scores borrowed from Bach and Vivaldi never remedy the poverty of inspiration (almost always pederastic, psychoanalytical, disproportionate in relation to the limited means of production).

But in this film, whose modesty is all its charm, it seems that these limited means alone could assure its success, and we think with a chill of the failure that this enterprise would have been, conceived and made according to the norms of American production, which becomes mediocre and pretentious as soon as it tries to escape from the traditional themes that it knows how to handle royally. (RCH)[59]

Compare this review, willing to recognize all the film's defects but still granting to it genuine passion in its construction and execution, with any of the daily reviews of the period, and you will find that Truffaut was once again going against the established critical grain. Today Oboler is primarily remembered as the person who produced and directed the first independent 3–D theatrical feature, *Bwana Devil* (distributed by United Artists, 1953) (as opposed to de Toth's *House of Wax*, the first major company 3–D release). Truffaut sees that *Five* is, and must be, a commercial enterprise, but he is moved by it, respects it, refuses to dismiss it on the grounds of its "amateur . . . mise-en-scène." Though specks may indeed cover the lens in several sequences, this is really nothing to be concerned about.

Truffaut values, above all, integrity. He reviles "scores borrowed from Bach and Vivaldi [that] never remedy the poverty of inspiration" in other "16mm and 35mm experiments," but in this film, "modesty is all its charm." "A limited means alone could assure its success" Truffaut reminds us; in the hands of a major studio, with the creative constraint that an "A" budget brings in terms of front-office interference, "this enterprise would have been . . . mediocre and pretentious." Truffaut does not even mind that the acting is "limited [and] almost devoid of invention." For him, the film is a success, in part because it follows one individual vision instead of being made by committee, as so many "A" films are. In its present incarnation, Truffaut finds the film "completely effective" and feels that Oboler "has succeeded in constructing his scenario *perfectly* [my emphasis]." That one word sums up Truffaut's view of the "B" film: capable of perfection despite the superficial imperfections of indifferent acting, shaky shots, "blurry photography," and limited financing.

---

* Specks on the film reveal that sometimes they neglected to clean the lens! (RCH)

2 A Private Pantheon

Of all directors yet mentioned in this volume, Fritz Lang is one of the most curious examples of an "A" director finding a creative haven in the world of the "B" film. Truffaut's long love affair with Lang is everywhere evident in his numerous reviews of Lang's works. However, as a "director for hire," Lang often had to compromise with his producers. As Lang told Peter Bogdanovich in Bogdanovich's book *Fritz Lang in America*, the production of *While the City Sleeps* (1956), for example, was not without its difficulties. Lang and his editor, Gene Fowler, Jr., had to contend with front-office interference on an almost daily basis.[1] Truffaut is quite sensitive to these difficulties in his appraisals of Lang's later films, even without specific knowledge of them. Truffaut recognizes the truth in what Lang was to tell Bogdanovich nearly ten years later: "I was hoping that if I made somebody a great financial success I would again have the chance—as I had with *M*—to work without any restrictions."[2]

Unfortunately, this great commercial success eluded Lang, and certainly not without reason. Lang was never really in tune with "popular" audiences, and he used the existing platform of the genre film as a starting point for the dissemination of his own ideas, no matter how unpopular they might be. The "bitterness" (Truffaut's word) that one finds in such late Lang films as *The Blue Gardenia*, *While the City Sleeps*, *The Big Heat*, *Human Desire*, and *Beyond a Reasonable Doubt* guaranteed their relative lack of popularity with contemporary audiences (though *The Big Heat*, superficially appreciated solely as a gangster melodrama, did well at the box office). However, the uncompromising harshness of Lang's moral universe gives these films a depth and resonance that keeps them alive today, while most other '50s "programmers" have faded in memory. Truffaut recognizes this and implicitly agrees with Lang's view of 1950s American culture. In a 1956 essay for *Arts*, Truffaut examined Lang's concerns in his later Hollywood films and found Lang's work as a whole an act of "dry, clear, pitiless criticism."

If I were to name the most patently underestimated filmmaker, Fritz Lang would instantly come to my mind. Cinema historians and critics admit that his German works have some value and even tolerate some

41

of his American films, but they deny him any genius when he "signs" spy movies (*Chasse à l'Homme* [*Man Hunt* (1941)], *Cape et Poignard* [*Cloak and Dagger* (1946)]), westerns (*Le retour de Frank James* [*The Return of Frank James* (1940)], *L'Ange des Maudits* [*Rancho Notorious* (1952)]), war movies (*Guerillas* [*American Guerrilla in the Philippines* (1950)], or simple thrillers (*Règlements de compte* [*The Big Heat* (1953)], *La Femme au gardéna* [*The Blue Gardenia* (1953)]).

For all those who really like Fritz Lang, none of these recent films is unworthy of *Die Nibelungen* (1924) or of *Fury* (1936), in spite of the rough look that a second-rate production automatically has.

Of course, Fritz Lang never was given the benefit in Hollywood of the independence that one or several dazzling financial successes procure for lucky, more adaptable filmmakers, whose minds are more in tune with those of their audience. He must express himself through badly built scripts full of implausible facts, the dialogue of which he has to hurriedly rewrite two days before he starts shooting. His reputation as an uncompromising director, and his bad temper, force him to change producers often.

If the films he makes today look more commercial than his other films, it is because Fritz Lang has become, as he grows older, sterner and thus further from the audience. He probably never was sentimental, but in the films he made as a young man, he didn't disdain cinema effects, plastic effects, script effects. Fritz Lang was lyrical, full of humor, and prodigiously inventive; *Les Espions* [*Spies* (1928)] and the two *Mabuses* (1922) show an astounding zest. Hitchcock owes Fritz Lang a lot— a lot. . . .

Fritz Lang, as he was developing, purified his style as Renoir, Hitchcock, and Hawks did. Lyricism and humor gave way to bitterness and sour criticism. Hardly any effects left, but a unique mastery and technical sureness. Yes, I dare write that today Fritz Lang is greater and above all deeper, even if he pleases less.

. . . No films are harder on American civilization than Fritz Lang's; if one doesn't realize it, it's because there never is any satire involved but just dry, clear, pitiless criticism. The beautiful Technicolor *American Guerrilla in the Philippines* (1950) that Fritz Lang made after the war, with Micheline Presle and Tyrone Power, on the subject of the battles in the Pacific Ocean, was "dragged through the mud." People howled that it was just mean American propaganda. They did not understand all the hatred the old monocled German had put in the last shot of the picture: in the island "freed" by the marines, the population, won over to Americanism, is lined up in front of the sea as if for a family picture: all the civilians wave, with their right hands, little paper stars and stripes, while they put small Coca-Cola bottles to their mouths with their left hands. Doesn't this last scene say more than a long pamphlet? Fritz Lang, thus, never got over nazism. In Hollywood, he always refused to join

left-wing political groups, but when the "Hollywood Ten" were ar-
rested, he is the one who set about collecting money from all his colleagues to pay for a lawyer, even though he was convinced they would
all be electrocuted, and that he would be too! (BFH)[3]

Lang in the 1950s is indeed "sterner, and thus further from the audience." He holds his audience, and the society they represent, in contempt.[4] What Truffaut admires in Lang's later film, then, is not so much
the execution of the work but the hatred Lang feels for American society,
which is so eloquently expressed in *The Blue Gardenia* and, as Truffaut
notes, in the horrendous final shot of the often-dismissed *American
Guerrilla in the Philippines*. Lang uses the generic conventions of the
war film, the crime film, and even the western as a vehicle for social
criticism. If he settles for a second-rate physical production at times, this
does not bother Truffaut. Practically alone among critics of the period,
Truffaut equates Lang's work in the 1950s with his better-known films
of the 1920s (*Spies* and the two *Dr. Mabuse* films). Lang remains a vig-
orous original, no matter what his budgets dictate in terms of sets, actors,
and shooting schedules.

In the same issue of *Arts*, Truffaut also examines a western by Anthony Mann and John Ford's *The Searchers*. The Ford review is perhaps
one of the most interesting and revealing essays translated in this volume. Mann is superior to Ford, in Truffaut's eyes; Ford is "senile and
repetitive." What Truffaut really objects to is the suffocating patriarchy
that informs the construction of all of Ford's westerns, a patriarchy
championed most vigorously by Sarris, for whom Ford is the first figure
in his "pantheon" of American directors, and later by Tag Gallagher in
John Ford.[5] Gallagher, too, fails to satisfactorily address the racism and
sexism that Ford simultaneously embraces and defends (the only possible words) in his work. In Truffaut's own pantheon, John Ford holds a
quite subsidiary position to Anthony Mann. If Mann's work fell off a
good deal in later years (with the partial exception of *El Cid* [1961]), at
this point in time, Mann seems a more worthy *auteur* in the young critic's estimation.

The Last Frontier by Anthony Mann.

It is to Anthony Mann that we owe the purest westerns of the last
years: *The Naked Spur (L'appât)* [1953], *Bend of the River (Les Affa-
meurs)* [1952], *The Far Country (Jesuisun aventurier)* [1955], *The Man
from Laramie (L'Homme de la Plaine)* [1955]. Mann plays a straightforward game and never cheats with the rules of the genre; he calls a horse
a horse and doesn't try to make us believe he is shooting anything but
a western. Nevertheless, it is a good Shakespearian night that falls over
the fort in which the whole action of *The Last Frontier* takes place.

More clever than John Ford, Anthony Mann makes westerns less literary and less theatrical but more subtle. The characters seem more real and the relationships between them more true. In *The Last Frontier,* Victor Mature (who isn't always up to what he has to do, the only weakness of the movie) is an uneducated and wild scout who is forced to render some services to the garrison, where he is [barely] tolerated. After kissing, against her will, the colonel's wife, he will become her uncouth lover, the one she needs to make up for the colonel's lapses, the colonel whose mind is inexorably shaken up a bit more every day.

If Anthony Mann is a young filmmaker in spite of the fact he is nearly fifty, it is because he came to directing after being a theater actor and then a stage manager, then "talent scout" and producer. Of course, he is not yet as consecrated by the Oscars, the festivals, and the critics, but Marilyn Monroe is thinking of him to direct her in *The Brothers Karamazov* and he is, with Alfred Hitchcock, the favorite director of James Stewart, with whom he made nearly ten films.

The Last Frontier only makes the mistake of having a stupid French title, *La Charge des Tuniques bleues (The Charge of the Blue Coats),* and of having been released only in a rather badly dubbed French version. But that is not a good enough reason to ignore this beautiful movie, perhaps its author's best. (BFH)[6]

Compare this sympathetic notice to Truffaut's scathing dismissal of *The Searchers* and, by direct implication, the balance of Ford's late westerns in this next piece, which immediately followed the review of *The Last Frontier* in *Arts.* For Truffaut, *The Searchers* is mere "entertainment," which "bores us."

The Searchers (Prisonnière du désert) by John Ford.

John Ford, if Hollywood was a garrison, would be a warrant officer. Let's give our preference to General Fritz Lang, Colonel Anthony Mann, Lieutenant Robert Aldrich, or even Sergeant Raoul Walsh and Quartermaster-Sergeant Allan Dwan.

John Ford symbolizes an age of Hollywood, the one when good health prevailed over intelligence, craftiness over sincerity. This age has gone; Elia Kazan's and Nicholas Ray's movies make more money than John Ford's, poetry triumphs over entertainment.

Good health is a virtue, of course, but that is not enough, and John Ford, senile and repetitive, bores us. Always strong and daring heroines, eternal caricatures of Lillian Gish, always the husband giving them a big slap on the butt, always the same traditional old story and the manly brutality.

The starting point of the film is excellent: John Wayne, for five years, looks for two women kidnapped by Indians. Since money for these outmoded productions has become less, we don't have the right anymore, today, to the purple passages we used to be offered, but only to their *accounts.*

In *The Searchers,* the camera always arrives *after* the battle is over, with John Ford's train arriving late, to shoot the still-smoking ruins, still-warm corpses, and footprints or hoofprints. And since John Ford doesn't know how to film passing time, we feel as if two days, instead of five years, have elapsed between the first picture and the last one, and we regret the shabbiness, which is a vice this time.

The colors aren't ugly, and if you see the movie at the Rex Theater, the fact that you are allowed to smoke, not to mention the bewildering "fairyland of waters" [this is a reference to a bizarre stage presentation that preceded the screening of the film itself], makes up a little for the Fordian boredom. (BFH)[7]

In view of Ford's current canonization, this piece comes as something of a surprise. Most criticism directed against Ford's late westerns can be found, for the most part, in the daily press of the period, and no one today takes these contemporary notices too seriously (nor should they). Truffaut's own review is brief, cursory, and does not go into the detail and depth one might wish. There are points in Truffaut's analysis that might profitably be disputed, foremost among them Truffaut's contention that it is money, rather than design, that is behind Ford's decision not to show the massacre that triggers the film's action in the first reel. There seems no error in showing the result rather than the action that led to the result; Godard would later do much the same thing in *Le Mépris (Contempt)* and *Week-End (Weekend),* showing the result of car crashes in both films without documenting the activity of the crash itself. Yet it is worth pointing out that in Truffaut's own films, we are almost never given these "images after the act." In *Jules et Jim (Jules and Jim),* we see the car plunge off the bridge; we are witness to cremation as a step-by-step process. In *Tirez sur le Pianiste (Shoot the Piano Player),* bullets hit, corpses fall, violence is shown as an active agent that inexorably leads to specific results. So perhaps it is Truffaut's own prejudice against showing "still-smoking ruins" that colors his attack on this aspect of Ford's mise-en-scène. But as Truffaut notes, "John Ford symbolizes an age of Hollywood . . . when good health prevailed over intelligence, craftiness over sincerity. This age has gone." Ford, along with Hawks, had been recycling the same characters, situation, and dialogue for many years, using John Wayne as a cinematic presence so comfortable with his own on-screen persona that he has no need to create a new one, or even to embellish his "traditional . . . manly brutality."

Truffaut is getting tired of seeing the same scenes transplanted from one film to another, without any new material to give these "stations of the cross" added resonance or justification. One wonders if Truffaut would still stand behind his positive assessment of Kazan's films as "poetry," but in citing his own pantheon of "western" directors at the beginning of the review, complete with their appropriate military rank, Truffaut is clear that for him, Ford is a "warrant officer," inferior to Walsh or even Allan Dwan, both competent Hollywood professionals. Truffaut also finds fault with Ford's cinematic syntax, stating flatly that Ford "doesn't know how to film passing time," and criticizes the general "shabbiness" of Ford's visual structuring. The color of the film may not be "boring," and Truffaut is pleased that one can smoke if one wishes to, but none of this really compensates for the "Fordian boredom" that seems to suffocate Truffaut to the point that he can't wait to escape from the cinema.

Inasmuch as Truffaut dedicated his luminous tribute to the process of filmmaking, La Nuit américaine (Day for Night, 1973), to "Dorothy and Lillian Gish," it cannot be that Truffaut objects to the past, to the Victorian vision of a director like D. W. Griffith, or to the image projected by the Gish sisters in their films. What Truffaut objects to are Ford's "caricatures" of Lillian Gish, Ford's attempts to recreate and live within a world that has long since vanished. Ford, above all, offers nothing new, nothing inventive, nothing even remotely original. He recapitulates and restates, with increasing stubbornness, the values and social systems of the American frontier.

An index of this is Ford's 1953 remake of Judge Priest (1934), The Sun Shines Bright, in which he recasts Stepin Fetchit in the same role the actor played in the original film and Charles Winninger in the role originally created by Will Rogers. In both films, the structure of the white patriarchy is upheld over all other systems; blacks in both films (not just Fetchit) must appeal to Winninger or Rogers for aid and assistance; women are seen as peripheral characters, gossips, or objects of adoration, to be sought after and acquired. In 1934, one might argue that the film was a reflection of the period in which it was made, as well as a remembrance of the Old South; even then, the racist and sexist fabric of the film, though countenanced by the society of the '30s, is still offensive. To recreate the film in 1953 as a personal project, Ford went to Republic studios to make The Sun Shines Bright and worked on the film as coproducer; again, for better or worse, a director was using the facilities of a "B" studio to realize a project no other studio would support. Ford's intense desire to make the film is symptomatic of his embrace of the past, in opposition to all other value systems. It is not only Ford's style of filmmaking that is "outmoded," it is his view of the world.

However, by 1973, Truffaut's position on Ford had changed radically; indeed, he sought to completely repudiate his initial critical evaluation. In "About John Ford," a brief essay that appeared in the journal Action and which was subsequently reprinted by Truffaut in The Films in My Life (with the date altered to "1974"), Truffaut now finds Ford "royal," stating that "John Ford knew how to make the public laugh . . . or cry. The only thing he didn't know how to do was bore them."[8] This is quite an about-face from Truffaut's 1956 assessment that Ford "bores us." Seeking to account for this change of heart, Truffaut admits in the later essay that "for a long time when I was a journalist, I criticized his conceptions of women—I thought they were too nineteenth century—but when I became a director, I realized that because of him, a splendid actress like Maureen O'Hara was able to play some of the best female roles in the American cinema between 1941 and 1957." Truffaut closes the essay with the notation, "and, since Ford believed in God: God bless John Ford."

There is more, yet this later essay seems remarkably imprecise, and the passage quoted above never directly addresses the problem of Ford's "nineteenth-century conception of women." Is Truffaut suggesting that Ford's patriarchal stance in some way *allowed* O'Hara to do some of her best work in films? That Ford's Victorian instinct liberated the actress while simultaneously confining her within the rigors of Fordian narrative? Perhaps the essay can be partially, even wholly, explained by the fact that it was intended as a memorial to Ford, who died in 1973. Yet there seems no way to deny the fact that Truffaut's critical stance here had undergone a complete reversal, echoing, to my way of thinking, the reflexive romanticism of Truffaut's late films, which in themselves were softer, less urgent than the director's first efforts as an *auteur*.[9]

Before his climactic 1973 "about face," Truffaut is fairly consistent in his dislike for Ford's work. As charted by Walz, Truffaut "dismisses" (Walz's word) Ford's *Mogambo* in *Arts* 485 (October 13–19, 1954)[10] and then attacks Ford with even greater venom in a review of *The Long Grey Line* (*Arts* 527 [August 3–9, 1955]). Truffaut views *Mogambo* as "sentimental," and he affords it only scant consideration, as Walz contends.

Mogambo (*Mogambo*) [1953]
American film by John Ford.

Clark Gable and Ava Gardner are made for each other, but they do not know it. Clark Gable and Grace Kelly are not made for each other, but they think they are. Ava Gardner, a flighty and charming adventurer, will bring them all to their senses and reestablish the sentimental balance of one and the other.[11]

In his commentary on *The Long Grey Line*, according to Walz, Truffaut declaims Ford's "manifest technical incompetence" (Walz's phrase) and then (again quoting Walz) "lists Ford's films and claims not to like any. He concludes by stating that Ford is overrated, less important than Walsh, Mann, and Vidor."[12]

However, in 1955, Truffaut wrote two generally favorable notices on Jean Mitry's early critical text, *John Ford*, one in *Cahiers du Cinéma* 8.45 (March 1955), and another in *Arts* 506 (March 9–15, 1955). In *Arts*, according to Walz, Truffaut refers to Mitry's book as "indispensable."[13]

Also in 1955, Truffaut briefly recommends a revival screening of Ford's *Tobacco Road* in *Arts* 515 (May 11–17, 1955). Then comes Truffaut's attack on *The Searchers*. After that, there is literally nothing in Truffaut's writings on Ford until "About John Ford" in 1973.

What went on in this long gap between Truffaut's public pronouncements on Ford is anyone's guess. Nevertheless, it seems more than a little odd that Truffaut would choose to reprint only the hagiographic "About John Ford" in *The Films in My Life* and completely ignore, except in passing mention, the extensive corpus of writing against Ford he created in the mid-1950s. Certainly this is a revisionist strategy: it also gives us no real clue as to how Truffaut's critical reevaluation of Ford took place. Is Truffaut's 1973 assessment of Ford an accurate indication of his final feelings toward the director? Or is it a sentimental marker, a salute from one filmmaker to another, even if the writer is not particularly fond of Ford's work? Truffaut's repudiation of his initial critical work on Ford remains one of the most mysterious and inconsistent acts of Truffaut's career as a writer. There is no gradual awakening, no shift, just a sudden denial.

Truffaut's Cinema Diary

Truffaut's critical commentary is always wide-ranging because, during this period, the director-to-be was truly an omnivorous moviegoer. Unhampered by artificial distinctions of "A" or "B," Truffaut saw everything he could, regularly met with directors and screenwriters, and spent many hours in the Cinémathèque Française, using their collection of films, scripts, and stills to delve deeper into the history of cinema. One gets an idea of the breadth and depth of Truffaut's moviegoing experience from his "Petit journal intime du cinéma," which appeared from time to time in the pages of *Cahiers du Cinéma*.

In the material quoted below, Truffaut credits himself as the author of the journal; on another occasion, he credited "Robert Lachenay" as the diarist and included a photo of Lachenay to complement the deception.[14] The journal entries demonstrate that Truffaut was already acquiring quite a name for himself as a critic, and the young writer's connection with *Cahiers* and *Arts* offered Truffaut the chance to meet many of the most important filmmakers of the period, including Renoir, Rossellini, Hitchcock, and Bunuel. Here, then, are some selected excerpts from these "diaries."

Private Cinema Journal
by François Truffaut
*Tuesday, June 1
    13:00—I am accompanying [André] Bazin and his parrot to the Gare

de Lyon. They are leaving for Tourrette-sur-Loup, close to Vence, in order to take a rest from three months of fatigue in Sao Paolo and Cannes. . . .

21:00—Bunuel shows one of his latest films to a few friends and some friends of friends: *Robinson Crusoe,* with which the author of *El* [also known in the United States as *This Strange Passion*] takes for the first time to color (cinematographer: Alex Phillips). A good movie, excellent Technicolor.

*Wednesday, June 2

18:00—Cocktails at the Vendôme for the release of *El.* I always get extremely bored at this type of get-together, where everybody gives me the impression of being drunk . . . except myself. A big lady holds Bunuel by the neck—to the great confusion of the latter—and she yells roundabout: "He's a genius, he's a genius." Without doubt this movie *[El]* has something inspired: its key sentence is most likely the following: "the happiness of fools exasperates me."

*Friday, June 4

A very beautiful novel of Audiberti's, *Les Jardins et les fleuves (Gardens and Rivers),* is dedicated to Molière, to Chaplin, and to Jouvet. A lot in it concerns cinema. A book that should be read.

Jacques Flaud announces the results of statistics recently undertaken concerning the disenchantment of moviegoers: (1) 64 percent of the French go to the movies and 36 percent don't go anymore, of whom 30 percent went before the war and 6 percent never went. (2) 80 percent of French moviegoers choose their program deliberately. (3) 80 percent of French moviegoers go to the movies with company (how many among those in "delightful company"? That's something the rigid figures of statistics do not convey). I have to confess that I am indifferent toward this apparently pessimistic survey. All I see is that Autant-Lara is shooting four movies, one after the other. Becker two; and Gance is going to make a movie after a twelve-year silence; color is spreading; true or false, quality pays off right now and I claim that everything is as good as can be in the best of the cinematographer's worlds.

11:00—Doniol and I meet Bunuel in the Elisian "Select." A survey that I am carrying out on some film directors brings me to ask them the indiscreet question about never-to-be-proposed films since they are impossible to shoot. "I can say so," says Bunuel, "because I know that I will never be able to shoot it. It would be a rather realistic movie, but the characters would behave like insects: the heroine like a bee, the priest like a beetle, etc. . . . it would be a film about instinct." To Doniol, who questions him about *El,* he declares: "We had a good time shooting *El,* we never stopped laughing." Comparable to Renoir's words: "One has to have a good time while making movies; that is very important."

*Saturday, June 5

The great Alfred has arrived at the Côte d'Azur where, for the last three days, he has been shooting his new film, *To Catch a Thief,* with

Gary Grant, Grace Kelly, Charles Vanel, Brigitte Auber, Roland Lesaffre, Georgette Anys, Jean Martinelli, Michel Piccoli, René Blancard, Jean Hebey, Dominique Havrey, and Gérard Buhr. In VistaVision.

Jean de Létraz has died. I always thought he could have the best French scriptwriter. Let me explain: his screenplays were often sickening, sometimes low, and always vulgar. On hearing them, your laughter stuck in your throat, and you left the theater humiliated and disappointed; but the plot construction, the interrelations among plot events—in a word, the workmanship was irreproachable. I am convinced that the scripts of *Thérèse Raquin, Les Orgueilleux, La Minute de vérité,* etc., would have lost their gratuitousness and especially their clumsiness if mended by him.

*Sunday, June 6

French cinema must ignore the day of the Lord since, today, Sunday, the whole crew—or almost everybody—of *Ali Baba* is working on the "F" platform in Billancourt. I find everyone filled with respect for Fernandel, who proved himself as a purist yesterday. The dialogue involved the following: "So, I am leaving to Mecca," and "Fernand" rectified it himself: "So, I am leaving for Mecca." They are filming one scene in which Vilbert has to fall in the water from a height of 1.5 meters. At this moment, a thick pile of mattresses replaces the water that will be in the reverse shot. Vilbert falls and dislocates his knee a little; yesterday it was his shoulder. Fernandel spends his day making fun of Vilbert, who does not reply. The atmosphere of *Ali Baba* is very pleasant, and Becker, who pretends to be compassionate, is not immune to the fun.

*Monday, June 7

Jacques Audiberti has accepted an invitation to prepare an article for *Cahiers* every month, "Audiberti's Note," in which he will deposit his remarks as an dedicated moviegoer.

*Tuesday, June 8

In July, Gance is going to film *La Tour de Nesle,* with Pierre Brasseur and Sylvana Pampanin—in color. Producer: Fernand Rivers. On the phone Gance told me how excited he was: "*The Tower of Nesle* is *Lucrèce Borgia* as a student left back for the third time."

Otto Preminger has started shooting a second film in CinemaScope: *Carmen Jones.* The cast will be 100 percent black. Real exteriors in South Carolina, in Chicago, and in New York.

With *Land of the Pharaohs,* which he is shooting in Egypt (and in CinemaScope) from an original script by Faulkner, Howard Hawks has rediscovered the actor he used in *The Thing* and *Big Sky:* Dewey Martin. (Warnercolor process.)

In England, James Mason will be *Colonel Chabert* under the direction of Herbert Wilcox.

Jean Renoir will shoot *French Cancan [Only the French Can]* for which he is now writing the script and the dialogue. Shooting will take place beginning August in Eastmancolor.

René Clément is preparing a film in CinemaScope: *Barrage contre le Pacifique*; a Franco-Anglo-American coproduction.

*Wednesday, June 9

An appointment with Rossellini at 12:30 p.m. in the Hotel Raphael. I wait in the bar, fifteen minutes, half an hour, forty-five minutes; he arrives, he is charming; we visit. I find him bitter, a little depressed because of an odious press campaign that has lasted three to four years already: "It is morally very exhausting to have to work when despised." [15]

*Thursday, June 10

In "La Gazette Littéraire," Michel Beccarie writes about the book *Mémoires d'une starlett* by Gaby Bruyère: "Gaby Bruyère certainly talks a little too often about her hips, her breasts, and her thighs, but after all, those are her working tools, and she asks God's forgiveness for having to use them too openly." In short, a pair of thighs has to be either open or closed.

*Friday, June 11

I crossed paths with Ingrid Bergman—who was humming—in the halls of the Opera. Photographers are coming in for the press conference. A lady that I can see only from the back brings a microphone close to Rossellini's mouth; she must call this "an interview," although you hear only her. I don't know exactly why, but I think irresistibly about *The Rules of the Game*. Now I know: the interviewer is Lise Elina. "We are on the airfield of Le Bourget, etc."

*Saturday, June 12

A few minutes with Renoir in the Théâtre de Paris during a pause in rehearsal for "Julius Caesar." He tells me how much he enjoys working on *French Cancan:* "I wrote a first script; then I remade it into a second one, which is much better, which is very funny. Oh! It will be very nice."

6:00—a little walk on the set of *Ali Baba*; there is a basin filled with water. I walk around it carefully, and I am surprised no one falls into it. "But," says one of the assistants, "you should have been here three days ago. First it was the producer, Adolphe Osso, who came to see Becker; on the poorly lit set, Becker holds out his hand, Osso advances to shake it, and 'splash!' in the water; a little later the same happened to a gardener. Both of them kept a dignified expression."

9:00—We are only five—among us Henri Langlois—to watch *La Tosca* in the Cinémathèque's small screening room. It's film directed by Carl Koch, which was started by Renoir; true, the program was not announced in the papers. That's really too bad.

*Thursday, June 17

At the chemistry museum, a "Homage to United Artists" was presented by the Cinémathèque Françoise. Lots of people, and of the best; all sorts of Mauriacs: François, Marie-Claude, Claude; Preston Sturges, Bunuel, Becker, Grémillon, Pierre Prévert, etc. . . . Henri Langlois opens the session with a recital of the history of United Artists. Then it is time for the screenings: a reel of the great *Orphans of the Storm* by Griffith, a reel of *The Black Pirate* by Douglas Fairbanks, and especially three reels of *The Gold Rush,* which we will be able to see in its entirety—in a few years. The second part of the screening is modern. First, ten minutes of *High Noon* [1952] (that will be the only excerpt not applauded all evening; isn't that moral?), two well-chosen reels of [Renoir's] *The River,* and finally a half-hour of Bunuel's *Robinson Crusoe.* All in all, an excellent evening.

*Friday, June 18

Le Cardinet, the movie theater with the most intelligent programming in Paris—together with the Studio Parnasse—advertises this week *Story of a Love Affair* [*Cronaca di un Amore,* Michaelangelo Antonioni's first feature film, made when the director was thirty-eight years old]. I owe it to history to point out that, when this movie was projected at the "Rendez-vous of Biarritz" in 1949, Jacques Rivette and I extolled it to the skies, and that we were also the first French journalists to interview Antonioni. Now, I will feel that much better about it when I state that we were deceived. In four years, I have seen *Story of a Love Affair* four times, and each time I liked it a little less; this time my disappointment is total. Few bad movies abuse us more than once or twice; the problem here is that *Story of a Love Affair* is not a bad movie; but it is an imitation of a good film, like a caricature of all the directors we love, from Bresson to Preminger, not to mention Renoir, Borzage, Rossellini, and so many others. What insincerity, what simulation, what a deception!

*Monday, June 21

I had the chance to see "privately" *River of No Return,* Preminger's first film in CinemaScope; it may not be the best Preminger, but it is definitely the best of the six CinemaScopes I have watched so far; between *Niagara* and *River of No Return,* Marilyn has learned to sing; a gorgeous Marilyn who rows down the river in jeans and a corset.

*Tuesday, June 22

As a direct result of the (well-deserved) success of *Touchez pas au Grisli* and the (not too undeserved) success of *Les Femmes s'en balancent,* these films are going into production in France: *La Peau des autres* (Jean Sacha), *Chéri Bibi* (Paul Mesnier), *Bonnes à tuer* (Henri Decoin), *Les Veuves* (Clouzot), *Série Noire* (Pierre Foucaud), *La Mort peut attendre* (Chr. Stengel), etc.

*Wednesday, June 23

Our friend Eric Rohmer, whose excellent scenario for *La Roseraie* (*The Rose Garden*), published in Number 4 of *Cahiers,* we remember—presented his short film in 16mm at the Maison des Lettres, taken from

Bérénice by Edgar A. Poe; this is, without any doubt, one of the best amateur films, one among few that hardly suggest that their format represents a shortcoming. A vogue for 16mm film should be started again.[16]
*Thursday, June 24

    "What's the matter?"

A young man with his hair freshly greased approaches a pretty, although slightly vulgar, girl. He wraps his arms around her and tries in vain to kiss her on the lips. He gets angry: "Listen, what would you say if you loved a girl who . . . well, if you were about to see your dentist?" By means of an art that we love, here we are at the dentist's office: "Scientific tests prove that, in seven cases out of ten, Whatchamagate instantly gets rid of bad breath, in the mouth," the last words being spoken under the breath, as if regretfully, like a required obscenity, as if this operetta dentist realized the ugliness of the role he is playing. This little film, with a thousand variations, takes on an even more abject air when the girl is the one chosen as victim. When will they finally decide to throw into prison the man whose idea it was to poison the evening of thousands of fine folks by telling them, in veiled terms, these disgraceful little stories?
*Saturday, June 26

I have held in my hands the manuscript of the most beautiful book on cinema. It concerns a monumental text on Jean Vigo, his life and his oeuvre. In forty-eight typewritten pages, the author P. E. Sales Gomes has reconstructed the day-to-day filming of *Zéro de conduite*. One hundred pages more are devoted to *L'Atalante*. How can one not be upset by the text about Vigo's death? It would be deplorable if this work does not get published, all the more so since critical unanimity has been reached on the *auteur* of *L'Atalante*. I am convinced that when this book is published—and it must be published in its entirety—one could not write two lines anymore on Jean Vigo without referring to it.
*Sunday, June 27

I have watched *La Belle Ensorceleuse* (*I Married a Witch* [1942]) again in the Studio Parnasse. One never laughs, and smiles little. The work strikes one first because of its dryness, the absence of all verve. The best script trick will never replace a last-minute invention, an improvised eccentricity. That's why we do not follow our elders when they pay homage to Jean Renoir and René Clair at the same time. Not one film of Clair equals Renoir's *Tire au flanc* [1928] in drollery and in inventiveness. And, for the last ten years, René Clair has taken on too much the role of official entertainer. He makes films for old ladies who go twice a year to the movies, in an old chauffeured Delahaye, one of the two times to see the latest masterpiece of Sir Laurence Olivier! Our youth prefers, I think, and rightfully so, friend Hulot over Sir René Clair.
*Monday, June 28

At the celebration of Luis Mariano's tenth birthday, Alfred Hitchcock

. . . received a few columnists in his apartment at the Hotel George V. This forty-five-minute conference will hold such a place in the history of cinema that the readers of *Cahiers* will not be surprised when we keep coming back to it, and this not later than in the next issue. Since I do not for anything in the world want to steal the thunder of my friend Claude Chabrol, who, according to plan, will tell you all about this not very ordinary event, I can only deplore the nonfunctioning of the wall plugs at the George V, since I could not possibly connect our lie detector (that's what we call our tape recorder); the truth serum did not circulate, the little lamp was not lighted, the red light was not turned on. While waiting for the next issue, please refer (for laughs) to your favorite gossip-columnist (not one of them was absent from the roll call).

*Tuesday, June 29

Hitchcock yesterday, Hitchcock today. At the Cinémathèque, for the first and only time in France, his last silent movie, *The Manxman*—preceding immediately the famous *Blackmail* in chronological order—is being shown. It is certainly a very fine movie, in which many scenes clearly foreshadow *I Confess.*

*Wednesday, June 30

I would like to take this opportunity to say everything that goes through my head (insofar as it is of course related to the cinematograph) in order to say some good things of a not-so-well-known director, Norbert Carbonnaux, and his still-unreleased movie: *Les Corsaires du Bois de Boulogue.* I do not know Norbert Carbonnaux, but I have seen his movie and I have found out that the scheming distributors are planning to release it in the middle of August, when nobody will be around to watch it. *The Pirates of the Bois de Boulogne* is a very funny movie, different from *Hulot* but equally interesting, and one senses that the people who made it must have lots of more and more comical ideas in their heads, [each funnier than the last]. While I am on the topic, I am worried about the fate of another film, also French and also comical, that received the successive titles of *Le Toubab, Monsieur Dupont homme blanc,* and *Le Sorcier Blanc.* Why has this excellent film, unusual and charming, with an abundance of rare inventiveness, not yet been released, even though I saw it, finished, more than two years ago? The film's director is Claude Lalande.

The least pseudo-psychological or pseudo-police or pseudo-phenomenological or pseudo this or that rubbish is being offered on the cinema circuits, while two likeable good movies, and above all, dammit, extremely *funny* movies, are bullied by the distributors. What does that mean?

8:00—Apparently, it has been an agitated afternoon at the "Film Standards Commission." Hitchcock's *Dial M for Murder* has been projected; the representatives of various ministries, Justice, National Education, etc. . . . were asking for the scene of the murder to be cut. Anyone who has heard about this movie or anyone who knows the script realizes that the film loses its entire raison d'être if this scene is amputated. Professional indignation reached its height with everyone being enthused about Hitchcock's work; it took another replay of the murder scene to convince these gentlemen finally, and we have to believe there is justice since the movie obtained its visa in the end, with the exception of one vote.

*Friday, July 2

Certain readers wonder why—with the exception of four or five greats—we hardly treasure French cinema in our hearts, whereas many American "B" directors (Anthony Mann, Douglas Sirk, Raoul Walsh, etc.) are praised kindly in the columns reserved for "Notices about Other Movies."

I have before me a press clipping from *France-Soir* dated Tuesday, June 29, that might make things clear to them. With regard to *Fils de Caroline Chérie*: "*Cécil Saint-Laurent had had the foresight to write in his script a battle in* [deep canyons] *and to make his heroes cross very photogenic streams. But before shooting, Jean Devaivre prudently had a peasant—who volunteered as a guinea pig—check the temperature of the water as well as the violence of the stream that appeared to be capable of swallowing a whole army. As he was only pulled out with great effort, half-frozen and choking, the skirmishes will take place on a flat and dry location.*"

This refusal to "set things up," this backing out before a difficulty, this thumbing the nose at danger, in a word this cowardice condemns us never to see a good adventure movie made in France again. And yet, Jean Devaivre is perhaps the only French series director to have shot a good detective film *(La Dame d'onze heures)*. All of Jeanson's intellect was necessary to make sure that no one would notice that *Fanfan la Tulipe* was filmed according to the same principles of the hidden torrent. However, isn't it by dint of retreating from the stream that French cinema will fall down the precipice?

*Saturday, July 3

[The following comments appear under a photograph of Abel Gance.]

We are living in a year of cinema in which few evenings are as exciting as the one yesterday at the Cardinet Theater. The occasion was the inauguration of a cycle of screenings, along with an exhibition, dedicated to Abel Gance. First we watched excerpts of *Napoléon*; the astonishing sound version that is not well known. Then Abel Gance himself commented in the dark on the remarkable experiments with his process, the "pictograph," projected for the first time in public. Finally, the admirable movie *Un Grand amour de Beethoven* was shown. Gance had had the painful surprise of seeing amputated certain of the scenes to which he was most attached; "if the veins of a film are cut, the blood cannot possibly circulate," he said. In spite of these most scandalous mutilations, the movies of Abel Gance maintain a strength and an effectiveness that has increased in time. There is not one shot that does not determine a moment of film history. His Beethoven, extraordinarily played by Harry Baur—evokes Rodin's Balzac lifting up with him the earth in which his feet are implanted. Let's mention finally that, because of the Cardinet retrospective that will last until mid-August, *La Fin du Monde, La Folie du docteur Tube,* and excerpts of *Napoléon, La Roue, La Capitaine Fracasse,* and *J'accuse* can be seen again.

*From Arles—Sunday, July 11

Yesterday evening, 8,000 spectators were present at this city's Roman arena to view the unique production of *Julius Caesar,* staged by Renoir. André Bazin and Maurice Scherer [Eric Rohmer] will talk to you in more detail about this memorable evening in Arles. Jean Renoir is a filmmaker, the filmmaker before everything and everyone; that's why I would not give up one shot of any of his movies for this nevertheless admirable spectacle. It must be moving for the author of thirty-five masterpieces in film format to have the opportunity for the first time to be present at the public's reactions to a spectacle that's in the process of unfolding. But has he not experienced any uneasiness when seeing the actors escape him—the actors to whom he knows how to communicate, when they are in front of the camera, to all of them at once and one by one, shot after shot, the precise measure of his genius? I imagine he would answer as does Camilla [in Renoir's *Carrosse d'Or (The Golden Coach)*]: "a little."

The most fervent admirers of Renoir had come by hitchhiking, on scooter; anonymous and yet familiar faces who had met at one movie theater or another where, for a year, the author of the *The Golden Coach* has shown himself a few times. Two soldiers had come especially from Baden-Baden; there were also former students of the I.D.H.E.C. and of Vaugirard, the intern from *Ali Baba,* Marguerite Renoir's assistant, and numerous devoted "fans" from ciné-clubs.

Renoir has placed among the extras all those who were not able to obtain a role; all this is extremely cordial. Three months of work have ended in this excellent evening. Henceforth, Renoir is going to dedicate himself to the preparation of his next film, *French Cancan,* which he will make in Paris in October. (BFH/SK)[17]

In these brief diary jottings, Truffaut demonstrates again his love for all films, but particularly for those films that might be considered "fugitive" works, made under duress and underappreciated by the mainstream critics. He even addresses the issue of his affection for "B" films directly, admitting that often his column finds more to praise in the films of Anthony Mann than in the most polished, lavishly budgeted French production. Truffaut has his idols, Gance, Hitchcock, and Renoir among them, but in all cases he chooses the objects of his admiration rather than following critical tradition.

Remakes

Truffaut's immersion in the American "B" film was so complete that he could unhesitatingly spot an indifferent "remake" reworking the concerns of its more illustrious predecessor. In the case of Vincent Sherman's *Affair in Trinidad*, the film owes debts to *Gilda* (1946; Dir. Charles Vidor), *Notorious* (1946; Dir. Alfred Hitchcock), and *Key Largo* (1948; Dir. John Huston), among numerous other possible candidates, and Truffaut locates all of these borrowings within the work. Still, he dismisses *Affair in Trinidad* as a minor exercise of no particular import, while using the opportunity to offer an argument against the commercial (as well as critical) success of *Gilda*. For Truffaut, *Gilda* is a manifestly cynical enterprise. "Isn't it time to admit," Truffaut asks, "that *Gilda*'s qualities were primarily negative, and that it owed more to cunning, even to foxiness, than to sincerity—the essential virtue of American cinema?" There is little doubt that much of *Gilda*'s resonance, even today, resides in its "going against the grain" of generic assumptions, and that the bisexuality of George Macready's character in that film (for one immediate example) was a calculated attempt to shock and disorient contemporary audiences, weary from World War II's endless war-centered and/or escapist product mill.

Gilda's primary quality is its sense of cultural displacement, of people outside of war. One memorable moment in *Gilda*'s narrative occurs when Glenn Ford's character interrupts his recitative of the "romantic" triangle that is the center of the work to remark, "Oh, and about that time the war ended," suggesting that in the aftermath of war, the importance of that conflict as the center of all attentions is justifiably diminished and any references to it must necessarily be elegiac or glibly offhanded. Yet *Affair in Trinidad* lacks even the freshness of calculated invention. *Affair* is only a knockoff of a "constructed" genre, the disillusioned post-World War II film. Rather than being possessed of the genuine cynicism and world-weariness present in these informing works, *Affair*'s machinations are synthetic and do not rise from the conditions that created the earlier films. This is not surprising, in that *Affair* was produced in the early 1950s, when the war had already begun to recede into the realm of fabulism; the more deeply felt works (for all their commercial calculation) that so strongly influenced *Affair* were made right after the war.

The plot of *Affair in Trinidad* does indeed bear more than a casual resemblance to the narrative structure of *Gilda*. Rita Hayworth (seen in *Gilda* to great effect) is once again a nightclub singer, and Glenn Ford, this time cast as her brother-in-law, is her costar in the enterprise. Together, the two team up to discover the identity of the person who murdered Rita's husband. Stephen Geray provides background support in both *Gilda* and *Affair*. Much of *Affair*'s running time is devoted to Hayworth performing on the floor of the club, in a deliberate attempt (or so it would seem) to remind the viewer of her "striptease" sequence in *Gilda*. Though Truffaut finds "there is nothing in it for the misogynists," one is hard pressed to agree with this assessment. The film relies almost entirely upon the presentation of Hayworth's body to "entertain" the viewer and is notable for its extreme objectification in body display. *Affair* is yet another example of the male spectatorial gaze that underlines classical Hollywood cinema.

Affair in Trinidad (L'Affaire de Trinidad) (1952)
American movie by Vincent Sherman.

Without any doubt, the comparison of this movie with *Gilda*—which it seems to want to reflect—is hardly flattering for it. But isn't it time to admit that *Gilda*'s qualities were primarily negative, and that it owed more to cunning, even to foxiness, than to sincerity—the essential virtue of American cinema?

I admit being sensitive to virginity such as found in the perverse Rosalind in *The Lady from Shanghai,* and in the even more perverse Gilda. Here, Rita Hayworth calls herself Christopher; she is a widow, and mourning becomes her as much as the warm feelings she has [presumably toward costar Glenn Ford].

The scenario, not only closely inspired by *Gilda* but also by *Notorious* and by *Key Largo,* is less clever.

Finally, there is nothing in it for the misogynists, in this movie whose chief virtue is virtue itself. (SK)[18]

Truffaut's briefer notices on films are striking in two characteristics: they waste no time getting to those aspects of the film that most intrigue the young critic and are often so epigrammatic that they require the reader to, in a sense, "complete" the notice. Three very short critiques for issue number 484 of *Arts* demonstrate Truffaut's use of this "gestural" technique, which shows respect for his readership while simultaneously (and not unconsciously) elevating Truffaut's position as a critic. In Truffaut's capsule review of Robert Wise's 1953 *The Desert Rats*, another "carbon copy" film that reworks (as Truffaut notes) the central conceits of Henry Hathaway's 1951 film *The Desert Fox* (while simultaneously recycling James Mason in the role of Rommel), Truffaut does little more than note the similarities between the two films, allude to censorship problems that prevented French audiences from seeing *The Desert Fox*, and then redact a brief portion of the film's narrative. It is left up to the reader to divine Truffaut's opinion of the later work, although by noting that French audiences are permitted to view *The Desert Rats* "in exchange" for *The Desert Fox*, it certainly seems as if Truffaut views Wise's film as a second-best proposition. Truffaut feels that *The Desert Rats* delivers to French audiences "a Rommel without prestige or glory," and he demonstrates the inherent ridiculousness of any censorial enterprise. Wise's film is inherently compromised by Hollywood's desire to please all factions of its viewing audience, on both a national and international scale.

The Desert Rats (Les Rats du désert)
American film by Robert Wise.

We will never see *The Desert Fox* in France, a film by Hathaway, which is forbidden by censure because Rommel appeared as a nice guy in it.

So here, in exchange, is *The Desert Rats,* in which, just as in the former film, James Mason takes on the role of Rommel, but this time as a Rommel without prestige or glory. Whereas Hathaway's film starts out in October 1942, right before the battle of El Alamein, Wise's movie begins in April 1941, and it is located at Tobruk, where, for eight months, a company of Australians, surrounded in a fortress, succeeded in defending the place against the elite troops of the African Korps. (SK)[19]

More than this Truffaut does not tell us. He does not have contempt for Wise's film, but he also holds no great admiration for it. Do we really need to be told any more? Truffaut, cognizant of the shared knowledge of his constituents, can let the matter rest here. The title of Wise's film should tell us a good deal about the project: Rommel, a "fox" in 1951, has become a "rat" by 1953.

Truffaut's review of Pinoteau's *Le Grand Pavois*, in the same issue of *Arts* is more cursory still. Truffaut asserts that the film's "topic, in its flexibility and its lovable pretentiousness, has nothing damning in itself," but it is left to the viewer and reader to discover whether or not Truffaut feels that the film succeeds in preventing its sentimental theme from spilling over into bathos. One gets a feeling of Truffaut's grudging admiration for the work, if only because he does not dismiss the work altogether (something we have certainly seen that he is capable of doing). As with the brief review of *The Desert Rats,* this notice could be interpreted in a number of ways, and Truffaut seems pleased to have us do our share of the critical labor.

Le Grand Pavois (The Great Bulwark)
French film by Jack Pinoteau.

In the course of a crusade on the training ship *Jeanne d'Arc,* a marine officer regains his faith in a profession he was ready to abandon.

Such a topic, in its flexibility and its lovable pretentiousness, has nothing damning in itself. (SK)[20]

But is the film "damned"? This very brief notice shows us Truffaut at his most personal and idiosyncratic. So slight that it barely qualifies as

a critical notice, these few lines nevertheless give us the theme and plot
of the film and gently remind us that this pretentious topic has been
tackled before. Is Pinoteau's film successful? Probably not. Reaching for
very little, the film still fails to accomplish what it sets out to do. Is it
really necessary to acknowledge both the film's failure as well as the lack
of ambition of its predecessors?

The last film Truffaut considers in issue 484 of *Arts* is *Little Boy Lost*
(1953; Dir. George Seaton). An embarrassing ode to the American colo-
nial instinct, the film stars Bing Crosby, driven by conscience to return
to France at the end of World War II to seek out his son conceived during the war. As Truffaut notes, the authorities initially present Crosby
with "a little starving boy . . . [whom Crosby] does not recognize." Yet,
the film ultimately offers its audience the traditional patriarchal closure
afforded by a "happy ending." Truffaut tells us that "despite everything,
[Crosby] ends up by taking the boy back to the U.S., where little boys
eat their fill."

This phrase damns the film more effectively than any critical broad-
side ever could. As with the final shot of Lang's *American Guerilla in
the Philippines*, in which the natives line up with American flags along
the shoreline, Truffaut correctly excoriates this insidiously complacent
signification of America's vision of peace and plenty for all. Unlike Lang
in *American Guerilla*, Seaton is entirely unconscious of any ironies his
scenario contains. Truffaut is not. "The little boys who eat their fill" are
not only those children victimized by the war but also the Bing Crosbys
of the world who have never really grown up. These "little boys" have
had one last chance to flaunt their irresponsibility during World War II,
as soldiers "liberated" country after country, while simultaneously dis-
placing the native social fabric with their own values and desires (as
evidenced by Crosby's wartime "romance" with a woman who is now
conveniently dead, thus avoiding any question of moral responsibility
toward the child's mother). Not even the skillful and luminous Gabrielle
Dorziat (so memorable in Cocteau's 1948 film of *Les Parents terribles*)
can redeem this film, which sinks beneath the combined weight of its
treacly narrative and its crushingly neolithic sense of mise-en-scène.

Little Boy Lost (Le Petit Garçon Perdu)
American film by George Seaton.

An American journalist [Bing Crosby] comes back to France after the
Liberation, in order to find his son, whose French mother has passed
away. They present a little starving boy to him, whom he does not recognize. Despite everything, he ends up by taking the boy back to the
U.S., where little boys eat their fill. (SK)[21]

What is also remarkable about these three notices, other than their
abruptness and brevity, is the complete lack of any consideration by

Truffaut of cinematographic values. Camera placement, lighting, editorial structures, movement within the frame—none of these factors seem to concern the young critic. If Truffaut requires his public to "complete" these brief commentaries, he also indirectly states, through omission, his lack of interest in the mise-en-scène employed by Seaton, Pinoteau, and Wise in these films. In the case of *The Desert Rats*, Truffaut is dealing with the work of a director whom he manifestly admires, for Wise is the director of the "Bressonian" (Truffaut's word) *Born to Kill*.

In Truffaut's review of Don Weis's 1953 *Remains to Be Seen*, an MGM musical comedy/murder mystery starring June Allyson, Van Johnson, Angela Lansbury, Louis Calhern, and Dorothy Dandridge, we can see the other side of Truffaut as critic: champion of the underappreciated artist. *Remains to Be Seen* is based on a stage play by Howard Lindsay and Russel Crouse, as adapted by future-best-selling novelist Sidney Sheldon. *Remains to Be Seen* betrays its theatrical origins at nearly every turn: it is obviously a photographed stage play. The film is also undermined by MGM's flat, brightly lit house style of the period, which is functional yet works against the establishment of an individual signature. One might reasonably expect Truffaut to dismiss the film as competent but unmemorable. Weis is self-effacing, so much so that at times his presence seems evanescent. Yet he has a light and buoyant touch that Truffaut finds attractive. As with Truffaut's reviews of *Tuna Clipper* and *Niagara*, June Allyson's skirt seems one of the principal attractions of the film for the young critic; nor, characteristically, does Truffaut deny that this is the case.

Remains to Be Seen (Drôle de Meurte)
American film by Don Weis.

Cahiers du Cinéma has lately omitted mentioning an excellent American comedy entitled *Dream Wife (La Femme rêvée)* (1953), directed by Sidney Sheldon, who was until then known as scenario-writer. Neither do we know much about Don Weis, who is responsible for the direction of the charming film *Remains to Be Seen,* based on a script of the same Sidney Sheldon. Everybody loves June Allyson, the young woman who has her sex appeal in her voice, even though this does not ignore the fact that she is pleasant to look at as well. I particularly recommend one of her skirts: the one with vertical stripes, split on the side. Van Johnson always does well as a victimized character. Ending with June Allyson, let us remind ourselves that she played one of her best roles alongside Bogart in an admirable film—which *Cahiers* again has forgotten to mention: *Battle Circus* [1953] *(Le Cirque infernal)* by Richard Brooks. Three other movies by Don Weis are in the making; June Allyson will again star in one of them; in another, Debbie Reynolds—whose gray pleated skirt that she wore in *Singin' in the Rain (Chansons sous la Pluie)* [1952] nobody has forgotten. Many good hours to look forward to. (SK)[22]

As with Truffaut's appreciation of *Niagara*, as well as Beaudine's *Tuna Clipper*, much of Truffaut's admiration for the film seems to reside in June Allyson's skirt, and not Weis's mise-en-scène. Yet Truffaut goes out of his way at the end of the notice to note that Weis has three new films forthcoming. It is a mood that attracts Truffaut to *Remains to Be Seen*, as well as the presence of Weis, whom he senses in each shot. Weis's *Remains to Be Seen* belongs to that most problematic of all cinema ventures, the adapted stage property. Truffaut has no particular dislike for theatrical presentation in films. Renoir's *Golden Coach*, a meditation upon the process of theatrical presentation and acting styles, divided into strict three-act structure, is a film that Truffaut greatly admires. But if a film is to be theatrical, then it must be reflexive, acknowledging its source, and embrace (rather than seek to escape) the staging that first gave it an audience. Weis's relaxed, obedient, and smoothly assured camera work in *Remains to Be Seen* never ignores the many entrances, exits, crosses, and bits of staged business in the source play. Weis capitalizes on the original staging, and his film seems all the more sincere because of it. Surely this is a quality that Truffaut prized more than any other: that a film remain faithful to its subject, staging, and conception. Weis's film fulfills these requirements, and Truffaut deems it a modest yet genuine success.

In the case of the American melodrama *The Glass Wall*, a film by the director Maxwell Shane, Truffaut finds much less to like. Gloria Grahame's "beautiful eyes" are assets of the film, but obviously these attributes alone are not enough to save this ponderous cold war film from being a failure. Truffaut, while harboring the instincts of a "fan" in his idolatry of American actresses, particularly "maudit" personalities, refuses to abandon his critical standards, even in the case of Gloria Grahame, whose other work (particularly in Fritz Lang's *The Big Heat* [1953]) he greatly admires.

The Glass Wall (*Les Frontières de la vie*) [1953]
American film by Maxwell Shane.

If, as is the case for most of the *Cahiers* writers, the beautiful eyes of Gloria Grahame make you die of love, then wait a little longer, until another movie is released, because this movie can only make you hate them. I am exaggerating on purpose, because how can one hate Gloria? *The Glass Wall*, the wall in question, is—in case you want to know— the façade of the U.N. ["l'O.N.U."]; and that's that. (SK)[23]

In issue 581 of *Arts*, Truffaut offers a brief consideration of Norman Krasna's *The Ambassador's Daughter* (1956). Oddly enough, Krasna, who produced, directed, and wrote the original story for this film, also wrote the story for Fritz Lang's *Fury* (1936).[24] *The Ambassador's Daughter* is a very slight film, a fact that Truffaut acknowledges in the second sentence of his review, and one that Truffaut finds "pretty-pretty," rife with commercialism (the continual references to Christian Dior's costuming throughout the film), and predictable. Truffaut is able to guess the ending of the film "within ten minutes." As for Krasna's visual instinct, Truffaut finds it obvious and unimaginative: the artificial "symmetry" Krasna pursues in the film becomes mere "fussiness."

The Ambassador's Daughter (La Fille de l'Ambassadeur) by Norman Krasna.

A G.I. who can't wait to kiss a girl is worth every bit as much, she claims, as a plenipotentiary minister. That's the moral of this minor work that rehashes, with the sexes reversed, the thesis of *Roman Holiday,* which is the same as that of "Puss in Boots." We are a bit tired of these pretty-pretty stories, whose ending we guess within ten minutes. If Christian Dior, whose name appears everywhere in this film, did not finance *The Ambassador's Daughter,* let's say that the authors are a little over-thankful. Dior, as a matter of fact, designed the dresses that don't succeed in making us believe that Olivia de Havilland is a young girl, much less the daughter of an ambassador, and Myrna Loy her little sister. Norman Krasna's very ordinary mise-en-scène is worried about symmetry to such a point that it becomes fussiness: candlestick on the right, candlestick on the left. Everything is centered on the middle of the screen. In keeping with this impeccable axis, seven extras on each side, etc. You could choose not to see *The Ambassador's Daughter,* or you could only see the first half—the best. (BFH)[25]

It is not so much the lack of ambition displayed by *The Ambassador's Daughter* that dismays Truffaut; it is the lack of intelligence or novelty that is more of an affront. Truffaut, as we've seen, admired some very simple films, such as Beaudine's *Tuna Clipper.* In Truffaut's review of *Pete Kelly's Blues,* a film by that peculiarly obsessed American director, Jack Webb,[26] Truffaut does not dislike Webb nearly as much as he finds fault with Krasna. Both are inescapably minor *auteurs;* yet the comparison between the two men is all the more apt since Webb wrote, produced, directed, and acted in *Pete Kelly's Blues* and Krasna wrote, produced, and directed *The Ambassador's Daughter.* Webb is "more skillful than gifted, more sincere than brilliant, more likeable than prestigious"; Truffaut also notes that since Webb learned his trade in "television, he is not reluctant to look straight at the camera, that is to say look us straight in the eyes."[27] Webb is "shrewd," but he is not without talent: Truffaut cannot restrain himself from liking *Pete Kelly's Blues,* and even he admires the cynical calculation that informs its construction.

Pete Kelly's Blues (La Peau d'un autre) by Jack Webb.

We know that American cinema likes biographies. We also know that

American cinema has been given the benefit, for the past fifteen years, of Orson Welles's influence. Here is thus an ingenuous and kindly Wellesian biography of an apparently not too famous and not too glorious musician, Pete Kelly, who, as early as 1917, dedicated himself to New Orleans jazz band music.

Jack Webb is a filmmaker who is more skillful than gifted, more sincere than brilliant, more likeable than prestigious. Which is to say that his film is nice to see. He is, this good fellow who vaguely looks like José Ferrer, in every scene and nearly in every shot. Since he learned his trade working for television, he is not reluctant to look straight at the camera, that is to say to look us straight in the eyes.

Jack Webb, who is a shrewd man, knows perfectly well that one-half of the young audience likes jazz and the other half likes fights. So he made a film about jazz with fights. Janet Leigh is not that unpleasant to look at, but why on earth does she look so mean?

One can easily see *Pete Kelly's Blues,* which Jack Webb wrote, produced, directed, and performed himself. [This last sentence seems open to interpretation: Truffaut here may be saying that the film is easy to see because it is playing nearly everywhere in Paris, since the film was released in a "saturation booking" pattern, blanketing all the popular theaters simultaneously for a period of several weeks; or he may mean that the film is "easily see[n]" because of the simplicity of its construction.] (BFH)[28]

However, Truffaut cares much less for the work of another actor/director, Ray Milland. Milland won the Academy Award for Best Actor in 1945 for Billy Wilder's *The Lost Weekend.* Milland also made at least one creditable film as a director (which I suspect Truffaut liked a great deal more than *A Man Alone*), the post-apocalyptic thriller *Panic in Year Zero* (1962), starring Milland, Jean Hagen, and Joan Freeman. *Panic in Year Zero,* made for American International, was nevertheless damaged by the inclusion of a preexisting music score by Les Baxter, originally created for another film. This score worked entirely against the mood of Milland's film. Milland fought against the use of the music, to no avail; an example, if one were needed, of the downside of low-budget filmmaking.

A Man Alone, made for Republic, is every bit the formulaic western that Truffaut feels it to be. In every film he directed, Milland was forced to use his services as an actor as a bargaining chip. Even then, it was only the marginal studios, such as American International or Republic, that gave Milland a chance to direct. In Milland's case, he most often found, not freedom of expression at the minors, but the drudgery of the "B" picture assembly line at its most stultifying.

A Man Alone (Un Homme traqué) by Ray Milland.

As an *auteur,* I don't care too much for Ray Milland because of what

I can read on his face, even when he is impersonating a character: conceit, duplicity, solemn stupidity, and all sorts of other petty and unpleasant things. One can make mistakes, and I was willing to change my mind when I saw Ray Milland, who directed himself in *A Man Alone*. Alas! Never was he less genuine, more unbearably a sinister show-off than in this film, the script of which is a bunch of clichés. Hunted down, this mysterious cowboy is innocent. He must, in order to avoid being lynched, hide and discover who is guilty of what he is accused of. Where does he take cover? In the sheriff's house, no less. The sheriff is dying on the second floor while, on the first floor, his daughter plays around with our wretched hero. Ray Milland isn't any better as a director than he is as an actor. Do we have to use the word mise-en-scène for this story, which is recorded as a TV programme would be? Mary Murphy, the heroine of *l'Equipée Sauvage,* is, like Janet Leigh, an interesting actress, but she is hard to direct because of her harshness; she is pretty bad in this movie, in spite of her nice figure. It is no use to go and see *A Man Alone,* or to stake anything on Ray Milland's career as a director. (BFH)[29]

Truffaut's assessment, though harsh, seems appropriate. Milland's work as a director is remarkably even, though his work as an actor demonstrates more range than Truffaut seems willing to give him credit for. Of Milland's other films as a director, perhaps *The Safecracker* (1958) is one of his better works. The opening sequence of that film, in which Milland, as the title character, breaks into a seemingly deserted mansion to rifle through a wall-safe, is a beautifully composed series of tracking shots, well designed and executed. *Hostile Witness* (1967) is also not without its compensations, but on the whole, Milland's work as a director is perhaps the most marginal of any *auteur* considered in this volume. Still, as Truffaut notes, "one can make mistakes," and even in the case of an actor he does not particularly care for, Truffaut demonstrates that he is willing to consider the film seriously if briefly.

Comedy

Truffaut was displeased with much traditional French farce, yet he had a surprising affection for that most traditional of Gallic comedians, Fernandel, though perhaps this is not that out of place. Fernandel's multiple "turn" in *The Sheep Has Five Legs* (1954) recalls Alec Guinness's work in *Kind Hearts and Coronets* (1949; Dir. Robert Hamer) and prefigures Jerry Lewis's *The Family Jewels* (1965; Dir. Jerry Lewis), in which Lewis (as an actor) tackles not five but seven different roles. Truffaut's review of *The Sheep Has Five Legs* is of interest because Fernandel's physical comedy is directly linked to the work of Lewis, whose films are much admired by a number of the *Cahiers* critics. Yet if Truffaut admires

Fernandel, he is less taken with Lewis. Fernandel indulges in burlesque, but he is not offensive.

Le Mouton a Cinq Pattes (The Sheep Has Five Legs)
French movie by Henri Verneuil.

An old man who feels his death is nearing (Fernandel) asks a relative (Delmont) to find his five good-for-nothing sons, who are quintuplets. The first one manages a beauty institute (Fernandel), the second one washes windows (Fernandel), the third one is a journalist (Fernandel), the fourth one commands a ship (Fernandel), and the fifth one is a priest (Don Fernandel). All this, as one may guess, constitutes the object of six sketches on the theme of "noblesse oblige." (SK)[30]

In contrast, Truffaut finds Jerry Lewis calculating, cloying, and manipulative. Interestingly, he also tags Lewis as a misogynist, which is ironic in view of Truffaut's own fetishistic regard of the feminine. Yet Truffaut correctly identifies Lewis's appeal to his audience. Lewis is the perpetually bewildered infant, alternately enraged and appealing, his feigned stupidity a mask for barely concealed viciousness. Because of this, audiences regard Lewis with effortless condescension. As Truffaut notes, "the sight of triumphant stupidity is designed to liberate the most inhibited spectator."

Yet women (and children; that is, children other than Lewis) are treated with even greater contempt in Lewis's work than in the persona of the comedian himself. In Truffaut's words, the feminine in Lewis is, "finally, monstrous, barely good enough to be hit in the stomach by car doors." In his examination of Norman Taurog's 1956 Martin and Lewis vehicle Pardners, Truffaut holds up to the reader the "furiously misogynous" instinct that informs the basic structure of Lewis's comedy and the work of "most comics and cabaret artists."

Pardners (Un Pitre Au Pensionnat) starts with the parody of a thriller: "Here is Los Angeles . . . everything seems to be quiet there, doesn't it? Well, not at all, there's going to be a robbery and a murder!" We fade into a very skillful transposition of The Major and the Minor [1942], a film of Brackett and Wilder's, in which Ginger Rogers pretended to be a little girl. Pardners shows us the same scene in front of the ticket office in a station: "A half-price ticket, please, sir, I'm eleven years old!"

Jerry Lewis's comic persona is based on degeneration; scriptwriters create for him foolish stories that concentrate on character defects, the symptoms of which he mimics all too well. In Sailor Beware [1951; Dir. Hal Walker], he was a navy man allergic to women's makeup, who is nevertheless chosen by forty overheated girls to be the referee in a kissing contest. In Artists and Models [1955; Dir. Frank Tashlin], the clev-

erest of all his films, he transposed the world of comic strips into everyday life.

What causes the audience to laugh here are the misadventures of a
character who's more stupid than they are. The general public wants to
see an exceptional person, but genius, or simply intelligence, bothers
their eyes like a cinder would; it annoys them and makes them ashamed.
They would rather see the exceptional stupidity of a Bourvil farmer, of
a Fernandel from Marseilles, of two twits, of a pair of friends like Laurel
and Hardy. . . .

The sight of triumphant stupidity is designed to liberate the most inhibited spectator.

All this illustrates only the "heads" side of the coin, the "tails" side
being even stranger.

Jerry Lewis most certainly plays the fool, but it's in order to get something out of it; you should not imitate the lady who understood nothing
of *La Traverseé de Paris,* and declared, as she left, "It's idiotic, but I
laughed a lot." Jerry Lewis, his scriptwriters, and his gagmen are evi-
dently cultured, subtle, intelligent, and refined. They also happen to be
ferociously misogynous, as most comics and cabaret artists are.

The trick is thus to pretend the gagmen are making fun of Jerry Lewis,
but, by means of his eccentricities, women and children first are held
up to ridicule. That's why gagmen never miss an opportunity to make
the heroines of the film ridiculous: they are mean, silly, vulgar, possess-
ive, gold diggers, blunderers, and, finally, monstrous, barely good enough
to be hit in the stomach by car doors. . . .

The script by Sidney Sheldon—director of a charming movie *Dream
Wife* [1953]—is more than ingenious, only slightly spoiled by directing
which is skillful, but which curbs the shock effects instead of logically
taking them to a purifying frenzy. Jerry Lewis, pretending he is a little
boy, is tucked in by a beautiful but very silly creature whose essential
worth is to smile like Gloria Grahame; another stuck-up girl pokes around
in his pants pockets and finds a diamond, thus combining business with
pleasure.

All this is not very attractive, and one might even become indignant,
by virtue of the fact that anything that doesn't go all the way is despicable. But this is due to the director rather than to the scriptwriter. For
example, I'd like to see a movie, directed by Frank Tashlin, in which
Jerry Lewis would pretend he is a cat; no lines for him, just a few "meows"
and a lot of saucepans tied to his tail, plenty of fur being stroked the
wrong way and a few thrashings from his mistresses after some mischievous episodes. There would be in such a film a good chance for
something new, and an opportunity to handle the subject more completely, without neglecting the element of parody *(La Belle et la Bête).*
To remain with parody while coming back to the Clown [the original
French title of the film translates as "The Clown in the Boarding School"],

let's admire Lewis's dazzling caricature of Humphrey Bogart, toward the end of the movie, in which Lewis contracts his jaws to uncover his teeth in rigor mortis, with, of course, his little fingers at his pants belt, his jacket wide open, scratching his left ear with his right hand.

I don't share the severity of my friend Claude Mauriac concerning Dean Martin. He plays with Jerry as Tom does, as a ventriloquist plays opposite his dummy, with the apprehensive smile of Pygmalion, the sorcerer's apprentice for whom things are becoming too much to handle. His songs are well "in place," and he is as tanned as Cary Grant.

If from time to time you like sitting on a stool in front of a hamburger and a Coke in a shiny snack bar, while enjoying a certain smile that a girl who could serve as a model for the *Esquire* calendar is sending your way, you could see *Pardners* with pleasure. (SK)[31]

Truffaut's review of *Pardners* lays bare a number of Lewis's most repellent (yet undeniably effective) representational strategies. Truffaut's review of *Sailor Beware,* mentioned in his review of *Pardners,* demonstrates that even at first blush, Truffaut had already isolated much of the mechanism of the Martin and Lewis "mystique." Or, more precisely, the *Lewis* mystique: Dean Martin's appearance in *Sailor Beware* goes unmentioned in Truffaut's review.

Although Truffaut does not take the film to task with the same precision with which he dissects *Pardners,* he still notes that, for Lewis, "women . . . cause, as everyone knows, the perdition of all American Marines." Further, in a paraphrase of Victor Hugo, Truffaut states for the first time the themes he will embellish in his notice on *Pardners:* " 'the poorest, the powerless perhaps / suddenly become free from seeing Jerry appear.' Or, 'A madman always finds a virgin to admire him / One often needs someone more depraved than oneself.' "

Sailor Beware (La Polka des marins) [1951]
American movie by Hal Walker.

Jerry Lewis, a new comedian, puts on the face of an American "avant-gardiste," very effeminate, with a short hairdo and bangs. It goes without saying that he is also overpowered by all the known signs of degeneracy: a fat chin, thick lips, and the hint of a goiter. He crunches everything put in his mouth—even a thermometer (which he mistakes for a candy cane). His blood is colorless and his extremely acute sense of smell allows him to detect women from a distance of 300 feet. But he must not approach them, even less hang around with them, because sniffing their makeup can cause him to die by suffocation. Indeed, he is also troubled by allergies that manifest themselves through sneezing and instant swelling of the mucous membranes, as soon as a woman comes near. As a Marine enlistee, he disguises himself during a stopover, once as a rickshaw-boy and once as a hula dancer.

Of course, he becomes a Don Juan in the army. He's chosen to judge a kissing contest; he comes through it when, as the result of a bet, he gets a long kiss from Corrine Calvet. At the end, in accordance with the axiom "heal bad with bad," he becomes normal, like everyone else, like you and me! Nevertheless, he returns to the submarine, in order to be better protected from women, who, as everyone knows, lead to the perdition of all American Marines.

This movie, made with the official cooperation of the United States Marine Corps, is loaded with black humor that's not all involuntary. The film may give back some confidence to American—and other—spectators who are deprived of physical attractiveness by nature. Therein lies the objective of this new comic strategy. One might say, parodying Hugo:

> The poorest, the powerless perhaps
> suddenly become free when they see Jerry appear.

Or,

> A fool will always find a youth to admire him.
> We often have need of folk more defective than ourselves.*

Etc. . . ., etc. . . . , etc. . . . (RCH)[32]

The affection with which Lewis is regarded (better yet, the distanced respect he is afforded) stems more from his use of the camera in his work as a director (particularly in *The Bell Boy* [1960]) and his innovation of the "video tap" (a device that allows a film director to instantly review a shot on videotape, after each take) rather than the comic persona Lewis fashioned for himself in these early films. This persona remained essentially unchanged, even after Dean Martin's departure from the act. Lewis, for all his modesty, belongs to an old and not particularly distinguished branch of comedy, that of the cabaret artist who debases himself because it makes his linking debasement of women more "acceptable" to his male audience. Lewis's comic stratagem in these early films is derived more from burlesque than anything else; one thinks of the scene in *Raging Bull* (1980; Dir. Martin Scorsese), in which Robert De Niro, as the aging Jake La Motta, pale and overweight, hosts a New York strip show with tired comedy—allusions to his fallen state of "non-masculinity"—and then presents a series of scantily clad, exploited dancers to the unresponsive audience. If this is comedy, Truffaut finds it distasteful in the extreme, or perhaps he despises it because it lays the misogynistic mechanism behind such comedy bare. Certainly the Marx Brothers, whom Truffaut admires, treat the various women in their films as little more

---

* The first line seems to be from La Fontaine, but I have been unable to locate the specific source. The second line from La Fontaine's fable *Le Lion et le rat* says "*smaller*" than ourselves in the original French. Reference: Norman B. Spector, ed. *The Complete Fables of Jean de la Fontaine, edited, with a Thymed Verse Translation.* Evanston, IL: Northwestern University Press, 1988. Book II, fable II, line 2, 74–75. (RCH)

than props, from the forced pomposity of Margaret Dumont to Harpo's wordless assaults on a series of anonymous chorus girls. Perhaps Truffaut liked the Marx Brothers more because of their cerebral wordplay, and because they heaped equal amounts of scorn on both the men and women in their films, despite their undeniable streak of misogyny.

In Lewis's work, however, his hatred of the feminine reaches a certain sort of appalling purity. Lewis makes himself as unattractive as possible, and then, as a consequence, is given license to portray the rest of humanity in an even more unflattering light, if such a thing is possible. Katz claims that for the critics of *Cahiers du Cinéma* and *Positif*, Lewis's films "reveal something profound about America which Americans themselves fail to understand,"[33] yet as with most American critics, he fails to specify what that something is. Yet it seems significant that in *The Nutty Professor* (1963), Lewis's reworking of *Dr. Jekyll and Mr. Hyde*, the Hyde persona (whom Lewis names "Buddy Love") is an exaggerated matinee idol, complete with slicked-back hair and an artificially nonchalant manner.

Lewis's films are designed to make one uncomfortable—it is only the least sophisticated filmgoer who is put at ease. Lewis reserves his greatest contempt not for himself, or for the women and children in his films, but rather for his audience. This is reflected in the self-imposed insularity of such later Lewis films as *Which Way to the Front* (1970), which almost totally eschews plot and character motivation for a series of gags based on greed, narcissism, and male bonding. Even in his later critical writings, Truffaut failed to jump on the *Le Roi Crazy* bandwagon, leaving the adulation of Lewis to Godard and the other *Cahiers* critics, while he remained relatively silent on the subject.

The Old and the New

Truffaut, not surprisingly, was often at odds with the sensibilities of the censors, who seemed to prize all that Truffaut deplored in the cinema, particularly in the case of *La Belle Otéro*, a film that displays a directorial style "devoid of the least inventiveness." *La Belle Otéro* is a film that really isn't even worth a clever phrase or two, or even active disgust; yet the state film censors found the film "wholesome, moral, and entertaining." Truffaut lets the censors damn the film for him, effectively damning the current state of commercial French cinema practice as well.

La Belle Otéro [1954]
Franco-Italian movie in Eastmancolor, by Richard Pottier.

We know from reliable sources that the censor's committee, after previewing this film, gave it a real ovation and addressed the members of the cinema profession in the following words: "We would like to see movies like this every day; it is a wholesome, moral, and entertaining movie, without vulgarity."

Indeed, *La Belle Otéro* is inoffensively insipid. As a passionate Gypsy, born in Spain, "she" comes to Paris, walks around, and seduces an American multimillionaire, who takes her to New York, a city far too puritan for her taste.

Maria Félix is pretty, the movie sumptuous, the direction devoid of the least inventiveness, and the spectator is most likely disappointed. (SK)[34]

While deploring what he perceived as the less adventurous, old-line commercial French cinema, Truffaut was continually heralding the new. In particular, his stirring defense of Roger Vadim's first feature, *Et Dieu Créa la femme*, demonstrates that while Truffaut seems unaware of the objectification inherent in the enterprise (and in this, I side to some degree with Mauriac's objections, quoted within the article; more on this later), he still prized Vadim's freshness and praised the director's use of the CinemaScope frame, which is indeed quite striking for a first film.

Much of Truffaut's admiration for Vadim's work resides in the "presence" of Brigitte Bardot—films with Monroe or Bardot in Truffaut's pantheon mysteriously step outside the bounds of conventional *auteurism* and become products of their stars rather than their directors. While much of the following review is a defense of Vadim, the article itself is titled "B. B. Is the Victim of a Plot."

Truffaut takes critics to task for failing to appreciate Bardot as an actress or a screen personality and Vadim as a director, yet there is no point in denying that much of his attraction to the film resides in his fascination with the sexual icon of Bardot, who ruptures, as did Monroe, the fabric of the repressive 1950s. No doubt the semi-improvised air of the film appealed to the young director-to-be as well, yet it is a *Bardot* film above all other considerations for Truffaut: Vadim's participation seems highly secondary.

B. B. Is the Victim of a Plot

We too often see a film lazily criticized to feel we have to throw a Bernanosian fit, but nothing can give you a more bitter distaste for criticism than reading the press reviews of a film.

It is a fact that every film is judged from its appearances. Robert Bresson's *Un condamné à mort s'est échappé,* having all appearances on its side, gained from a unanimously flattering criticism, but the reviews, rather than speaking of Bresson's film, concerned another film invented by the critics that could be imagined halfway between *La grande illusion* and *Rififi.*

Et Dieu créa la femme (And God Created Woman), having all appearances against it, hardly found any defenders save The Three Masques from *Franc-Tireur,* André Bazin, Doniol-Valcroze, your humble servant, and, of course, Robert Chazal.

I have always planned on getting people to measure, by means of an article, the gap that separates the way cinema is made from the way cinema is judged; and cinema the way it is seen by those who make it, from cinema the way it is seen by critics. This last group, in a film, generally take only the script into account, giving it a value by comparing it to novels that they might have come across. About mise-en-scène, about the direction of actors, about the "tone" of the enterprise, about its style, they won't say anything or they will bluff, since they are unable to understand the methods employed by a film's *auteur.*

An example? *Et Dieu créa la femme,* like Joshua Logan's *Picnic,* is essentially influenced by Elia Kazan's *East of Eden* [1955], by the style of its mise-en-scène, by the use of color, the performing, and even the script. Now, Simone Dubreuilh enumerates without hesitation *Duel in the Sun, Gilda, Susanna,* and *La femme à abattre,* which are irrelevant here, while Louis Chauvet discloses the quintuple influence of Anouilh, Grémillon, Hunebelle, Raoul André· and John Berry!

Jean de Baroncelli sees in Vadim's film a "vaguely licentious melodrama," and it would be a "purely commercial enterprise" for André Lang, whose *Voyage à Turin* is certainly a metaphysical work.

As to Miss Claude Garson, the rewrite desk at *L'Aurore* should have tried its hand at the summary she makes of the script beginning with: "The subject takes place in Saint-Tropez."

In most French movies, the action takes place inside, and the outside shots, which are very rare, are only used to link together the interior setups, because French cameramen and filmmakers are afraid of nature and feel better at ease in a studio sheltered from sun, rain, and wind. Vadim's film is thus one of the very rare films in France—with Max Ophüls's *Le plaisir*—to give considerable room to nature, sea, sun, and wind. Thirard deserves, for his daring photography, the warmest praises. CinemaScope is used here with an amazing skillfulness, particularly if one realizes that Vadim had never even made so much as a short film before directing this feature.

One could also note the cleverness of the dialogue directed in the same manner as Becker's in *Casque d'or,* an anti-theatrical laconicism that gives the film a great reality.

The most important bone of contention is, of course, the "tone" of the film, and that is where I'm most shocked by the opinion of the whole of the press. I don't understand how, after having so rightly stigmatized American cinema, its prudishness, its hypocrisy, its system of sentimental conventions (the young leads who will necessarily get married, while the comic supporting actor will marry the maid, these four characters required to be virgins), my colleagues were not able to appreciate the frankness of Vadim, who, perhaps for the first time in cinema history, dares to show us a young married couple behaving like a young married couple, that is to say, patting each other, playing like children (or animals, it doesn't matter), and making love during the day (indeed!). One can, if need be, reproach the script for its dramatic developments—even though one has to tell a story so that critics won't get bored!—but the reality in the detail is obvious. (There's no reason why cinema should indefinitely lag behind literature, and one just has to watch *Et Dieu créa la femme* as one would read a novel of J. M. Caplan's, for example the excellent *Conqueror,* a novel that is unusually precise in its detail!)

Basically, Vadim's real boldness is to make his movie begin where others' films end, with the wedding. I also like the fact that nearly all the characters of the movie are likeable, even the "bad ones," and the freshness of certain ideas: Brigitte Bardot lifting in her arms a little girl who wants to grab a newspaper placed out of her reach, for example.

As for me, after seeing 3,000 movies in ten years, I can no longer stand the insipidly pretty and false love scenes of Hollywoodian cinema and the filthy, licentious, and no less fake love scenes of French cinema.

That's why I thank Vadim for directing his young wife into repeating, in front of the camera, everyday gestures, innocuous gestures, like playing with her sandal, or less innocuous ones but just as real; instead of copying other movies, Vadim wanted to forget cinema in order to "copy life," to obtain real intimacy, and except for the slightly complacent ending of one or two scenes, he has reached his goal perfectly. (The dying Hollywoodian cinema was able to recover by reacting against censors: *The Man with a Golden Arm, Attack, The Moon Is Blue,* etc. It falls to us to compete with American filmmakers by being a bit less allusive and crafty on these questions of sex, where they are very backward!)

All this naturally brings me to Brigitte Bardot, who, being unlucky enough to appear in three films in a month, sees a league forming against her, an army of gossipers who, not sufficiently versed in mental arithmetic, find themselves counting on their fingers that three times thirty million is far from what they will ever earn with their witty little news items, their miserable underfed-from-childhood intellectual lines.

That is where the misunderstanding lies; the audience does not give a damn about the director and doesn't even know his name. People go to the movie theater to see their favorite star. Shortly before they get there, the mealy-faced critic arrives, showing the ticket-taker the green card that allows him to get in free; the critic knows the director's name, but that's all he knows, and, supported by this knowledge, he pretends to ignore the stars who are nothing but "instruments in the director's hands" and so on and so forth.

He doesn't suspect for one second, my critic brother, that good directors came to cinema because they loved actors and actresses and the pleasure one finds in directing them. *It is in this manner that films made out of love for actors are judged by people who don't love actors* [Truffaut's emphasis].

The critic arrives in the movie theater, his eyes glazed over, his view obstructed by foolish prejudices. He will willingly blame the film for not being consistent with what he was expecting, instead of being delighted that it is consistent with what the director seems to have wanted. That's how Simone Dubreuilh, who does not like Martine Carol, reproached her for not being a credible *Lola Montès*. Now, I admire Max Ophüls for being clever enough, since he had to film *Lola Montès* WITH [Truffaut's capitalization] Martine Carol, to shift the interest of the subject and to change it into a kind of biography of Martine Carol, a poetic essay on the state of an actress imprisoned by modern forms of show business, on all the cruelty and all the bitterness that glory brings in the twentieth century, transposed into the last century; scandal for scandal's sake, overwork, publicity to the point that it looks like a circus show, private life spread out in front of the audience, etc. Max Ophüls filmed *Lola Montès* this way because he is sincerely touched by the constraints of an actress's career. Simone Dubreuilh didn't like *Lola Montès* because she doesn't like actresses.

It's for punning's sake, and without checking it in the least, that the anonymous columnist of *L'Express,* where approximation reigns, wrote: "and God created B. B. . . . but gave her only one expression." It's enough to place side by side six or seven photos of Brigitte Bardot [in the film] to be sure of the contrary; you could even go and see the film, but maybe this is asking too much. . . .

Elsewhere, Brigitte Bardot is blamed for . . . *her diction* [Truffaut's emphasis], but Louis Chauvet is the only one left who believes that an actress is a lady who articulates better than others, as in primitive tribes it is believed that in order to be a writer, one has to have a very legible handwriting. (It's true that Louis Chauvet owes his Interallié prize to his downstrokes and the Fifi title to his upstrokes.)

Let's remark incidentally that the critics' animosity is exerted only on pretty girls, never on the others. Marilyn Monroe was sneered at because she didn't read much; she is now sneered at again because she devours the classics. Françoise Rosay, Edwige Feuillère, Gaby Morlay, Betsy Blair, Greer Garson, and Bette Davis are never said to be the least-spontaneous actresses on earth, and all sorts of prizes are regularly rewarded to them. Who would dare to give Marilyn Monroe an Academy Award for her performance in *Bus Stop?*

The most irritating argument in this anti-Bardot campaign is Claude Mauriac's: "What can we think of a husband who, although working for cinema, displays with such complacency his spouse's body, publicly offered to the eyes in its quasi-nudity for an hour and a half?" What indeed can we think of this husband? That he loves her and that he is entirely proud of her, that is, *including her body* [Truffaut's emphasis], especially since she is a movie actress!

Dear Claude Mauriac, I suspect you didn't bother seeing in the *Ciné-mathèque* the extraordinary *Charleston* [1926], an erotic dance by Catherine Hessling, filmed by her husband, Jean Renoir, or his *Le Petit Chaperon Rouge* [1929], unreleased because of the censors, in which the big bad wolf, Jean Renoir himself, chases through the woods and finally eats his young wife, Catherine Hessling, perched, in lace panties, on a 1925 bicycle![35]

If this humble plea for a pretty woman and her director has gradually changed into getting even, I apologize, since I just meant to compensate for unfair critical overkill and to place in fairer perspective a film that most certainly is not a masterpiece but that rises clearly—from a moral point of view as well as from an intellectual or aesthetic point of view— above the average. (SK)[36]

Many of the points that Truffaut presents in this review are valid: the lack of knowledge possessed by most reviewers; the fact that cinema operates as a consequence of the "cult of personality"; the insularity then shown by mainstream French cinema; and the "prudishness" and "hypocrisy" of the "sentimental conventions" then present (and *still* present) in American filmmaking.

It is easy to see how Truffaut got carried away with this review. Vadim's approach to the scenario was, for the period, "bold," containing a "freshness of certain ideas"—mostly small details of "everyday gestures" that Vadim substituted for a conventional scenario. There is also a certain grandeur in the making of such an intimate film with the Cinema-Scope and Eastmancolor apparatus; this makes the film at once lush and splendid, even as it retains a narrowness of focus. Bardot was, as Truffaut suggests, overexposed, making "three films in a month" as a popular film actress, but *And God Created Woman* launched her as an international star. In a sense, Vadim's approach to his subject matter in this film echoes the neorealists, who were forced to make films on a shoestring, using actual locations and only a few professional actors. Vadim, however, was above all a sumptuous stylist, and the deeply textured tones of flesh and fabric in *And God Created Woman* are at once seductive, decorative, and strikingly well organized.[37]

Truffaut, impressed by the "freshness" of Vadim's conception and the undeniable stylishness of his execution, gives his wholehearted support to the film, and if Vadim's later work does not live up to this film, that is something Truffaut cannot be held accountable for. However, what Vadim and Truffaut both miss (and what Vadim still seeks to explain today) is the fact that the film's visuals are resolutely anchored around Bardot's nude body, and were it not for the voyeuristic nature of the enterprise, and the sexual repression they manifest in both American and European culture, the film—for all its flair—would have been just another program picture of the period. For *And God Created Woman* is, indeed, as are many of the films in this volume, a "B" film, made possible because of Bardot's involvement with the project. This bought Vadim freedom on a tight budget, and he used it, but the film is still an exploitational venture, and it exploits both Bardot and its intended audience.

This said, one must remark upon the viciousness of Truffaut's attack on his "critic brothers." "The mealy-faced critic" who condemns the film, and by extension, other adventurous cinematic projects, is, after all, Truffaut's colleague in the strictest sense of the word. But Truffaut disassociates himself here with great ferocity from his fellow reviewers. These other critics are governed by "foolish prejudices"; they are "irritating," "bored," "unable to understand the methods employed by a film's author." Truffaut also displays more than a certain amount of contempt for his readers: "you could even go and see the film, but maybe this is asking too much," he asserts.

Truffaut *does* correctly note the critical tendency—still all too widespread today—to denigrate "pretty" actresses while reserving praise for those performers who present a more plain appearance to the audience. "Who would dare to give Marilyn Monroe an Academy Award for her performance in *Bus Stop?*" Truffaut asks. Bardot is being penalized by her beauty, something that persists to this day in all aspects of popular culture. Beautiful women are seen primarily as objects. Men may be handsome yet still retain an intellectual identity. Truffaut is disgusted at this hypocrisy, and rightly so.

Yet Claude Mauriac's objection to the film, which Truffaut dismisses, is not, to my mind, entirely without merit. "What can we think of a husband who . . . displays with such complacency his spouse's body, publicly offered to the eyes in its quasi-nudity for an hour and a half?" Mauriac wonders. "What indeed what can we think of this husband? That he loves her and that he is entirely proud of her, that is, *including her body*, especially since she is a movie actress," Truffaut responds. Mauriac's objections are couched in the "protective" power of the patriarchy, as if Bardot had no voice or choice in the matter; certainly Mauriac upholds this patriarchy, and its power to affirm or deny, with his comments. Yet if Vadim is "proud of her, that is, *including her body*," it does not necessarily follow that the presentation of this body to the public gaze must be construed as an act of love. As Vadim's later work affirms, *And God Created Woman* is conceived and executed as an act of exploitation. *Charleston* and *Le Petit Chaperon Rouge* share this problematic structure, even as an aura of unreconstructed innocence pervades Renoir's two shorts, much more so than Vadim's first feature. The misogynist impulse that would eventually lead to the ritual slaying of a group of young cheerleaders in Vadim's 1971 film *Pretty Maids All in a*

Row (one with her head stuffed in a toilet) is already present in *And God Created Woman*, although it lurks outside the edges of the frame.

Vadim is a sensualist and a stylist, but he is also, although he vigorously denies it, an enthusiastic adherent of the patriarchal cinema structure. It is sad that the liberation of sexual affairs began with the exploitation (even if it was consensual exploitation) of the feminine, which then led into the first stirrings of feminism, as the mechanisms of this exploitation became unavoidably apparent. One wonders what Truffaut would make of this film today, or its 1988 remake. In many ways, Vadim's story is one of the saddest in this volume: he has never lived up to the promise of this, his first film, a film that inspired both Truffaut and Godard, as well as Rohmer, Chabrol and others, to make their first films as directors, and thus launch the French New Wave.

3 A Passion for the Cinema

Truffaut's review of *Doctor in the House,* one of a series of seven *Doctor* comedies made in Britain during the 1950s and early 1960s, and the first in that series, is not of particular interest in and of itself. However, in juxtaposition with Truffaut's review of *The Quatermass Xperiment,* the notice takes on added resonance. In these few lines on *Doctor in the House,* Truffaut expresses his admiration for the "good humor and excellent comedians" in the film and declares his fondness for "English humor." All in all, he finds that the film has "lots of spirit." He says nothing of Ralph Thomas as a director,[1] but inasmuch as the film is a series of "gags and characters," perhaps this is not necessary. The film belongs to a tradition of broad British farce shared by the *Carry On* films of the '50s, '60s, and '70s, such as *Carry On, Nurse* (1960) and *Carry On, Doctor* (1968), both directed by Gerald Thomas. In no way can it be compared to the earlier, and better, Ealing comedies, or to the Peter Sellers/Terry Thomas comedies *I'm All Right, Jack* (1960; Dirs. John and Roy Boulting) or *The Wrong Arm of the Law* (1962; Dir. Cliff Owen). *Doctor in the House* was released in France under the title *Toubib or Not Toubib.*

Doctor in the House (Toubib or Not Toubib) [1954]
British film by Ralph Thomas.
  This is a historical documentary—hardly romanticized—about British medical schools. It contains no plot, no suspense, no drama, but a series of gags and of characters, calm good humor, and excellent actors—in particular, Kenneth More, one of the drivers in *Genevieve* [1953; Dir. Henry Cornelius], playing the role of a student who voluntarily fails his exams since his unwise grandmother has left him 1,000 pounds in her will as long as his studies last. All lovers of English humor have to see this movie, which has lots of spirit. (SK)[2]

  Compare this relatively enthusiastic notice with Truffaut's dismissive review of Val Guest's *The Quatermass Xperiment,* released in France under the title *Le Monstre.* The review is not only unsympathetic to the

film immediately in question; it dismisses British film as a whole with
the sweeping claim that "a film is a born loser just because it is English."

The Quatermass Xperiment (Le Monstre) (Mr. Cactus) [1956, British; Dir:
Val Guest][3]

Unproductive week, awfully unproductive. We had placed all our hopes
on *The Quatermass Xperiment,* although we knew it was an English
film. It is not yet that the British will surprise us by sending us a good
film; this one is very, very bad, far from the small pleasure we get, for
example, from the innocent science fiction films signed by the American
Jack Arnold.

The subject, worthy of Lovecraft or Poe, can make us think of Kafka's
"Metamorphosis": a rocket crash-lands in a little village in northern England; the crew has mysteriously disappeared, except for one who has
become mute and whose only remaining human characteristic is his appearance, and that barely.

In fact, a substance has taken possession of the survivor, who is not
quite himself anymore and who, in his turn, absorbs everything as he
goes along: plants, animals. At the hospital, his hand settles on a cactus
and it disappears. A bit later, the unfortunate wife of the man helps him
escape from the hospital, to protect him from a doctor's proposed experiments, and when she wants to take his hand to comfort him a little bit,
she only finds, at the end of her husband's arm, an aggressive cactus;
she runs off yelling, but we don't feel sorry for her since she isn't pretty.

Our friend has become a monster; in a few hours he has grown considerably bigger, after absorbing a few lions and miscellaneous wild animals at the zoo.

The situation is hopeless. All mankind may disappear for good, as the
monster scatters cells here and there which are liable to reproduce
boundlessly.

But the monster has a soul, since he is found taking a nap on some
metallic scaffoldings in Westminster Abbey; all that is left to do is connect the whole city's electrical power to the scaffoldings, turn the switch
on, and the poor beast disappears in front of our half-closed eyes.

Nothing much new here, since the plant-thing has been wonderfully
used by Howard Hawks in the best movie of the genre, *The Thing from
Another World* [1951],[4] the only really intelligent science fiction film. As
a matter of fact, *The Thing* ended on an electrocution that was much
more ingenious than this one.

But the subject could have been turned into a good film, not lacking
in spice; with a bit of imagination, they could have come up with one
or two nice love scenes between Mr. Cactus and his wife, maybe a chase
scene, goodness knows what else. We've had the woman as sex object;

next could be the man as plant, the cactus hubby that you have to water regularly and keep up, or some such thing.

None of this is in this sadly English film, which avoids difficulties and takes us from office to office, from phone to phone, while the monster runs around the city, hidden from our eyes, although he is the one we would like to see on the screen from start to finish.

Imagination! A whole film! Imagination is what English cinema most cruelly lacks; in the cinema of that country, where stars look like their queen, everything is grey and ineffective, slow-witted and arduously painstaking. The British cinema is made of dullness and reflects a submissive life-style, where enthusiasm, warmth, and zest are nipped in the bud.

A film is a born loser just because it is English. Even a good script filmed by a good director and performed by good actors in England will most likely end up as a bad film. Why? This is the only mystery that English cinema has in store for us. (BFH)[5]

Certainly *The Quatermass Xperiment* is a cheap film, but this has not prevented Truffaut from appreciating similarly inexpensive films in his other reviews. What is more telling is total dichotomy presented by these two notices. Truffaut finds *Doctor in the House* amusing because it is, in its own mild manner, a sex comedy. It relies upon a series of painfully antiquated burlesque jokes for its structure. As Truffaut notes, "it contains no plot, no suspense, no drama, but a series of gags and characters." One can be momentarily amused by the films in the *Doctor* series, but even as one laughs, one is aware of being compromised. The film is perhaps too gentle to be termed directly misogynistic, but it certainly relies upon feminine objectification for most of its humor, and soon becomes tiresome.

This same spirit of critical misogyny pervades Truffaut's notice on *The Quatermass Xperiment*, but in a much darker sense. "We don't feel sorry" for the transformed astronaut's wife, Truffaut asserts, "because she isn't pretty." This is an uncalled-for slap, not worthy of Truffaut's critical instinct as a whole. Yet it is indicative of the manner in which Truffaut approached both films he approved of and films he disliked. Truffaut's lack of affection for science fiction also colors this review, and indeed his dislike of the genre seems to dredge up his least attractive critical tendencies.

The Quatermass Xperiment represents a failure of the imagination for Truffaut, but is this really the case? Val Guest's direction is methodical, it is true, and relentlessly tied to the narrative. The monster is absent from the film for much of its running time. This is due primarily to reasons of economy, but it is also designed to withhold from the audience the visage of "the dreaded other," a strategy essential to any Gothic thriller or science fiction film. One could say the same of the carefully linear narrative of *The Thing*, in which a group of scientists walk from "office to office, from phone to phone, while the monster runs around . . . hidden from our eyes, although he is the one we would like to see on the screen from start to finish." Truffaut has, as he admits, viewed *Quatermass* through "half-closed eyes." His view of *The Quatermass Xperiment* seems ineluctably colored by the phantoms of misogyny, generic preference, and cultural antagonism.

Criticizing the Critics

If Truffaut had little patience with those films that he perceived as being mediocre, he had even less patience with those critics who, in his view, were less than perceptive in their analytical efforts. Truffaut's attack on Jean d'Yvoir, a writer for the rival critical journal *Télé-Ciné*, is notable for the complete condescension with which Truffaut treats d'Yvoir's work.

So savage was Truffaut's denunciation of both d'Yvoir and *Télé-Ciné* that André Bazin, as editor of *Cahiers du Cinéma*, felt obliged to soften the blow with a few introductory remarks, which nevertheless fail to take much of the sting out of Truffaut's rebuke. In attacking the work of Renoir, d'Yvoir had clearly strayed onto what was, for Truffaut, sacred ground. Truffaut saw d'Yvoir's work not only as a repudiation of the values in Renoir's films but of the values that Truffaut prized in the work of other filmmakers.

Bazin's preface follows:

Téle-Ciné (#27–28, March–April 1953). We have not often commented on *Télé-Ciné*, a magazine significant for its certainly useful efforts, which are in any case pleasing and praiseworthy. We particularly have in mind the issue on *The Work of Robert Bresson* (#25, 1951) and the one on *The Economic Problems of European Cinema* (#32–33, 1952). We would like to mention that *Télé-Ciné* is of Catholic inspiration (though not of Catholic obedience) and that its primary goal is to publish short film analyses for use by Ciné-Clubs, and more generally by people who view cinema for cultural ends. This preamble was necessary in order to accompany the sincere but perhaps excessively severe account by François Truffaut of the magazine's latest special issue.—A. B.
[Truffaut's remarks:]

It is a curious homage that *Télé-Ciné* pays to Jean Renoir. *Le Bled* [1929] becomes a "melodrama in favor of colonialism." "The scene where Boudu [in *Boudu sauvé des Eaux* / *Boudu Saved from Drowning* (1932)] cuckolds Lestingois is irresistible" and the Resistance, which is the subject of *This Land Is Mine* [1943] constitutes a "pretentious theme." Few movies of Jean Renoir find grace with Mr. Jean d'Yvoire, in whose eyes, on the contrary, "Delannoy's images are irritating because of their ambiguity."

Nana [1926]: "A slow style, has inter-titles—excerpts from Zola in a pretentious style that rings false."

Marquitta [1927]: "This conventional topic is accompanied by mediocre direction."

Tire au Flanc [1929]: "Rather disjointed vaudeville, forced comedy. Some amusing scenes. Through the window, the engaged prisoner sees his beloved courted by the rival." (!)

Le Tournoi dans la Cité [1928]: "This pseudo-historical drama in Renaissance costume reminds one a little of *Miracle des Loups* by Raymond Bernard, without however possessing its qualities."

La Nuit du Carrefour [1932]: "A work of little significance."

Madame Bovary [1933]: "Very mediocre work with debatable casting."

Les Bas-Fonds [1936]: "Pseudo slave masquerade."

La Bête Humaine [1938]: "A nonchalant and flat dramatic progression."

Swamp Water [1941]: "It's a film drawn from a successful series novel, which any good *metteur-en-scène* could have filmed; and in spite of the melodrama, it has all the characteristics of a respectable 'western.' "

This Land Is Mine [1943]: "The worst film of his American career."

The Diary of a Chambermaid [1946]: "One senses an impression of uneasiness, and sometimes of boredom."

The Woman on the Beach [1947]: "A hardly credible story, the drama is melodrama."

Une Partie de Campagne [1936; released in 1946 in France; 1950 in the United States]: "Among the actors appear Jean Renoir and his wife, moreover in a rather mediocre manner."

The Golden Coach [1952] "The dialogue constitutes one of the weak points of the movie." "Could it be then that Renoir is a Populist, incapable of viewing the ruling class other than through a keyhole, with the eye of a servant?"

The technical jargon is worth mentioning; the prettiest pearl is this one (in *La Grande Illusion* [1937]): "The framing of shots is rarely gratuitous."(!)

One could also reveal the errors that fill each list of credits and dwell upon the involuntarily comical aspect of the review that treats *La Règle du Jeu* [1939]. What's the use? (SK)[6]

Truffaut goes on to state that only a review of Renoir's *The River*, in the same issue of *Télé-Ciné* but written by another critic, gives the reader an impression of what the "enterprise might have been" had that "enterprise" been a legitimate (in Truffaut's opinion) overview of Renoir's work in film.

Truffaut's sarcasm in this review is tied to his enthusiasm for film as a medium and his passionate involvement in both films and filmmakers. This is not something he was able to sustain at the same pitch after he began his own career as a director, a fact he rather regretfully acknowledged some time later. In an interview for *L'Express*, given to Pierre Billard, Christiane Collange, and Claude Veillot and published on May 20, 1968, Truffaut noted that he was now less deeply involved in the public reception of the works of others. He could "no longer live like that for somebody's else's film."

Ah, all the same, I await films made by others with less impatience than in the past. There is, let's say, a film lover's purity you can't help but lose when you take to making films for yourself.

For example, in '47 or '48 I knew in advance that Orson Welles had shot a film called *Macbeth* in twenty-one days and that he was going to present it at Venice. I lived for that film. When they announced that Laurence Olivier's *Henry V* would show at the same festival, I was heart and soul for Welles. When they then announced that Welles was withdrawing his film from the competition, I thought: "Ah! the scum! That has to be a put-up job." . . . There you are. Today I no longer live like that for somebody else's film. It's impossible.[7]

The date of these remarks is interesting, coming shortly after the abortive attempt by Charles de Gaulle to oust Henri Langlois as secretary general of the Cinémathèque Française, a struggle that began officially on February 9, 1968, and concluded on April 22 of the same year.[8] Truffaut's comments in May would seem to suggest that he had outstripped his earlier work as a critic, and in many ways this is certainly the case. Langlois and Bazin had served as Truffaut's educators and mentors; he had responded to this by spearheading the attack against De Gaulle, ensuring, along with many other writers, actors, and directors, that Langlois would not be stripped of the enterprise he had built up from nothing, as the result of a governmental whim.

Yet by 1968 Truffaut had moved on from his earlier role as a critic. Truffaut's first film, the 1954 production of *Une Visite*, a 16mm short, was followed in 1957 by *Les Mistons*, and in 1958 by *Histoire d'eau* (the title being an obvious pun on the novel by the pseudonymous Pauline Réage; Godard coauthored this film with Truffaut); 1958 was also Truffaut's last year of intense critical activity. With the production of *Les Quatre Cents Coups* in 1959, Truffaut's critical writing dropped off sharply, from fifty-seven published articles in 1958 to twelve articles in 1959. One only has so much energy; Truffaut was now transferring his passion from criticism to practice.

It is this marvelous sense of passion that distinguishes Truffaut's critical work in these early years and sets it apart from the work of his more established contemporaries. One might consider Truffaut as a "guerilla critic"; his near-punk stance invites the reader to disagree with him while simultaneously placing him beyond the reach of such disagreement.

In later years Truffaut would occasionally have cause to regret the ferocity of some of his critical positions. In his collected letters, *François Truffaut Correspondance*, published for the first time in 1988 in French and in 1989 in an English translation by Gilbert Adair, Truffaut demonstrates that by the early 1970s, he was somewhat embarrassed by the tone of his more negative reviews. Responding to a letter from director Marcel L'Herbier, Truffaut seems sincere in his desire to distance himself from his unfavorable assessment of L'Herbier's films, which L'Herbier had apparently not forgotten. Truffaut writes:

I am sorry that your memory of my negative articles has remained so vivid, since I have come to realize in rereading them—for another book—that my good reviews have stood the test of time far better. . . . If, as a critic, I was not invariably kind to you, do believe me when I say I regret it, and the various prefaces that I have recently written, for Bazin's book as well as my own, will, I hope, help to answer the questions that one cannot help asking oneself concerning the function of a critic, as soon as one becomes the object of the criticism of others.[9]

Truffaut's comments in the second paragraph are particularly telling. His letters offer ample proof that Truffaut felt hurt when the same degree of critical heat was applied to his own works. For one example, Truffaut is visibly upset when critic Jonathan Rosenbaum, in a review in *Film Comment*, dislikes *The Story of Adèle H.*[10] In another instance, Truffaut writes a lengthy and obviously distressed defense of his work to novelist and critic Jean-Louis Bory, when Bory claims, in an article, that Truffaut has "sold out to the system."[11] Truffaut also admits (in his letter to Rosenbaum) that absence of many of his own negative reviews in *Les Films de ma vie* was influenced by this newfound respect for the feelings of others.

With regard to my book, *Les Films de ma vie,* it contains several negative pieces: on Albert Lamorisse, Anatole Litvak, Jacques Becker (Arsène Lupin), Mervyn Leroy, and René Clément. . . . Moreover, if I decided against publishing my negative criticisms of Yves Allégret, Jean Delannoy, Marcel Carné· etc., it is because these directors are now old men. . . . It's a situation you will understand better when you are a little older.[12]

As an example of Truffaut's most unfettered negativism, one immediately thinks of his review of George Stevens's *Giant* (1956). Truffaut never repudiated this notice, although he did not reprint it in *Les Films de ma vie.* Truffaut could be completely unrestrained in his contempt for the work of others when the spirit so moved him: this notice is brutal, lengthy, exhaustive, and amusing. It is also a review that the Truffaut of the 1970s would be wholly incapable (for better or worse) of writing.

Giant (Géant)
American Film by George Stevens (Stupid and Solemn).

Three hours and twenty minutes of deadly boredom tinted with disgust!

Every year, Hollywood offers us a substitute for *Gone with the Wind* [1939], with a few variations according to the tastes of the time. A large American family, three generations, a prestigious setting, a social transformation, a historical event. Generational conflicts in the house: "families, I hate you [a famous line from Gide's *Nourritures terrestres*]," and a bit later: "families, I don't hate you anymore. Long live Dad! The little horse is dead!" "You see, Sam, this land that stretches as far as the eye can see? Well, one day I'll grow corn on it!" UGH!

But I should expound my grievances more clearly.

Let's say that Edna Ferber's saga-novel, from which the film is adapted, has nothing to do with literature, and that works of this kind shouldn't even get reviewed, which is only natural. Things are very different with cinema, since films are born equal in rights, and *Giant* [1956] is presented to us as an ambitious work, and one as important as—for example—*La Traversée de Paris.*

What dooms this kind of movie at the outset, as well as the novels they are adapted from, is the fact that the genre is FAKE, built on a lie. *Giant,* which is solely a 200–plus-minute-long uninterrupted dialogue, refuses to be an adventure film; it wants to a psychological work, a social fresco, a monument of thought; well then, precisely what is most shocking in this is the lack of reality of the characters, the simplifying falsity of the social painting, the hypocrisy of the suggested moral, the vices of thought.

Anyone who has seen *Gone with the Wind* [1939], *Mrs. Parkington* [1944], *So Big* [1953], *The Green Years* [1946], and *The Best Years of Our Lives* [1946] can imagine the script. The characters are always etched in the same way, the heroine, Elizabeth Taylor, being particularly privileged, since the female audience is decisive for the commercial success of such a work. Let's note as we go along that only women find time to read these big thousand-page novels written by other women to kill time. The film is almost entirely made of scenes between Rock Hudson, rough but strong, uneducated but powerful, racist but brave, and his wife, pretty and clever, witty and generous, open to modern ideas, feminist and tolerant. Small fights that would deceive nobody, small, babyish reconciliations.

Then, there are the kids: "You mean that you . . . I mean that I . . .

no, our . . . well, that we are expecting a. . . ." Let's hope it's a boy to run the ranch. A few months later: "Oh! Isn't SHE pretty? Yes, but HE is so cute!" Yes, twins, a boy and a girl, it's more convenient for the scriptwriters and that makes the audience so happy! To show us that the son will have his Mom's character and that, instead of running the ranch, he will choose to be a doctor, he is shown to us as a two-year-old young-ster, screaming when his father sits him on a horse and rushing toward a doctor's black bag, dreamily stroking the stethoscope. To indulge in such jokes is really to play to the audience's lowest level of intelligence.

I didn't really like George Stevens's previous movies, especially *Shane* [1953]. The same vulgarity and the same fondness for easy effects are to be found again in *Giant;* in *Shane,* during a scene in which we under-stand that Alan Ladd and Jean Arthur share an impossible love, we catch a glimpse in the background of two cows rubbing snouts. At the end of *Giant,* behind a little Texan and little Mexican who are growing up side by side, we can see a black sheep fraternizing with a white sheep. It's by using in a repetitive way such glaring symbols that the film pro-gresses laboriously, this film so desperately stretched out that we would have time, between each cue, to go and have a cup of black coffee in the nearest café if the usherette of the Normandie delivered exit tickets.

Stevens is a cheat, a fraud. There is in *Giant* a fight set exactly like the one in *Shane;* if you look closely, you'll see that a piece of furniture always conceals the blow; the one who gives the blow is systematically framed rather than the one who receives it; our attention is diverted to the things flying about and every blow, invisible, is perceived by our ears, for it is one of these fights that make you laugh if the soundtrack is cut out. The whole movie is directed in that same way: avoidances, schemes, small tricks to film it the easiest way.

A slice of life between two slices of moral, and what a moral: *Giant* is made of three sandwiches.

To show the aging of the characters, the hair whitens from one scene to the next; after births and marriages and after deaths; a burial at dusk in silhouettes, that's the "sound and light" aspect, the water show, the dark continent of the matter. The songs: "Yellow Rose of Texas," "Auld Lang Syne," a few American hymns and funeral marches—in sum, everything that pleases people. Not an opportunity is missed to laud America to the skies: "their" big country, traditions, improvements, and modernism give rise to big empty sentences that we've already heard a hundred times: "My grandfather and father did it this way and our son will too. . . ." And racial questions are approached with the usual hy-pocrisy. Scarlett O'Hara whipped her Negro servants; that was twenty years ago. Elizabeth Taylor awakens to social awareness; for her a Mex-ican is nearly a man like every other man, but the black servant who's faithfully attached to her naively cries when the children cry and laughs when they laugh, for he is a big child, of course, and belongs to the good old tradition of "necessary luxury."

Rock Hudson's performance reminds one of Yves Vincent's, and I could not say who should feel the more insulted by the comparison. Elizabeth Taylor is affected as her part demands, but at least she is wonderfully beautiful and admirably dressed, which is important. Carroll Baker has much less glamour than in *Baby Doll* [1956], disguised as a young milliner.

There remains James Dean. He can be seen for twenty carefully scattered minutes in the movie. Stevens gave up directing him, and never could one feel so clearly in a movie the mutual contempt of a director and a star; whereas every other actor is directed within an inch (well or badly, but firmly), James Dean does exactly what he wants, with weariness it seems to me, for the flame that was burning in *East of Eden* and *Rebel without a Cause* is here strangely turned low. As a producer, master of his editing, Stevens kept as few shots with James Dean as possible. One conversation scene, where the camera doesn't leave Carroll Baker's face while James Dean speaks from off screen, proves it. *Giant* is the only James Dean movie I won't go see again.

I have to come to a conclusion: *Giant* is everything that is contemptible in the Hollywood system, especially when the said system works for the benefit of a prestige movie, deliberately conceived to win a few Academy Awards. It's a silly, solemn, sly, paternalistic, demagogic movie without any boldness, rich in all sorts of concessions, pettiness, and contemptible actions.

This dead film won't take away from us the idea that American cinema is the most alive cinema in the world when it offers us, for example, *Written on the Wind* [1956; Dir. Douglas Sirk], a small, successfully done *Giant*. (BFH)[13]

Truffaut's review of Ranald MacDougall's *Queen Bee* (1955) is also dismissive, though not written with the same ferocity as his review of *Giant*. *Queen Bee* is another "families, I hate you" film, and as such it shares many of the same defects as Stevens's film. *Queen Bee* is a film of "facile foulness," with "weak, very weak" acting, further compromised by MacDougall's direction, which Truffaut finds without "many cinematographic values." Truffaut is also not overly fond of Joan Crawford's technique as an actress. As he notes, she has a tendency toward parody, unless this is checked by an alert *auteur*. This "literary" film, whose structure is borrowed from "so many psychological novels," has little to recommend it and would still be a failure in the hands of a more kinetic, and competent, director. What Truffaut dislikes the most is the "conventional" line of the film's narrative, coupled with the laziness of *Queen Bee*'s visual construction. There is nothing to excite Truffaut's imagination here, but unlike *Giant*, there is also nothing that actively engenders his disgust.

Queen Bee (La Femme Diabolique) [1955] by Ranald MacDougall.

This seems to be a first film adapted, not from a play as one would swear on leaving the theater, but from a novel, as the advertising leaflet states.

Play or novel, all this, under the direction of Ranald MacDougall (whose future works I don't really feel like seeing), hasn't acquired many cinematographic virtues. The acting is not absolutely bad, but weak, very weak, including Joan Crawford's, who's always ridiculous when directed by a filmmaker who precisely fears ridicule. Not only is the mise-en-scène clumsy but also, because of its solemn awkwardness, it curbs the timid impulses of the script, dulls the rare clever details, and permanently endangers our acceptance, which is nonetheless strenuously courted by a devilishly pseudo-psychological text packed with facile black moments and deadly traps.

The conventional anathema, "families, I hate you," makes for a slightly indigestible and in the long run tedious cinematic food.

Let's see what it's all about: pretty Jennifer with too-small eyes comes to live at the house of some relatives she does not know. A nice family indeed: John, disfigured by a car accident, is a drunkard. His young sister kind of flirts with John's assistant, Jud, to whom she is more or less engaged. Suzy was John's deserted fiancée, until he turned to Eva. Eva—well, Eva is Joan Crawford, who resembles both an octopus and a spider. She pulls the strings, chooses her bed partners with a roll of the dice, untangles situations to everyone's complete undoing, sows ruin and desolation everywhere she buzzes about, reducing to despair hearts that—since they can't get themselves bronzed like trophies for her—break at her feet into a thousand pieces.

The American title of this grayish little work would suggest that Joan Crawford, in my mind an octopus-spider, represents, for the authors, some kind of queen bee. Do we have to dart to view her hives? I honestly don't think so. The posterity of *Mourning Becomes Electra,* from which the opening and ending scenes have been borrowed, of *La Vipère [The Viper],* from which the rest has been borrowed, and of so many psychological novels much too thick to be honest has endowed cinematographic art with a number of almost unreleasable offshoots, of which this film is one. (BFH) [14]

In both notices, but particularly in his review of *Giant*, Truffaut abandons any pretense of objectivity. He is, rather, the avenging angel, excoriating that which would violate the sacred. The opening line of his review of *Giant*—"Three hours and twenty minutes of deadly boredom tinted with disgust"—signals Truffaut's contempt for the film, for the fact that he must even waste time writing his review, and for those who are behind the creation of such a mediocre and unimaginative studio product.

Giant is seen by Truffaut as "a substitute for *Gone with the Wind*." The flaccid construction shared by both films is one indication of this (*Giant* ran 201 minutes in its original cut; *Gone with the Wind* ran 222 minutes). Both films are derived from "saga novel" texts (to use Truffaut's terminology), "and works of this kind aren't even entitled to a review." Both films deal with "a large American family . . . a prestigious setting, a social transformation, a historical event." In both films, "the characters are . . . stamped in the same way, the heroine [in *Giant*], Elizabeth Taylor, being particularly privileged." (Vivien Leigh's Scarlet O'Hara is, of course, the focal point for much of *Gone with the Wind*'s narrative structure.) Both films are sprawling, overproduced, and aim for "psychological" penetration. They aspire to be "social frescoes." And, although one could continue in this vein, I should perhaps end my comparison of the two films by noting that both *Gone with the Wind* and *Giant* won Academy Awards for their respective directors (Stevens for *Giant*, Victor Fleming for *Gone with the Wind* [Fleming is the director of record; as is well known, many other hands helped to create *Gone with the Wind*, including George Cukor, William Cameron Menzies, and B. Reeves Eason]).

The "ambition" inherent in such an enterprise seems to confer a certain amount of immediate splendor on *Giant*. The visual backdrop of Texas readily lends itself to the creation of a series of superficially striking compositions, and Stevens makes the most of the natural setting he works with in *Giant*. Yet the film emerges as "an over-200–hundred-minute-long uninterrupted dialogue," in which the locations are used in comic book fashion, as illustrative settings rather than integral landscapes. Truffaut notes Stevens's clumsy symbolism, his reliance upon a hackneyed and predictable script, the use of instantaneously recognizable icons in place of developed characterizations, and, above all, the "vulgarity" that permeates every frame of the film.

Giant is nothing if not grandiose in its conception; at the same time, it is hollow at the center, and "FAKE, built on a lie." Not only is the film's dramatic construction fraudulent; even the fight scenes and dramatic confrontations that form the bulk of the work are synthetic and unconvincing. Truffaut's deconstruction of Stevens's fight scenes is merciless in its accuracy and shows that even as a critic rather than a practitioner, Truffaut possessed a finely developed sense of what one could accomplish with misapplied montage. In all of this, as Truffaut notes, James Dean is the odd man out, refusing to be "directed within an inch" by Stevens. Dean occupies his few scenes in the film with authoritative nonchalance and does indeed display throughout the film his "contempt" for the project. It is, actually, no wonder that Dean's "flame . . .

is here turned strangely low"; the actor instinctively recognizes the film as the put-up job that it is and is discharging his contractual responsibilities with the least amount of energy.

Giant is "contemptible . . . deliberately conceived to win a few Academy Awards." Yet this "silly, solemn, sly, paternalist, demagogic movie," which today would be cited as a "button-pusher" within the industry (playing, as it does, upon our most superficial emotions and refusing to allow us any latitude in our response), was an enormous commercial and critical success upon its initial release and is still highly regarded by many critics to this day. Truffaut's review of *Giant* is one of his more important "negative" notices, in that it shows that at least one contemporary critic refused to be seduced by the external trappings of this overblown production. Truffaut concludes his review with the statement that "this dead film won't take away from us the idea that American cinema is the most alive cinema in the world," mentioning Douglas Sirk's *Written in the Wind* as an alternative (and antidote) to Stevens's pomposity.

Ranald MacDougall, however, is not even worthy of detailed dismissal as an *auteur*.[15] Truffaut doesn't "really feel like seeing" MacDougall's "future works," and indeed, MacDougall directed only four more films of which the best is probably *The World, the Flesh and the Devil* (1959). In the first paragraph of his review of *Queen Bee*, Truffaut puts his finger on MacDougall's principal failure as a director. "One would swear upon leaving the theater" that this "first film" is "based on a play." *Queen Bee* is static, resolutely lacking in usual impact, and tediously linked to its conventional text. MacDougall does nothing to liberate his actors and actresses; rather, they all seem trapped within the confines of the frame. Although Stevens's compositional sense is limited to pompous effects (he is particularly fond of placing a performer in the foreground of the shot, against a stark horizon in the distance), there is at least the attempt to do something with the camera. MacDougall doesn't even attempt to borrow (as Stevens does) a visual style. *Queen Bee* is claustrophobic to no discernible benefit, a film that seems stillborn even as it unreels inexorably on the screen.

Hitchcock

An *auteur* much more to Truffaut's taste was Alfred Hitchcock, whose work was a continual source of fascination and inspiration for the critic/director. Of all the directors Truffaut praised, Hitchcock holds a special place in Truffaut's personal pantheon. Hitchcock alone was the subject of a book-length interview by Truffaut, published in 1966 in France as *Le Cinéma selon Hitchcock* and in 1967 in English translation as *Hitchcock*.[16]

The project began, as Truffaut notes in his introduction to the volume, with a 1955 interview at the Saint-Maurice Studios in Joinville. Truffaut and Claude Chabrol arrived during the post-synchronization of *To Catch a Thief* hoping to watch Hitchcock at work. According to Truffaut, both he and Chabrol were so thrilled with meeting the renowned director that they failed to watch where they were walking and wound up falling into a pond, much to Hitchcock's amusement.[17]

Truffaut decided to expand the interview with the director and arranged for a series of marathon taping sessions, using Helen G. Scott as translator during the taping.[18] What emerged was a signal volume, one of the first book-length interviews with an *auteur* of major importance, and a book that opened up a good portion of both Hitchcock's and Truffaut's creative processes to the general public.

Long before this volume, however, Truffaut wrote on Hitchcock in *Arts* and *Cahiers* at considerable length. A look at Truffaut's critical writings in the early 1950s reveals that only Jean Renoir received comparable attention. Hitchcock is the subject of, or is made reference to, in no less than forty-eight of Truffaut's early critical articles. Renoir comes next, at forty citations. Robert Aldrich, André Bazin, Jacques Becker, Godard, Ophüls, Rossellini, and Preminger are also the subjects of sustained analysis, but in each case, Truffaut writes, on the average, only twenty articles per *auteur*.[19]

Thus, in terms of sheer quantity of analysis, it is clear that Truffaut, from the first, was fascinated with Hitchcock's work, both formally and as a humanist. It is well to remember that in the early 1950s, the case for Hitchcock's importance as a director had yet to be made. Hitchcock was considered a popular entertainer, with a penchant for thrillers, whose love of "effects" and set pieces overshadowed any social or psychological concerns. Truffaut realized, almost from the start of his career as a critic, that this preliminary assessment was unfair and unjust.

Nor was Truffaut particularly taken with Hitchcock's first period of filmmaking in Britain, preferring the director's Hollywood films in the 1940s to such films as *The Thirty Nine Steps* (1935) and *The Lady Vanishes* (1938). While contemporary critics viewed Hitchcock's early films in this country as a diminution of the director's initial works, Truffaut, writing in the early 1950s, saw such films as *Rebecca* (1940), *Suspicion* (1941), *Notorious* (1946), and *Under Capricorn* (1949) as the apotheosis of the director's work to date.

Here is Truffaut's notice on the rerelease of *Rebecca*.

Rebecca
American movie by Alfred Hitchcock.

This first American film of Alfred Hitchcock signals a turning point in his career. As soon as it was released, *Rebecca* revealed its superiority not only to the successful novel on which the film was based but also to previous films Hitchcock had made in his native England. And yet, in the light of the twelve or thirteen films since 1945 from the same director, attentive Hitchcock fans will appreciate this *Rebecca* even more in its rerelease, as it foreshadows in an extraordinarily precise way *Suspicion* and especially *Under Capricorn,* considered overall his masterpiece. By this first Hollywood production, themes appear that will be found in all "Hitchcocks of the second period" [America in the 1940s and '50s]: suspicion, the fascination of one person with another, safety in the confession of a secret. The rerelease of another Hitchcock movie is awaited with impatience: *Notorious. Rebecca* has to be seen. Above all, it has to be seen a second time. (SK)[20]

Ironically, although *Rebecca* won Best Picture in the 1941 Academy Awards, the award went to producer David O. Selznick rather than to Hitchcock. John Ford won Best Director for *The Grapes of Wrath.*[21] This notice reveals not only Truffaut's devotion to Hitchcock as a director; it also sets the stage for a defense of Hitchcock's most problematic works. Even in the present day, there are not many admirers of Hitchcock's work who would consider *Under Capricorn* "overall the director's masterpiece." Nor do most cineastes completely dismiss Hitchcock's British films.

In reality, this review of *Rebecca* is less interested in the film itself than in extolling the virtues and delights of post-1940 Hitchcock. Tangentially, in its last sentence, the review urges the viewer to see *Rebecca* at least twice, and, by extension, to extend the same consideration to Hitchcock's other works. Truffaut was well aware that Hitchcock's reputation (and skill) as an entertainer mitigated against the serious appreciation of his works. Hitchcock is a perverse moralist, a man in the grip of certain thematic obsessions, as well as a director who is compelled, above all else, to please his audience.[22]

Alfred Hitchcock may not declare the seriousness of his intent in a pronounced exterior fashion, but his films are undeniably personal documents, storyboarded down to the last detail and then realized by an array of technicians who did nothing more than follow the director's blueprint. Truffaut, in all his mentions of Hitchcock, seems simultaneously awed and mesmerized by the director's facility and depth; these early reviews are no exception. Of the many reviews this volume could consider, I have chosen his reviews of *Lifeboat* (1944) and *The Trouble with Harry* (1955). While many could argue, and certainly with some justification, that these films do not represent Hitchcock's finest work, they are two films that Truffaut was quite taken with.

Truffaut's review of Alfred Hitchcock's *Lifeboat* is interesting because it appears so far after the actual production of the film. Truffaut thus has the distinct advantage of comparing it to much of Hitchcock's later work as a director. I do not agree with Walz's assessment that Truffaut finds the film "not Vintage Hitchcock . . . a banal psychological drama,"[23] because it seems clear to me in this review that Truffaut merely fears that such a thing will happen and is delighted when it does not.

While the film "does not start very well," it soon becomes an intriguing series of ambiguities for the director, and Truffaut delights in stating the polarities presented, without making any real attempt to unscramble them. Above all, Hitchcock cites *Lifeboat*'s resistance to the then-common critical strategies; while the mechanism for potential symbolic substitution seems present in the work, for one example, Truffaut is pleased to discover that the work resists the temptation of falling into any such system. Hitchcock makes films "to disturb," and that's exactly what Truffaut finds in this work: a "disturbance" of audience expectations and thus a film that is, at base, absolutely serious.

Lifeboat (Lifeboat) by Alfred Hitchcock.

How could one review this movie after seeing it only once? This time, we lack the plot that brings about the misunderstandings, the humorous trappings, and lastly the alibi, with which Hitchcock regularly satisfies the most frivolous part of his audience, as well as the most demanding. *Lifeboat* (1944) is like roast beef without gravy, and whoever does not get enthusiastic about the movie will be bored to death.

The film does not start very well. A "great" and wealthy female reporter, an engineer with left-wing ideas, a young army nurse, a powerful manufacturer, a wounded sailor, a Christian Negro steward, and an English lady carrying her dead child in her lap are stranded on a lifeboat. At this point in the movie, there is nothing very Hitchcockian about the movie, except the apparently impossible challenge of the three dramatic unities—ninety minutes in a lifeboat, hats off!—and the style of framing and acting, brilliant as usual. But we are now ready, if not for the worst, at least close to it: the theatrical and psychological conflict among eight characters whose origins and mentalities are completely different. "My God!" we catch ourselves whispering in the dark, and the name of John Steinbeck (who came up with the idea for the situation but did not take part in writing the screenplay) intensifies our suspicions.

A quarter of an hour into the film, a last castaway appears; he is hoisted up into the boat, and his "Danke Schön" is sufficient evidence that he belonged to the crew of the German submarine that sank the American ship on which our eight survivors were sailing. From now on, we feel better. Nothing of what we feared is going to happen. The simple psychological conflict is replaced, not exactly by a plot, but by a succession of small unexpected events linked by a philosophical discussion. If Good and Evil are not named, it is precisely because they are in the center of the discussion, which deals with nothing else. As in most of his films, Hitchcock uses a lot of critical or objective details, startlingly clever and true, but without giving us either a conclusion or the capacity to find one on our own.

Among those nine characters—each of them contemptible at one point and sublime at another—which are the good ones and which are the bad ones? Who is wrong and who is right? What crime have they committed? There again, we just cannot grasp the point, which constantly slips between our fingers. *Lifeboat* is the opposite of a generous film, but I do not think that it is pitiless either. Everything looks as if Hitchcock were—or would like to be—clear headed. Each scene proves something, the next scene "erasing" the previous demonstration. I thought about André Gide, about his *Prisoner of Poiters: Do Not Judge*—first of all it's impossible, and secondly, it's not your position to do so.

Alfred Hitchcock makes films as Gide writes books: "to disturb."

All sorts of abstract and theoretical ideas do not necessarily lead to the reassuring symbols they suggest: the international journalist, after losing her movie camera, her mink coat, and her typewriter, agrees to give up her luxurious bracelet to bait a fish, but she keeps her lipstick on.

Among Hitchcock's films, *Rope* [1948] and *Trouble with Harry* are the ones closest to *Lifeboat,* but the themes dealt with—especially "interchangeable guilt"—classify it with the rest of his work, and the absence of humor, here, makes it appear more serious. (SK)[24]

Right at the outset, Truffaut demands to know how anyone could properly "review this movie after seeing it only once?" What interests him about *Lifeboat* is precisely that it lacks so many of the plot devices we have come to expect from the director: "The situation that brings about the misunderstandings, the humorous trappings, and lastly the alibi." Admitting that "whoever does not get enthusiastic about the movie will be bored to death," Truffaut deftly analyzes the inherent weaknesses in the film's construction, while simultaneously demonstrating that Hitchcock refuses to fall into any of the "traps" he has set for himself.

As Truffaut notes, "the film does not start very well." The usual cross-section of people, endemic to any disaster film, are stranded on a lifeboat. " 'My God!' we catch ourselves whispering in the dark; and the name of John Steinbeck . . . intensifies our suspicions." Truffaut is obviously not an admirer of Steinbeck's work, and at the film's outset, it seems that *Lifeboat* will turn into a predictable series of psychological and social confrontations, along the lines of *Abandon Ship* (1957; Dir. Richard Sale), *Five Come Back* (1939; Dir. John Farrow), or *The Towering Inferno* (1974; Dirs. John Guillermin and Irwin Allen).

As Truffaut correctly observes, it is the introduction of the excellent Walter Slezak as the U-boat commander that shifts the film into altogether different territory. "From now on, we feel better," Truffaut writes. "Nothing of what we feared is going to happen. The simple psychological conflict is replaced, not exactly by a plot, but by a succession of small, unexpected events linked by a philosophical discussion." Further, "all sorts of abstract and theoretical ideas do not necessarily lead to . . . the reassuring symbols they suggest." What makes *Lifeboat* "clearheaded" is Hitchcock's refusal to underscore the obvious. He allows "small unexpected events" to happen, but these "events" do not always lend themselves to a "conclusion." When Tallulah Bankhead loses her 16mm portable movie camera near the beginning of the film, one might expect Hitchcock to indulge in a certain amount of ironic meditation on the transience and permanence of film and the ways in which it distances us from the events it presents, whether tragic, comic, or mundane. But he does nothing of the sort.

The incident, as with other "events" in the film, is presented in a matter-of-fact, throwaway manner. The camera is lost, and one can think of it what one wishes. As Truffaut notes, Hitchcock shows us these actions "without giving up either a conclusion or the capacity to find one on our own." It is precisely this moral multivalence that distinguishes Hitchcock as a director from the more pedestrian melodrama disaster specialists.

"Among those nine characters—each of them contemptible at one point and sublime at another—which are the good ones and which are the bad ones?" Hitchcock refuses to be drawn out. The most pronounced instance of this may be the scene in which Slezak convinces the dying, hallucinating William Bendix to go over the side of the boat. Bendix, a common sailor in the film, is convinced that his "sweetheart" is waiting for him at Roseland; Slezak does nothing to discourage the delusion. When he is later reprimanded for his conduct, Slezak insists that he did it for the good of the group. True? Self-justification? And Slezak's eventual murder, at the hands of all the other members of the party: is this a reasoned act or mob violence? As Truffaut notes, "if Good and Evil are not named, it is precisely because they are in the center of the discussion that deals with nothing else." It is this moral complexity in Hitchcock's universe that fascinates Truffaut, an ambivalence in all things that also illuminates much of Truffaut's own work as a director.

The Trouble with Harry is an altogether different matter. Truffaut wrote two notices for the film. One is a very short analysis, done as one of a group of brief reviews; the other is a detailed examination of the film and of Hitchcock's intent in making it. As Truffaut notes, the humor of *The Trouble with Harry* catches in our throats. Even as we laugh, we are filled with a vaguely unsettling feeling that we shouldn't be so amused. More than anything else, this film displays Hitchcock's princely contempt for his audience. There are, indeed, "three or four films in a film of his"; he is "the most demanding and secretive filmmaker." The inaccessibility of this droll comedy has put off many viewers since its initial release. To Truffaut's credit, he understood the complexity and darkness of this film from the first, and he finds *The Trouble with Harry* at once

threatening, contemptuous, and anti-humorous. It is also, not incidentally, "a little metaphysical fable" created for the public's consumption,
a fable that intentionally goes over the heads of most audiences.

Here is Truffaut's brief notice of *The Trouble with Harry*; one short
paragraph heralding the film's first run in Paris.

The Trouble with Harry—A little metaphysical fable about a corpse.
Alfred Hitchcock has made a film against humor, against funny stories,
and against laughing audiences. He nevertheless puts the audience in
his pocket, along with his contempt for them. Hitchcock has become, in
the past few years, the most demanding and secretive filmmaker. There
are always three or four films in a film of his; he can be understood on
a first level, then on a second, sometimes on a third, but the rest remains
difficult to understand, temporarily. (SK)[25]

The last sentence, in particular, is telling. "The rest remains difficult
to understand, temporarily." Whatever one may think of the film, it is
certainly a subject for further research. Without specifying the precise
content of the many "levels" of *The Trouble with Harry*, Truffaut nevertheless gives an accurate impression of the depth of the work; mysterious, ineffably personal, and a film that only tangentially considers the
needs and desires of the viewer. When the film opened, public reaction,
notes Donald Spoto, was "confused."[26] Yet, perhaps because of Truffaut's favorable notice, both here and in the more detailed review that
follows, *The Trouble with Harry* "played [in Paris] to packed houses for
half a year," in Truffaut's own words. "I was never able to figure out
whether it was entertaining to Parisians or whether the audience was
made up entirely of British and American tourists. I believe it wasn't too
successful in other parts of the world."[27]

Characteristically, Hitchcock accepts Truffaut's praise with practiced
diffidence, stating that the film's problematic commercial reception was
due to the fact that "the distributors didn't know how to exploit it. It
needed special handling."[28] As with much of Hitchcock's work, *The
Trouble with Harry* is considerably ahead of its time, and it was made
possible by the fact that Hitchcock was then on a winning streak, with
the success of *Rear Window* and the "anticipated success of *To Catch a
Thief*."[29] The budget for *The Trouble with Harry* was one million dollars,[30] a rather large budget for such an intimate film, devoid of either
spectacle or a large group of characters. To Hitchcock's credit, he filmed
the project because he was taken with its "understatement,"[31] and the
commercial and critical reception of the film seemed, to him, a matter of
scant consideration. By the mid-1960s, with the success of *Dr. Strange-
love* (1964; Dir. Stanley Kubrick), *The Loved One* (1965; Dir. Tony Rich-
ardson), and *Lord Love a Duck* (1966; Dir. George Axelrod), to name just
a few films of that era's "black comedy" cycle, the humor of *The Trouble*

with *Harry* would be much more in tune with public tastes. In 1955, however, when the United States was just recovering from the McCarthy era and the effects of the Korean War, such a cavalier display of societal rupture was not wholeheartedly embraced by general audiences.

Truffaut's more involved discussion of *The Trouble with Harry* goes into much greater detail than his short notice and gives the reader a brief plot synopsis (without disclosing the ending) and a feel for the location and thematic concerns of the work. Truffaut also takes the time to locate *The Trouble with Harry* within the context of Hitchcock's other work, tracing Hitchcock's evolution as a social commentator and storyteller. As Truffaut notes, *Harry* is a comedy of "destruction," and the humor of the film "turns against the audience," "to the greatest jubilation of the author." Hitchcock purposefully underwrites the ground on which the film operates with each succeeding scene. The film continually questions itself, proceeds as if in a dream, and cheerfully violates the then-prevalent conventions of narrative progression. All in all, *The Trouble with Harry* is an unusual film, not only for Hitchcock, but moreover for the American cinema in the mid-1950s.

The Trouble with Harry [1955] by Alfred Hitchcock.

One nice fall morning in a forest in Vermont, little Arnie discovers the corpse of a stranger named Harry. An old, retired captain who was hunting in the area, a spinster, and Arnie's pretty mother (Harry's widow) one after the other think they've killed Harry. The fact remains that this corpse, which must be buried and dug out repeatedly, is rather clumsy. No use telling the ending of the plot here.

Alfred Hitchcock has mastered such a skill for cinematic narrative that he has become, in a few years, much more than a good storyteller. Since he passionately loves his job, does not stop shooting, and managed long ago to solve all the problems connected to directing, he must, in order not to get bored or repeat himself, invent extra difficulties, create new disciplines for himself, so that we find, in his most recent films, an accumulation of thrilling limitations that are always brilliantly overcome.

Like *Rope* [1948], *Dial M for Murder* [1954], *Rear Window,* and *Lifeboat,* which will soon be shown in Paris, *The Trouble with Harry* obeys unity of time, of place, and of action. This rule of the game that Hitchcock invented for himself, and that he loves to elaborate upon and enrich from film to film, also affects his scripts above all, which he manipulates every which way until they fit in to the strict circle of his usual thematic concerns. As in *Strangers on a Train* [1951], *Suspicion* [1941], and *I Confess* [1953], the characters in *Harry,* as soon as they think they are or might be guilty, start behaving as if they actually were guilty, thus creating the misunderstanding on which the whole plot is built.

This shows how much Hitchcock remains true to himself even in this gruesome entertainment, which he shot in thirty days with a small budget[32] and no stars.

The Trouble with Harry is a funny film; at least that's what it intends to be, and it probably is since the audience in the Monte- Carlo laughed very loudly, especially those who understand English. I must admit that I personally do not see anything funny in this film, which, on the other hand, offers a major interest: it completes the portrait—that we can outline through his movies—of this above-average man whose humor is essentially destructive. *The Trouble with Harry* is a dead ringer for those stupid jokes that before being told need to be classified as "shaggy dog stories" if you want the audience to laugh. Hitchcock deliberately neglects to warn us, and even the joke, here, like a sponge dipped in water, becomes heavy with the weight of realism that seems to stick to everything that has been filmed. Hitchcock has shot a pun.

Absurdity is above all destruction: as the film goes forward, it destroys itself, each scene being a challenge both to logic in general and to the logic of the preceding scene. Would Harry's corpse eat its own feet, like the Baudelairean *catoblepas?**

Anyway, as in every film made by Hitchcock, the laughter turns against the audience and, please believe this, to the greatest jubilation of the author, because it is born of the unhealthy display of four characters who admit they do not have a "conscience" and act crazily, while their talk is confusing and smutty.

The Trouble with Harry, only a few of whose aspects I have examined here (what a film!), is directed with simplicity but also without flaws, as an excellent TV program would be.

The color is artfully wonderful: fall shades disclose a poetry that offers a mischievous contrast to the gruesome text and action.

This movie is a fable whose moral can hardly be defined before three or four years have elapsed, a necessary condition for us to have proper hindsight (Hitchcock's latest films always enhance our understanding of the older ones). Maybe it has something to do with Pascal's "sadness of a world deprived of God."

At the end of the film, which is also a penciled essay on laughter, Hitchcock rubs out his demonstration: little Arnie confuses yesterday, today, and tomorrow. The corpse that has been brought back into the open will be found again by Arnie tomorrow, but without anybody risking anything from the police since time has lost its meaning. *The Trouble with Harry* takes place in one day: is it yesterday, today, or tomor-

---

*An obscure reference: the *catoblepas* was a legendary antelope whose slender neck caused its heavy head to droop to the ground and whose look killed whatever it rested upon. (RCH)

row? Only Hitchcock knows the answer since that day "has not taken place" and was only born of his imagination. (BFH)[33]

Truffaut views *The Trouble with Harry* as a film that deconstructs itself, a film that violates its own manufactured reality even as it takes pains to create an illusion of an actual place and time. (Hitchcock shot much of the film on location in Vermont, in the small towns of East Craftsburg, Morrisville, Smugglers Notch, and Stowe, although inclement weather forced the crew to do more "interior/exterior" work than they had anticipated.[34] It is, at base, a comedy that seeks to undermine any comic intent inherent in its premise or execution, and this willful abrogation of responsibility toward the audience delights Hitchcock, as Truffaut points out. What *The Trouble with Harry* most prominently displays is its author's perversity. Having for so long been a prisoner of the "suspense" genre, Hitchcock here gives us a film that seems to contain elements of suspense and gallows humor and then decisively deprives us of our expected satisfaction at the film's key moments. *The Trouble with Harry* is considered by most observers to be a minor film in the Hitchcock canon, and there is no doubt that it is a slight, quiet work, devoid of the pyrotechnics implicit in the final reel of *Saboteur* (1942) or the violence in the shower murder in *Psycho* (1960). In this superficial respect, the film is an unusual one for the director, a quietly sardonic meditation on the mechanics of mistaken guilt, sexual attraction, and small-town insularity.

But this quiet reflection is what sets the film apart from Hitchcock's other work. The director told actress Mildred Dunnock during the shooting of *The Trouble with Harry* that one of his principal attractions to the project was his desire to shoot the turning leaves of autumnal New England in color. Even when bad weather forced the crew inside, technicians remained outside gathering up fallen leaves to be used on artificial trees for soundstage shooting.[35] This attention to detail is certainly not atypical for the director, but though the milieu of the film recalls, in some aspects, the quiet town of Santa Rosa, California, in *Shadow of a Doubt* (1942–43), Hitchcock in *The Trouble with Harry* is in a far gentler, more forgiving mood. The humor is dark, even black, but it is tinged with nostalgia and personal contemplation. The release of the film to the public seems almost a by-product of the film's production, so personal is the work in both content and conception. Yet for all its methodical, almost ethereal assurance, the film is still accessible for those who can view it against the backdrop of Hitchcock's other works. This, of course, is what *auteurism* is all about: a work seen in context. *The Trouble with Harry* emerges as an unexpectedly different film from a troubling and intentionally "disturbing" director, a filmmaker who will have a singular impact on François Truffaut, both critic and *auteur* in his own right.

John Huston

John Huston, while he interests Truffaut to some degree, is seen by the young critic as a figure of considerably less magnetism. "Will John Huston always be no more than an amateur?" Truffaut asks. In a lengthy appraisal of Huston's works, Truffaut comes to the conclusion, stated in the title of the following article, that while Huston may be "an excellent scriptwriter" he is undeniably "a second-rate director." What interests Truffaut the most in Huston's work is the theme of failure, of reaching beyond one's grasp.

Using Huston's adaptation of *Moby Dick* as a starting point, Truffaut considers Huston's career, as well as the director's personal background, to arrive at the considered opinion that for Huston, "work is more important than success." As Truffaut notes, "the theme of failure in Huston's works has become a commonplace for criticism." The protagonists in Huston's films often spend the entire running time of the work engaged in an activity that will ultimately prove futile. "Huston uses his wits in order to cause the enterprise to fail," Truffaut writes. "The gold, after months of mining, will be thrown to the wind at the end of *The Treasure of the Sierra Madre*; the Maltese falcon that is found proves to be fake," and so on. This theme of perpetual, inevitable, guaranteed failure in Huston's films seems less a "deep theme" to Truffaut than a mere "stratagem," a "pirouette" created by a "literary director . . . afraid of looking naive." Truffaut sees Huston as a director who tackles an enormous theme but who lacks the depth and psychological penetration to bring his films to life. "Fascinated by Melville's novel, fascinated by the monster, John Huston directed these operations as if they were about the exploitation of war loot, of a jewelry store robbery . . . or of the mining of gold." Huston misses "the real subject" of *Moby Dick*: "the revenge of Captain Ahab." Truffaut expresses some admiration for Huston's efforts, but he feels that "too often, John Huston offers us, instead of creatures made of flesh and blood, only colorless beings who come onto the screen to deliver one or two aphorisms before going out of focus." [36]

Truffaut thus finds Huston's thematic preoccupations no more than a pose. Huston, says Truffaut, "deludes himself with the thought that he gives subtlety to a script by evading the outcome that logic and dramatic psychology demand." This is why Huston remains a director of surfaces rather than of interior motivation. Now that Huston's career has come to an end, and particularly in view of the director's long "dry spell" in the '60s and into the early '70s (up to *Fat City* [1972]), Truffaut's assessment of Huston's skills and shortcomings seems on the whole accurate, if somewhat unsympathetic. Huston was a workmanlike director of acceptable craft and precision. His chief defect as a filmmaker, for Truffaut, was his lack of self-knowledge.

Will John Huston always be no more than an amateur?
John Huston, an excellent scriptwriter, is a second-rate director.

John Huston made one of his old dreams come true when he shot *Moby Dick* [1956]. He must have found in Melville's masterpiece the perfect synthesis of the themes he deals with from *The Maltese Falcon* [1941] to *Beat the Devil* [1954].

Moby Dick is a strictly unclassifiable subject and partakes in characteristics of every genre; it's a saga, a scientific document, a fantastic tale, an odyssey, and a metaphysical fable put together.

For Huston, it was unthinkable, in two hours running time, to transpose to the screen the 500 pages of the book. To a faithfulness to the letter, he says, he preferred a faithfulness to the spirit.

Everything that deals with the whale hunt is told in the film through a succession of eventful episodes, with new developments, like a series of nightmares. This huge blubbery heap of a whale, *"which represents the weight of a village of eleven hundred inhabitants, is covered with an epidermis more tender than a new-born child's skin and when the beast, captured, too monstrous to be hoisted up onto the ship's deck, is hung up along her flank, they peel it like a fruit and search her putrefying bowels for the marvellous ambergris, source of the finest products of perfumery."*

Fascinated by Melville's novel, fascinated by the monster, John Huston directed these operations as if they were about the exploitation of wartime looting, or a jewelry story robbery, or the digging of a tunnel, or the mining of gold.

But the real subject is the revenge of Captain Ahab (Gregory Peck) whose leg has been devoured by Moby Dick and replaced by an ivory leg carved from one of the tusks of the white sperm whale. The commercial fishing expedition, supported by outfitters who have invested their fortune in this ship, becomes an unusual adventure of life or death. Ahab, with the help of a colorful preacher (Orson Welles), has subdued the group of pagan harpooners. For the crew, Moby Dick soon appears to be the representation of terror, enlarged by superstitions, gossip, omens, and fabulous legends, and they think they see him everywhere . . . without ever finding him.

The Theme of Failure

After years of searching in the isolation of Southern seas, a voice suddenly exclaims: "He's blowing, he's blowing." Moby Dick is here, real, so very close to the ship that he smashes several of her whaleboats, and it is the fight between Ahab and Moby Dick that gives the impression of some kind of powerless challenge of man against the monster, agent of God.

The hunting of the whale, his capture, his cutting-up will not fail to remind the best "Hustonian" experts of the meticulous burglary in *Asphalt Jungle* [1950], the painstaking mining of gold flakes in *The Treasure of the Sierra Madre* [1948], the comical adventure of the passengers of the *African Queen* [1952], and the hunt for the precious *Maltese Falcon*.[37]

The theme of failure in Huston's works has become a commonplace for criticism since a study by Gilles Jacob was published four years ago in *Cahiers du Cinéma*: "*The tragedy of rapacity and the poetry of failure are two essential themes of the Hustonian world. The desire to obtain what is coveted, the need to possess by any means, even at the cost of blood, the taste of having more and more, set into motion a dark world that is hardened against pain, and that waits. The chase, "the 'key of G' of the cinema, is the incurable disease of the Hustonian hero, the drug from which he can't be detoxified. Fabulous falcon, gold mine, supreme power, political murder, beautiful Mexican women, horse-raising in Kentucky, torpedoing of a German gunboat, are all so many shining flames that attract him like a moth and lead him to his downfall.*"

If Huston, in spite of his technical failings, seemed to be the ideal director to film *Moby Dick*, it is because his characters pay less attention to the object than to its conquest. When you get to such a degree of stubbornness, the aim becomes just an excuse, to the point that, with a beautiful persistence, Huston uses his wits in order to cause the enterprise to fail; the gold, after months of mining, will be thrown to the wind at the end of *The Treasure of the Sierra Madre*; the Maltese falcon that is found proves to be fake, the real one remaining undiscoverable; the tunnel that the rebels have bored won't be any use, and so on.

Every film of Huston's ends on a similar pirouette and, rather than a deep theme, I see there, for my part, the stratagem of a literary director who, afraid at first of looking naive, deludes himself with the thought that he gives subtlety to a script by evading the outcome that logic and dramatic psychology demand.

Too often, John Huston offers us, instead of creatures made of flesh and blood, only colorless beings who come onto the screen to deliver one or two aphorisms before going out of focus.

A Yachtsman

John Huston was born in 1906 in Nevada, Missouri. His father was the actor Walter Huston who recently died and who, under the direction of his son, created in *The Treasure of the Sierra Madre* an unforgettable portrayal. John, after solid studies at Lincoln High School in Los Angeles, started a career as a professional boxer, but as he was on a tour, he took advantage of a stop to join a theatrical company as a supplementary actor. In 1925, we find him as a cavalry officer, then sports journalist. Then he divided his activities between drama and painting. Through screenwriting he came to cinema, around 1938.

One can see that John Huston didn't intend to take up cinema as a profession at all: one can also notice his taste for "out-of-the-way" professions. John Huston failed in his attempts to become a boxer, a cavalry officer, an actor, a painter, and a playwright. Well-off from the day he was born, he remained, in spite of his will, an amateur, a "yachtsman," always mingled with professionals, with "specialists" whose competence in their chosen fields he admired.

Walter Huston's son would have given away all the gold of the Transvaal to become, in his turn, a professional, a specialist, and it took him a long time to understand that only cinema—where his father was a star—could fulfill this desire.

It is not an exaggeration to think that John Huston has to thank the contacts he had with boxers, officers, journalists, actors, writers, and painters for not failing as lamentably as his heroes did. For Huston, work is more important than success, the conquering spirit surpasses the thing to be conquered, the object is nothing when compared to the efforts made to reach it.

The theme of failure, for Huston, is nothing but the subject of an old fable, since, after La Fontaine, his heroes discover that "work is a treasure." (BFH)[38]

Truffaut admired those comedians whose genius remained confined to their presence on the screen and who refused, resolutely, to "adapt" to the cinema. Chaplin used the cinema to record his incomparable technique as a mime, and the Marx Brothers viewed the cinema as an almost documentary medium. Truffaut's review of the revival of *Animal Crackers*, the second sound film by the Marx Brothers, contains a few factual errors. The team did not break up during World War II, but rather continued on with the uninspired feature film *Love Happy* (1949) and a failed TV series pilot, tentatively entitled *Deputy Seraph*.[39] Yet Truffaut's appreciation of the team as satirists and masters of the verbal assault is right on the mark. The visuals here are clearly subordinate, if not nonexistent.

Animal Crackers (Animal Crackers) [1930; Dir. Victor Heerman]: The Reprise of a Classic

If there is a genre of films in which the story counts little, then it definitely includes films animated by the absurd and funny presence of the Marx Brothers. *Animal Crackers* was, together with *A Night at the Opera* [1935], perhaps their greatest success. In the latter film, they performed a comic opera on Broadway, probably with a fair degree of success, since someone experienced the desire to bring it to the screen, without changing a single line of text, yet, for the rather flatly filmed action takes place on only one set. Yet, who would think of reproaching the four Marx brothers for this ease, this neglect with regard to the most fundamental laws of filmmaking, as they were the greatest American comedians of the prewar decade? *Animal Crackers* is the second Marx movie. At the time, there were four of them: Groucho, Harpo, Chico, and Zeppo. The last one left them pretty quickly; the three others had some great successes, and then the group broke up during the war. We know how comedians die young, how the verve quickly dies out, how the imagination is exhausted. A justification of the Marx's poetry of the ab- surd is no longer necessary. We see again—and with great delight—the blithering Chico, Harpo the mute—shameless pickpocket and silly fool— and most of all Groucho, the incarnation of low-down trickery whose insolence has become famous: "You're beautiful, I love you . . . like a million dollars," or "I had a wonderful evening, but it wasn't this one," or "I never forget a face, but in your case I'll make an exception," or finally "You like nature? Well, you certainly don't hold a grudge, after what it did to you!"

The Marx Brothers have not made films for more than ten years. The only thing left to do is to see the best of them for a second time in the same way as one goes on a pious pilgrimage. One laughs with this movie as much as one did twenty years ago. The extraordinary sequences of the bridge party and Harpo's arrival are as irresistible as they used to be. It is quite remarkable that the two best shows offered currently on the Champs-Elysées date back more than twenty years: *The Passion of Jeanne D'Arc* (1928) and *Animal Crackers* (1930). (SK)[40]

In their later films, the Marx Brothers would indulge in some decid- edly cinematic sight gags: the missing mirror sequence in *Duck Soup* (1933; Dir. Leo McCarey), or the speeded-up football game at the climax of *Horse Feathers* (1932; Dir. Norman Z. McLeod). Yet both of these gags have their roots in vaudeville, and throughout their long film career, the Marx Brothers would derive their ultimate authority from the stage. Truffaut recognized this, and recognized as well that there were only a few "recipes" for comedy, all of them, perhaps, derived from "a crafty transposition of the French vaudeville that triumphed on the Boulevard in 1925." We can perhaps forgive Truffaut the undeniable chauvinism of this remark, in that vaudeville's origin was certainly not confined to the French music hall.

In an essay on the history and variants of American comedy, Truffaut briefly outlined the history of movie farce and highlighted the careers of Ernst Lubitsch, Frank Capra, Leo McCarey, Preston Sturges, Don Weis, and George Cukor as some of the most important American comedy *au- teurs.* This informal overview of the comic film begins with the early Lumière Brothers' short, *L'Arroseur Arrosé* (*Watering the Gardener* [1895]), and continues up to the films of George Cukor and Garson Kanin, necessarily neglecting the work of many important American comedians, such as Harold Lloyd, W. C. Fields, Chaplin, Charley Chase, and others (all graduates, by the way, of the American and British vaudeville circuit).[41]

With great confidence, the trade press regularly announces the death of American cinema "which is no longer what it used to be." Did Hollywood reach its height before or just after talkies? Has the best of American cinema disappeared together with World War II? The truth is that it is impossible to agree on the matter; and discussions seem to take on the shape of a quarrel between generations.

As for American comedy, everyone deplores its disappearance without, however, explaining the phenomenon. The Golden Age of American comedy is situated between 1934 and 1939, but, to the extent that this genre has been around since the invention of cinema, one may say that American comedy is not dead, as the movies of George Cukor, Joseph Mankiewicz, Walter Lang, Norman McLeod, Don Weis, and a few · others prove to us every year again.

Like the western, comedy is as old as cinema itself. Is it necessary to recall that the first film with a scenario, *Watering the Gardener,* was a little burlesque comedy based on a gag?[42] In America, films of 1,000 feet were made around 1908 that told in ten minutes how a girl and a boy met, argued, reconciled, and got married (see *Scenes from Real Life* [1908]). From his early movies on, Griffith was interested in comedy (*The New York Hat* [1912], which can still be seen today in the Cinémathèque). And Griffith often directed Lillian and Dorothy Gish into comedy in many scenes of *Judith of Bethulia* [1913]. We could also cite the gags with which Douglas Fairbanks brightened *The Mark of Zorro* [1920] or *The Thief of Bagdad* [1924]. The beginnings of comedy have constituted the object of many never-ending debates. But could it not be that this genre—which everybody agrees is characteristic of Broadway— was a crafty transposition of the French vaudeville that triumphed on the Boulevard in 1925? And yet what a difference in tone between a vaudeville of Alfred Savoir and a film by Lubitsch!

As Jean Georges Auriol stated very well, American comedy owes as much to the Boulevard as to Mark Twain, to Chaplin as to Bernard Shaw, to Noel Coward as to Meilhac and Halévy, to Sheridan as to Swift.

When Love Triumphs

Very naturally, American comedy was destined to find its achievement, its themes, and its laws with the coming of sound film.

In 1934, Ernst Lubitsch was master in the domain of comedy. *Trouble in Paradise* (1932), with Kay Francis, Miriam Hopkins, and Herbert Marshall, was a great success and was followed by a film made up of sketches: *If I Had a Million* [1932; Dirs. Lubitsch, James Cruze, H. Bruce Humberstone, Stephen Roberts, William A. Seiter, Norman Taurog, and Norman Z. McLeod]. At this point, Frank Capra, born in Palermo, who emigrated to the U.S.A. in 1903, made *It Happened One Night* [1934], a movie that would be greeted as a masterpiece. Thanks to this movie—plagiarized a thousand times afterwards—Capra was considered a second Lubitsch. The story involved a journalist (Clark Gable) who, in his quest of a "sensational" newspaper story, accompanied the daughter of a multimillionaire (Claudette Colbert) in her escapade from home. It all ended in marriage. American comedy had then found its recipe. It always involved a couple that was separated by social class but for whom love triumphed. Two years later, Capra shot *Mr. Deeds Goes to Town* [1936], a variation of *It Happened One Night.*

The recent success of *Roman Holiday* [1953; Dir. William Wyler], a film whose scenario has borrowed the same exact situations of the two classics mentioned above, proves that undertakings of the same genre are still in vogue. But the screenwriters of *Roman Holiday* learned their lessons from an era that valued seeing the dark side of things more than rose-colored glasses; the obstacle this time is not money but ancestry. Audrey Hepburn is a royal heiress, Peck a journalist, and Wyler's best movie ends with a bittersweet memory of twenty-four intimate hours.

Another variation on the eternal theme of the couple: husband and wife adore each other, but because of a misunderstanding they decide to file for divorce. The legal waiting period is ninety days. The movie will recount these ninety days, and one hour before the expiration date or, if you prefer, five minutes before the words "The End," reconciliation takes place. (Example: *The Awful Truth* [1937] of Leo McCarey.)

From Preston Sturges to George Cukor

As the first reel of an American comedy unwinds, everyone knows how it will end; the story is always the same. Only the means to get to the climax differ. As such, comedies are exercises of style. Misunderstandings are impossible; a mistake concerning the hierarchy of genres is no longer made. Everybody praises the comedy that, using well-known procedures, introduces the most unexpected ideas, the most sophisticated new developments, and the most comical details in the story. Comedy felt at ease within the limits of convention, although it was convention that killed it. On themes of Frank Capra, Preston Sturges introduced the "demystifying and anti-edifying" comedy in Hollywood. To *Mr. Smith Goes to Washington* [1939], Sturges replies with *The Great McGinty* [1940]; to *Sergeant York* [1941; Dir. Howard Hawks] with *Hail the Conquering Hero* [1944]; to *I Am a Fugitive from a Chain Gang* [1932; Dir. Mervyn LeRoy] with *Sullivan's Travels* [1941]. Preston Sturges sent affectation and friendliness to the devil and replaced them with satire and cynicism. But the Sturges vogue only lasted a while, and Sturges's impertinence caused his unemployment.

With Lubitsch dead, and Capra and Sturges in the doghouse, only one of the "greats" of comedy is left: George Cukor, who was wise enough to team up with the best scriptwriter in Hollywood: Garson Kanin. Together, they reward American cinema every year with a masterpiece.

Thanks to these last pioneers, American comedy—an inexhaustible subject—has never stopped preparing marvelous evenings for us. (SK)[43]

Consider this essay in the context of another "generic" examination by the young critic, "The Professional Secret: Western and Comedy." The "professional" aspect that Truffaut alludes to here is not far from the ethic of Hawks, that consummate artisan who gravitated between westerns and comedies, as we have seen, with great effectiveness. However, this article does not concern itself with Hawks but rather with the work of George Cukor, who emerged in the previous essay as one of the last bastions of American comedy, thanks in part to his association with scenarist Garson Kanin.

What is peculiar, on reflection, is that Truffaut in his essay on comedy sees little hope for the extension of the "classic" Hollywood farce into the future. Yet, Tashlin, Hawks, Weis, and others are mentioned elsewhere by Truffaut (and Weis is even cited within the essay itself) as proof that "American comedy is not dead." The elegiac tone of Truffaut's history of the comic film is pervasive and unmistakable. If "American comedy is not dead," his essay does not spend all that much time celebrating the genre's most recent exemplars. This same tone of lost grandeur permeates Truffaut's essay on Cukor's work, an essay that seeks to deconstruct Cukor's (and Kanin's) comic structures and seems to suggest that Cukor belongs to a dying breed, a specialist in a comic style for which there are as yet no apparent heirs.

The Professional Secret: Western and Comedy

American cinema—was cinema not always American?—can be divided into three basic genres: (a) westerns, (b) comedy, and (c) thrillers.

The comedy and the western are opposed to each other in the same manner as a wild animal and a domesticated animal. The western borrows from primitivism; characters are forged of steel. It is a rough, simple, and virile genre. The whole story centers on respect either for the official law, symbolized by the sheriff's brass star, or for the unofficial, natural law supported by one's conviction or word of honor. Honor constitutes the basis of the western.

Comedy illustrates the complete contrary; its domain is the civilized world, its main subject matter the art of nuance.

Let us observe in passing that thrillers, or gangster movies, borrow their "extreme" characters from the western, and the modernity of the environment (revolvers, tuxedos, taxis, etc.) from comedy. In spite of their fundamental opposition, the western and the comedy actually meet in terms of worldview; the first in its exaltation of old virtues, and the latter in its denunciation of the customs of a mechanized world.

Decadence and Grandeur

When the cinema has existed a century, sociologists will not fail to get a handle on its history. I rather think their major discovery will be the following: European cinema will have treated the decadence of man, whereas American cinema will have untiringly exalted that same man. It suffices to engage in an easy game of comparisons; on one hand *The Last Laugh* [1924; Dir. F. W. Murnau], *Quai des Brumes* [*Port of Shadows,* 1938; Dir. Marcel Carné], *The Bicycle Thief* [1949; Dir. Vittorio DeSica], *Les Orgueilleux* [*The Proud and the Beautiful,* 1953; Dir. Yves Allegret]; on the other hand *Birth of a Nation* [1915; Dir. D. W. Griffith], *Lonesome* [1928; Dir. Paul Fejos], *Mr. Smith Goes to Washington* [1939; Dir. Frank Capra], *Sergeant York* [1941; Dir. Howard Hawks].

The whole history of Hollywood equals a long flirtation with heroism.

The Tears of Spencer Tracy

Progressive critics, and more generally those who have adopted the famous axiom "Nothing human is foreign to me," have made a serious mistake by repudiating American comedy for its defiance of conventions. When good comic authors chase away philosophy, it comes galloping back. *It Should Happen to You* [1954; Dir. George Cukor] tells the story of a charming scatterbrain [Judy Holliday] who uses her savings to rent a large billboard on which she has her name written: Gladys Glover.[44] Soon—is it any surprise?—she finds the fame that this un-called-for advertisement legitimized in advance. This is an innocent but excellent project that, perhaps involuntarily, treats glory via the absurd, in terms strictly similar to the famous reflections by Monsieur Teste on the same subject.

However, whether conventional or demystifying, joking or preaching, American comedy constitutes essentially an exercise of style, it's a genre where the genius of directors and actors asserts itself best. Therefore, I will end my Praise of Comedy with an example from George Cukor and Garson Kanin's best movie, *Adam's Rib* [1949]. The scene takes place in a lawyer's office; Katharine Hepburn and Spencer Tracy are filing for divorce and are dividing up their property. Next comes the inventory of their country home where they were happy. Tracy, his back to his wife, turns his face to the audience and starts crying. Katharine Hepburn, moved by this, approaches him and takes him to the country house, to their reconciliation. That evening, they fight again, and Tracy declares: "If you contradict me, I will cry just like this afternoon." And while his surprised wife watches him, he re-creates his mask of grief by "distorting" his countenance to the extreme; his shoulders are bent, his wrinkles become hollow and his eyes hazy; tears finally flow, and the good-natured public—having had a good cry themselves ten minutes earlier—applauds this feat of strength by a great actor. Does this not represent a beautiful example of cinema in its pure state? (BFH)[45]

Not only is the "professional" skill of Cukor praised here, but also the skill of Spencer Tracy, in a tour de force scene that strips away, in a curiously reflexive manner, the pretense of acting. Tracy "doubles" his tears not only for Hepburn but for Cukor, Kanin, and also for the film's audience. This foregrounds the presentational nature implicit in all filmic constructs in a manner that Truffaut finds both unique and refreshing.

However, Tracy's skill as an actor, Kanin's admirable ability as a scenarist, and even Cukor's directional skill are all only a portion of the territory the essay seeks to explore. Of all of Truffaut's writings, this short piece is organized in perhaps the most random fashion of any of his critical works. A point is introduced in one sentence, then abandoned in the next; assertions as to the nature of American and European filmmaking are hastily introduced, without discernable supporting arguments, and then dropped.

Truffaut begins the essay with a brief treatise on the oppositional nature of the comic and western genres, then demonstrates how the two sets of thematic and iconic conventions thus represented have successfully cross-pollinated each other. The "thrillers," Truffaut notes, "borrow their 'extreme' characters from the western and the modernity of their environment . . . from comedy." Thus the "gangster movie" can be seen as a series of "western" archetypes in different dress.

However, in the next paragraph, Truffaut contradicts one of his earlier pronouncements. "When the cinema has existed a century," Truffaut states, "European cinema will have treated the decadence of man, whereas American cinema will have untiringly exalted that same man." This is a direct contradiction to Truffaut's earlier comments on the comedies of Howard Hawks, which demonstrate, Truffaut feels, "man's degeneracy and slackness in modern civilization."

While it may well be that "the whole history of Hollywood equals a long flirtation with heroism," Truffaut's arbitrary division of American and European cinema along these rather simplistic boundaries seems a trifle superficial. Certainly, one can hold up Quai des Brumes and The Bicycle Thief as evidence of one set of thematic preoccupations on the part of European (or, more specifically, French and Italian) auteurs, just as one can point to the earnest populism of Birth of a Nation, Mr. Smith Goes to Washington, and Sergeant York as examples of a simplistic jingoism that informs the construction of much Hollywood studio product.

European films were equally capable of being frivolous (see the comedies of Fernandel) and derivative (cf. the "American-styled" crime thrillers of Eddie Constantine, discussed later in this volume). And what of Billy Wilder's *The Lost Weekend* (1945)? Or Fritz Lang's *Fury* (1937)? Or King Vidor's *Our Daily Bread* (1934)? One might argue that these admittedly atypical productions are modeled after European films (as indeed they are) or, in the case of Wilder and Lang, are the work of expatriates who brought the concerns of their country with them. Yet this arbitrary division still seems misleading, even if one might find the discussion it engenders ultimately illuminating.

Truffaut concludes his essay with brief discussions of two Cukor films, *It Should Happen to You* and *Adam's Rib*. What is examined here is not so much Cukor's technique or mise-en-scène but rather his tact in collaborating with Hepburn, Tracy, and Kanin, in breathing life into what Truffaut describes, without condescension, as "an exercise of style . . . in which the genius of directors and actors asserts itself best." It is the seamlessness of this collaboration that most affects Truffaut, particularly when he recounts the incident of "the tears of Spencer Tracy" as one evidence of the technique on display in *Adam's Rib*.

"Display" is what is most pronounced here, both in *Adam's Rib* and in Truffaut's examination of it. There is, after all, nothing particularly new in the narrative structure of the film. What elevates *Adam's Rib* above the ordinary is Cukor's extraordinary skill as a comic craftsperson, a director who knows when to intrude, when to guide, and when to step back and let his actors perform most of the work. Certainly one never thinks in terms of visual pyrotechnics when one thinks of Cukor. His style consists of an unobtrusive control of all the elements at his disposal, and in this he excels. *Adam's Rib* is a triumph of style over substance, but the technique used so effortlessly here is beyond reproach. It is almost as if the energy and ability with which Cukor rejuvenates these comic "stations of the cross" is sufficient to renew them, to allow us to see them from a fresh perspective. It is this transubstantiational skill that Truffaut celebrates here, and it serves as a transcendent apotheosis for the essay.

4 The Egalitarian Spirit

Garnett, Marshall, Mann, and Farrow

Cukor and Hitchcock are indisputably major figures in cinema history. Yet Truffaut afforded even the most minor *auteurs* an equal opportunity in his reviews. While these less important directors would not always get the same degree of attention as Lang or Renoir might receive in Truffaut's columns for *Arts* and *Cahiers du Cinéma*, the reader of these journals could be equally certain that the latest films of such American directors as Tay Garnett, George Marshall, Anthony Mann, John Farrow, and other "assignment" directors would be afforded their share of coverage. Then, too, Truffaut made it his business to attend screenings, often at his own expense, of the more popular French films, such as the programmers of Eddie Constantine, or commercial films by Pierre Louis or Jean-Pierre Melville, and report on them on a regular basis.

Truffaut gives only a few words to *Houdini* (1953), yet he still manages to locate the principal difficulty facing the production. Conjuring tricks, when filmed, are not illusions at all: they become, in the act of being recorded, part of the illusion of the film medium. This defect decisively robs *Houdini* of most of its intended impact on the screen where, as Truffaut notes, "nothing irrational astonishes."

Houdini (Houdini, le grand magicien)
American movie by George Marshall.
This movie tells the life and exploits of the famous illusionist and magician. . . . The failure of the project was predestined by the particulars of the film medium itself: indeed, the juggling as well as the magic lose all their impact on the screen, since cinema itself is made up of trick shots, the quality of appearance, love of appearance, and appearance of love. In cinema, magicians may work behind the camera (like Méliès) but not on the screen, where nothing irrational astonishes. Janet Leigh is charming, the Technicolor pleasant; is that enough? No. (SK)[1]

One of the most remarkable aspects of this review is its failure to even mention the production's nominal leading man, Tony Curtis. "Janet Leigh

111

is charming, the Technicolor pleasant; is that enough? No." Truffaut is stating a fact when he declares that "In cinema, magicians may work behind the camera, but not on the screen." *Houdini,* a typical George Pal production in its incessant reliance on special effects, is thus in every way a failure. Even the "pleasant" physical production of the film cannot save it. *Houdini* makes the extraordinary ordinary.

The Glenn Miller Story gets slightly better treatment: the film "constitutes a success," because "the scriptwriters have succeeded in justifying the incessant intrusion of tunes and songs," and "Anthony Mann . . . manages to gain our interest in a story of so little excitement."[2] On the whole, one gets the distinct impression that Truffaut liked *The Glenn Miller Story* in spite of himself, and he has Mann's adroit handling of a potentially indifferent project to thank for his interest, no matter how minimal.

The Glenn Miller Story (Romance inachevee)[1954]
American movie by Anthony Mann.

This film pictures the romanticized biography of the famous jazz composer Glenn Miller.

A more unrewarding genre than this could not be found. However, *The Glenn Miller Story* constitutes a success: the writers have succeeded in justifying the incessant intrusion of tunes and songs. The work of director Anthony Mann appears even more skillful; he manages to gain our interest in a story of so little excitement.

The Technicolor is of irreproachable quality and the acting—bringing together James Stewart and June Allyson—is excellent. (SK)[3]

John Farrow's *Hondo* gets an even warmer reception. "This is one of the best westerns of the moment," Truffaut enthuses, and he compares the film to George Steven's *Shane* (1953). Not surprisingly, in view of Truffaut's opinion of *Giant, Hondo* comes off as much the better of the two productions. "*Hondo* moves as rapidly as *Shane* moves little," Truffaut insists. "Moreover, it is a movie with fewer pretensions." It's sad that Truffaut didn't allow *Hondo* more extensive discussion; the film has all but vanished from memory, while *Shane* is still revived at regular intervals. John Farrow's work as a director is well known, but he is not immediately identified as a director of westerns.[4] Here, he works with one of the dominant lights of the American western, John Wayne, and from all accounts the results are eminently satisfactory.

Hondo (Hondo, L'homme du désert) [1953]
American movie by John Farrow.

This is one of the best westerns of the moment. Obviously, the writers of *Hondo* thought of *Shane* when writing this story of a young widow who, abandoned on her ranch with her son, receives protection from

John Wayne and marries him later on. But here the comparison stops, because *Hondo* moves as rapidly as *Shane* moves little. Moreover, it is a movie with fewer pretensions. The color is very beautiful; the Apaches are at the same time appealing and threatening in their toughness; John Wayne is calm and strong. (SK)[5]

Less appealing, however, is *Le Grand Bluff*, an Eddie Constantine "action/adventure" film made in 1957,[6] and never released in the United States. Constantine, a curious figure for a matinee idol, was born in the United States but gravitated to France, where he became an associate of Edith Piaf and cut a number of popular records. In 1953 he began appearing in films and almost immediately established himself as a Humphrey Bogart knockoff in a series of predictable low-budget films.

For a time, he became something of a cult figure in France. Perpetually clad in a trenchcoat, speaking his lines in a disinterested monotone, ceaselessly smoking unfiltered cigarettes, Constantine's pockmarked countenance and his gravelly voice were enough to ensure him a brief flash of fame. His career was on the wane in the 1960s, when Jean-Luc Godard picked up Constantine and his perennial character, Lemmy Caution, for his film *Alphaville: Une Etrange Aventure de Lemmy Caution* (1965), which restored Constantine to a portion of his former glory. *Le Grand Bluff*, however, comes at the tail end of Constantine's first brush with the public, and as Truffaut indicates, the joke is wearing thin.

Le Grand Bluff (A tiring nonchalance)

In *Le Grand Bluff*, Eddie Constantine plays the part of an American, Eddie F. Morgan, who's a professional gambler because he has a taste for risk. He settles in the Hotel George V without a penny, borrows a Cadillac and lives it up, pretending to be a businessman who has decided to spend a lot of money in France. Oil, no more oil, oil again, yes, no, yes, it's the old Hustonian game that can be traced back to *The Maltese Falcon:* failure, success, failure.

So it's a bad screenplay, neither more nor less bad than all those that Constantine has performed in. The producers used to surround him with second-rate elements and people used to say: And yet, it would be possible to make a good movie with Eddie Constantine. Today, he is very powerful, he is nearly his own producer, percentage on grosses and everything that goes with it, he chooses the script, the director, the musician, and the main actors. Everything remains second-rate and people think: Eddie Constantine will never make a good film.

He used to fight against stuntmen; today, stuntmen fight against one another, and Eddie watches them, disenchanted. His laziness brings on the ruin of the best moments. An example? At the end of the film, oil gushes out and all the main characters start dancing wildly under the shower of black gold, dripping but exuberant under the oil flood. Only one is missing: Eddie, who didn't want to get sprayed, and who is shown on one side, impeccable in a gray suit, stupidly smiling, suddenly seeming ridiculous to us among his friends black with mud.

That's how the affection we had for the nice, but false, gangster becomes blunted—after all, a Yankee accent and pimples are not enough anymore! This is not a personal feeling but a fact, and it suffices to check the grosses of Eddie Constantine's latest movies, all released by the same distributor: Balzac-Helder-Scala-Vivienne. We find in *Le Film français: Folies Bergères* [1957]: 81,844,370 francs (with Zizi Jeanmaire); *L'homme et l'enfant* [*Man and Child,* 1957]: 60,302,100 francs, and *Le Grand Bluff,* which, as its title points out, doesn't even reach 40 million! In other words, Constantine's stock is falling, and that's his fault since it rested entirely with him to take advantage of his huge success, two years ago: more elaborate scripts, better directors, there's no getting around it, Eddie Constantine wanted to make too many weak films too fast.

From [director] Patrice Dali, who was Orson Welles's assistant [on the production of Welles's *Othello* (1952)] (from whom he only borrowed his way of walking and some clothing details, his shirt cuffs turned over his jacket sleeves), from Jules Dassin and Sacha Guitry (he filmed, alone, the fights in *Si Paris nous était conté* [1955]), we expected more. We get painful humor, clumsily etched characters, quick but weak mise-en-scène, irregular direction of the actors.

Worthy of notice: the confirmation of Mireille Granelli's great gift. Her acting is completely unrealistic but inventive and graceful. She already attracted attention in *Pardonnez nos offenses* [*Forgive Our Trespasses*]. Pretty person, fresh face. Let's also note some funny lines in Yvan Audouard's dialogue, and the liveliness of "Moustache," whose cheerfulness delights me. (SK)[7]

Truffaut links the cinema of Constantine with the cinema of Huston; "the everlasting Hustonian game that can be traced back to *The Maltese Falcon:* failure, success, failure." Because of this thematic line with Huston, Constantine and his director in *Le Grand Bluff,* Patrice Dali (Dali actually served as one of five coproducers on Welles's version of *Othello*),[8] start with "a bad script, [yet] neither more nor less bad than all those that Constantine has performed in." But a bad script can be overcome. Look at the work of Edgar G. Ulmer, particularly *Club Havana* (1946), which had not even a "bad" script, but no script at all.[9]

Yet there is no inventiveness in this film, visual or otherwise. Significantly, of all the films discussed thus far in this volume, this is the first time that Truffaut measures the success of a film, and the rise and fall of Constantine's career, strictly in terms of box office receipts. In Truffaut's view, the precipitous decline of this "false gangster" is entirely "his fault since it rested with him to take advantage of his huge success." Constantine "wanted to make too many weak films too fast," and the result is that "everything remains second rate and people think: Eddie Constantine will never make a good film."

Truffaut details every fault of *Le Grand Bluff*; the transparent use of stunt men, the newfound laziness of the film's nominal star. Eddie Constantine's vogue in France was all but over: the actor left that country in 1958 and made a series of dreary *policiers* in England, Germany, and Italy, his fortune obviously on the wane. Only the intervention of Agnès Varda (who featured Constantine in *Cléo de 5 à 7* [1962]) and Godard saved the actor from professional ruin. Truffaut's devotion to the *auteur* theory is here indirectly vindicated. Eddie Constantine needed a director of intelligence and vision to shape, and reshape, his screen persona. Failing a strong outside hand, his work suffered. Of late, Eddie Constantine has managed to resurrect his tough-guy image, with some modification, in such recent films as *The Long Good Friday* (1980; Dir. John Mackenzie) and *Beware of the Holy Whore* (1971; Dir. Rainer Werner Fassbinder). More than most actors, Constantine seems to have exhibited a considerable lack of judgment in the management of his career.[10]

Nor is Truffaut any more impressed with Jean-Pierre Melville's *Quand tu liras cette lettre* (1953), another French "policier." Melville's career is inextricably linked to that of Jean Cocteau; he appeared as an actor in Cocteau's *Orpheus* (1950) and directed the screen adaptation of Cocteau's *Les Enfants Terribles* (1950).[11] (Melville, whose real name was Jean-Pierre Grumbach, took the name "Melville" from Herman Melville, in homage to the writer's work.) As Katz notes, Melville functioned almost exclusively as an independent production entity, and as such served as an example for the economical maiden productions of the *Nouvelle Vague*.[12] Melville also appeared as an actor in Godard's *Breathless* (1959).

The intense dislike that Truffaut feels for Melville's film is thus somewhat hard to reconcile. With *Bob le Flambeur*, a 1955 film that Melville directed and co-wrote, and *Le Doulos (Doulos the Finger Man)*, a film Melville produced, wrote, and directed in 1962 to his credit, most critics and historians regard Melville as a genuine if minor talent, whose career was truncated by an unwillingness to work within the French film industry. Truffaut, however, considers Melville "not even a good maker of bad films" and finds *Quand tu liras cette lettre* "a very badly made film, with all the defects of 16mm cinema." What seems to displease Truffaut the most is Melville's apparent ambivalence toward his subject. The film refuses to be either "lyric" or "sordid," and as a result the film is not "courageous," nor is it "a film to see."

Quand tu liras cette lettre (When You Read This Letter)
French film by J. P. Melville [Jean-Pierre Melville].

Since *Le Silence de la mer (The Silence of the Sea)* [1949] has going for it only the generosity of its subject, since *Les Enfants Terribles* was repudiated by the one who signed his name to it but claimed by its father [Jean Cocteau], we may consider that *When You Read This Letter* is J. P. Melville's first film that counts, the first made according to the usual commercial standards, with, it seems, a fairly high price tag. In any case, the proof is thus made many times over, the proof is there, in this film, that J. P. Melville is not an *auteur* of films, nor even a good maker of bad films. Jacques Deval must share the guilt. The young delinquent, a bit of a thief, a bit of a pimp, dishonors a girl, having seduced and abandoned her; in the end he is touched by grace for the love that he bears for—and possibly inspires in?—a nun who is also the real sister of the defiled little girl. There were two ways to tell the story: a lyric way, "Stroheim style," and a sordid way, "Ralph Habib style." Deval and Melville couldn't choose. The result is a very badly made film, with all the defects of 16mm cinema, without the nice aggravations, a permanent compromise between a "tone" that seeks to be high but succeeds only in being grotesque. Philippe Lemaire is far from bad, but Juliette Gréco is far from good. She says banal things in a tragic voice and tragic things in an everyday voice. A courageous film? No. A film to see? No. Am I being unjust? No (everyone tells me). (RCH)[13]

There is no substantive evidence that Truffaut ever modified his views on Melville, despite Melville's alliance with Godard (and indirectly Truffaut) in the early days of the *Nouvelle Vague*. Melville himself went on to bigger budgets and more mainstream films in the 1960s, using Alain Delon and Jean-Paul Belmondo. He died in 1973. While it seems to me that Truffaut is being unnecessarily harsh here, perhaps even a bit envious (certainly Truffaut's early films have a "16mm" aspect in their sparse production values), it is Melville's lack of daring that Truffaut ultimately objects to, and in this respect he may be right.

Les Enfants Terribles is a careful and meticulous film, distinguished more by Cocteau's scenario and dialogue than any visual inventiveness. Melville's *policiers* are surface works. They contain precisely what they seem to contain, and nothing more. There is a lack of resonance and involvement in Melville's direction, which is partly compensated for by the director's methodical technique. In his use of actual locations, small production crews, and (sometimes) nonactors of exceptional presence in his works, Melville has at least a superficial link to the neorealists. Yet this may not be enough. Melville seems to have had admirable impulses in the creation of his work, but, as his films in the 1960s and early 1970s indicate (he made his last film, *Un Flic* [*A Cop*], in 1972), Melville ultimately settled for less than he might have achieved. This may explain Melville's affection for Godard in his early days. Godard was creating the work that Melville himself was incapable of.

In contrast, David Butler's *King Richard and the Crusaders* (1954) is a "bad American film," but it "comes over better than a bad French film," because "the rhythm does not slow down . . . the color is gay and the scenario correct." The actors may have been "bored" making this film, but the spectator viewing the finished work is, beyond all other considerations, "comfortable."

King Richard and the Crusaders (Richard coeur de lion)
American movie in CinemaScope by David Butler.

We know that a bad American film goes over better than a bad French film. *King Richard and the Crusaders* confirms this. A childish scenario, simplistic dialogues. Who cares, since the rhythm does not falter, since the color is gay and the scenario correct? The spectator who watches this movie is "comfortable." Rex Harrison as a Saracen and George Sanders as Richard the Lionhearted must have been very bored, but it was in order to entertain us. And then there is the CinemaScope, by whose charm we still let ourselves be taken in, as we are not completely used to it yet. (SK)[14]

David Butler hardly deserves greater praise. The director of *Bright Eyes* (1934), *The Littlest Rebel* (1935), *Captain January* (1936), *The Road to Morocco* (1942), and other modest entertainments has no pretensions in his work. He keeps an eye on the budget and makes certain that his performers are centered within the frame. Truffaut is comparatively generous with this film because it does not pretend to be anything other than what it is; a rather ridiculous Hollywood costume spectacle, efficiently photographed on a lavish budget. One can be "comfortable" watching this film because there is no risk involved.

The same might be said of William Wellman's *The High and the Mighty* (1954), which has to be considered the forerunner of the recent spate of airplane disaster films. As Truffaut indicates, the film is almost an exact duplicate of Wellman's earlier production of *Island in the Sky* (1953). Both films were produced by John Wayne. Wayne stars in both films, and the same person, Ernest K. Gann, wrote the two screenplays. There is thus a curious linkage between Wellman, Wayne, and Gann in the creation of these two identically themed works, though *The High and the Mighty* has the advantage of superior production values. As with *King Richard and the Crusaders*, Truffaut is disinclined to be too harsh on the film, which is everything that Hitchcock's *Lifeboat* (1944) might have been, had that film succumbed to the "rudimentary psychology" that frames this work.

The High and the Mighty (Ecrit dans le ciel)
Aviation and Cinemascope

The High and the Mighty is technically worse than the earlier CinemaScope films of 20th Century-Fox, whose pictorial definition touches on perfection. Placing the action *a priori* in the least "CinemaScopic" location—namely inside a four-engined aircraft linking America to Japan—constitutes the movie's appealing challenge.

Besides that, *The High and the Mighty* strangely resembles a earlier film by the same director, William Wellman: *Island in the Sky*. Both movies are produced by the same actor who functions also as their hero, John Wayne. Films produced by actors have the disadvantage of being custom made to fit the producer-star. *The High and the Mighty* is no exception to this rule.

The endangered aircraft carries twenty-two people of varying social milieus; some are afraid, and some are not. With this film we see again the stereotyped structures inherent in this genre: cowardice of some, courage of others, good humor in this one, the nervous breakdown of another.

We are used to blaming American movies for the rudimentary psychology reflected by their characters; this trait is only a flaw if the scenario aspires to be psychological—which happens to be the case here.

It is perhaps inappropriate to come down too hard on this movie, which has, despite everything, the advantage of being rather well acted, and which is definitely well directed. Behind John Wayne are the following secondary actors: Claire Trevor, Robert Stack, Jan Sterling, Paul Kelly, Laraine Day, Robert Newton, and David Brian. (SK)[15]

Wellman is not always guilty of such a conspicuous lack of imagination. His career includes *Public Enemy* (1931), the first version of *A Star Is Born* (1937), *The Ox-Bow Incident* (1943), *Call of the Wild* (1935), *Beau Geste* (1939), and my own personal favorite, *Wild Boys of the Road* (1933). Wellman began in the lower echelons of motion picture production and worked at terrific speed, making five films in 1931 and 1932 and seven films in 1933 before graduating to "A" status with *Call of the Wild*, one of Clark Gable's more effective early films.

The High and the Mighty is not one of Wellman's better films, and Truffaut is correct in his assertion that it was tailor made to fit Wayne's screen persona, with predictably constraining results. The action is claustrophobic, and the ill-advised use of the CinemaScope lens merely makes Wellman's cramped compositions all the more overbearing. Characterization is nonexistent. Robert Stack, Jan Sterling, Paul Kelly, and the other actors represent situations rather than personalities. Depth and motivation are suggested by attire. The "twenty-two people of varying social milieus" go through a series of predictable emotions aboard "the endangered aircraft"; ". . . some are afraid, and some are not. With this film we see again the stereotyped structures inherent in this genre: the cowardice of some, the courage of others, the good humor of this one, the nervous breakdown of another." Yet Truffaut feels "it is perhaps inappropriate to be too hard on this movie," for the film is "well acted" and "definitely well directed." Wellman has taken a routine assignment and done the best with it that anyone has a right to expect. This is the essence of the contract director's *code*, and Wellman has faithfully discharged his responsibilities to his star, supporting cast, and audience.

Samuel Fuller, even more of an iconoclast than Wellman, was also occasionally forced to take on a project that seemed manifestly "foredoomed." The director of *Forty Guns* (1957), *The Steel Helmet* (1950), *Underworld U.S.A.* (1961), and the notorious *The Naked Kiss* (1965), Fuller was no stranger to low budgets. Yet Fuller always managed to invest something of his own personality into even the most hurried and physically compromised productions. *Forty Guns*, for example, was made very quickly and cheaply, as part of a program initiated by 20th Century-Fox to produce a series of low-budget features in black-and-white CinemaScope.[16]

Faced with these requirements, Fuller wrote, produced, and directed *Forty Guns* in less than two weeks, designing the film as a series of audacious tracking shots that glide through the streets of a dusty western town with forceful assurance. Even Barbara Stanwyck (as Jessica Drummond) and Barry Sullivan (Griff Bonnell) are powerless to reduce the intensity of the piece, though the interpretation of their roles is, as usual, exaggerated. Fuller incorporates the frenzy of their performances into the aggressive design of the film, and the result, typically for Fuller, is arresting, individual, and brutally effective.

Godard, in particular, was impressed with the conclusion of the film, in which John Ericson (Brockie), holding Barbara Stanwyck in front of him as a shield, dares Sullivan to shoot him. Sullivan calmly does just that, and Stanwyck falls to the ground, slightly wounded, while Brockie dies. What interested Godard was Fuller's variation on a classic cliché of the western "stand off." Leading men in westerns aren't supposed to sacrifice their love objects (for this is precisely the function that Stanwyck fulfills within the film's narrative) in order to restore normative social values. Sullivan's and Fuller's "coldness" here suggested that these generic conventions were ripe for revision.[17]

Fuller functioned most effectively as a loner, typically writing, producing, and directing his films, and preferred to work without the interferences of studio executives. Perhaps his experiences during the production of *Hell and High Water* (1954) played some role in shaping his preference for independence. Bella Darvi was forced upon Fuller, and while his direction is "certainly sincere," Darvi's performance kills the film from the first frame onward.

As Truffaut asks, "Why do they make her act? Why her?" Darryl F. Zanuck was grooming Darvi as a "star"; *Hell and High Water* was her debut. Truffaut correctly calls Darvi's work in the film "a disaster" (one of the strongest condemnations of a performer in all of Truffaut's critical

writings). The film is fatally compromised, and even Fuller cannot sal-
vage it. In the end, *Hell and High Water* is an unremittingly unpleasant
experience.

Hell and High Water (Le Démon des eaux troubles)
American movie in CinemaScope by Samuel Fuller.

An atomic bomb has exploded in the waters of the South Pacific. A
French professor (Victor Francen), who is a nuclear scientist, and his
daughter (Bella Darvi), convinced that the "Federal Union of the Oceanic
Republics" [sic] is behind this bomb, charter a submarine in order to
locate the mysterious atomic base. Montel Francen and Bella Darvi leave
for the South Pacific aboard the submarine, which is under the tough
command of Richard Widmark. First incident: a battle between two sub-
marines, followed by the landing on the suspect island. Finally, we see
the discovery of the atomic base, where an enemy airplane is ready to
take off. The plane is shot down and Professor Montel [Francen] dies,
leaving his daughter to the charge of Richard Widmark, who does not
seem too delighted about it.

Expectations were high for the first CinemaScope film of Samuel Fuller,
who was the youngest reporter, the youngest novelist, and the youngest
scriptwriter in America. Between 1942 and 1946, he served in the infan-
try and took part in the landings in Normandy and Sicily. With *The
Steel Helmet* [1950], a film made with two cents and one set featuring a
pagoda, Fuller made an excellent film with unprecedented violence, and
plenty of inventions and details. We also kept very good memories of *I
Shot Jesse James* [1949] and *Fixed Bayonets* [1951]. *Hell and High Water*,
Fuller's first film in color and in CinemaScope is a far cry from the quality of the weakest of the films just mentioned. As a militant anticom-
munist, Samuel Fuller has written a scenario of disconcerting naiveté
and thanks to the censors, Soviet spies have become agents of the "Federal Union of Oceanic Republics." But it was necessary to cut some of
the movie's scenes that did not leave any doubt concerning the nation-
ality of the spies in question.

Fuller's direction is merely adequate; color has been used in an amusing way, but without taste. Richard Widmark (it was his last movie at
Fox) is prodigiously bored; Victor Francen, with his feverish chin, par-
odies himself. The deplorable element of this enterprise is the acting of
Miss Bella Darvi.

Miss Bella Darvi represents one of those mysteries in cinema. We ask
ourselves, Why is she involved in acting? Why do they make her act?
Why her? Not that she's so unpleasant to look at, but as soon as she
moves, talks, walks, what a disaster! As far as making her cry, scream,
or smile, do not even think about it. It is im-pos-sible [emphasis Truffaut's]. I do not think I will hurt her by saying this, because I would bet

that she hates acting and that she feels as if she is being tortured in front
of the camera. (SK)[18]

Byron Haskin's *Naked Jungle* (1954) is only slightly more accomplished. Better known as a director of photography, especially adept in
process and miniature work, Haskin began directing films in 1927 with
Matinée Ladies. However, after his fourth film as a director, *The Siren*
(1928), Haskin returned to cinematography and did not make another
film as an *auteur* until 1947, when he directed *I Walk Alone*. His films
as director are not particularly distinguished, although he scored a sub-
stantial box office success with *The War of the Worlds* (1953), *The Conquest of Space* (1955), and his second-to-last production, *Robinson Crusoe on Mars* (1964). Most of Haskin's better "late" films were made in
conjunction with George Pal.

All of these productions relied heavily upon special effects, and in
this respect, Haskin is something like disaster specialist Irwin Allen. He
is comfortable with spectacle and destruction, yet he becomes ill at ease
when dealing with human protagonists. As Truffaut indicates, "the acting prize" in *Naked Jungle* goes not to Charlton Heston or Eleanor Parker
but rather "to the Marabunta," "an army of ants that, three of four times
a century, leave their home, fan out in front, and lay waste to everything
in their path."

Naked Jungle (Quand le Marabunta gronde) [1954]
American film by Byron Haskin.

Charlton Heston and Eleanor Parker enliven this film, the former with
his virile beauty and the latter with her grace, but the acting prize goes
to the Marabunta. What is the Marabunta? Don't count on the advertise-
ments to tell you. The Marabunta is the army of ants that, three or four
times a century, leave their home, fan out in front, and lay waste to
everything in their path: flora, fauna, human beings. Nothing can resist
the Marabunta: an oil dam, graves, or a river. And in the dark you catch
yourself scratching your neck; but the Marabunta doesn't come down
into the theater. This plague ruins the hero of the film, but it also causes
love to blossom between a very charming couple. (RCH)[19]

As one might expect, Truffaut says little of Haskin's mise-en-scène; it
appears to be adequate but unremarkable. Disaster films become tedious
when deprived of a human center. Haskin's spectacle of destruction,
Truffaut seems to be saying, succeeds in spite of itself. There is, after all,
limited suspense in an unremitting series of scenes of an inexorable plague,
particularly when one feels certain that it will ultimately (though at a
cost) be vanquished. Truffaut is surprised that the film works as well as
it does.

Cause for Alarm (1951) is another minor film, from the director best known for his work on the *Postman Always Rings Twice* (1946), Tay Garnett. However, Barry Sullivan and Loretta Young seem a poor pairing after Lana Turner and John Garfield; Truffaut dismisses *Cause for Alarm* with a few lines, while still acknowledging that all the film's "effects hit home, perfectly timed, and isn't that what counts?" In short, this is a film of craft and manipulation, not to be despised, but also not to be taken very seriously.

Cause for Alarm (Un jour de terreur) [1951]
American film by Tay Garnett.

A gentleman [Barry Sullivan] who is paranoid and bedridden imagines that his luscious wife wants to kill him. He then dies a fine death, or almost, by accident in any case, but not before he has sent, alas, a letter to the police accusing his wife.

In her attempt to retrieve the letter, Loretta Young (yes, it is she) piles blunder upon blunder, and we are beginning to think she'll get the guillotine when the famous letter comes back to her—postage due. That's the ultimate suspense, where the solidity of the scenario is sacrificed to effect. But all those effects hit home, perfectly timed, and isn't that what counts? (RCH)[20]

Truffaut is more generous to this film than most. Garnett's "perfectly timed" effects notwithstanding, the plot's premise is so thin that the suspense is barely sustained for the film's scant seventy-four minutes' running time. What Truffaut means when he refers to Loretta Young with the aside "yes, it is she" is open to some debate. Perhaps Truffaut is referring to Young's pronounced penchant for "victimized" leading roles. Remembering Young in Orson Welles's *The Stranger* (1946), certainly one of the director's lesser efforts, Truffaut is perhaps growing tired of her tendency to play the martyr with such one-note insistence. *Cause for Alarm* is a minor accomplishment for all concerned, barely deserving of the slight attention it is given by Truffaut's brief review.

Truffaut's notice on Hugo Fregonese's *Decameron Nights*, which Truffaut finds "an innocent, quick sketch," not only is forgiving in the area of the film's technical and aesthetic defects but also implicitly condones the film's often brutal and blatant misogyny. In any event, the film is not American but British. As noted in chapter three, Truffaut had a peculiar distaste for British filmmaking, making his approbation of *Decameron Nights* all the more surprising. It's also amusing to note that Truffaut could find, at this stage of Joan Collins's career, that her screen presence is, for him, "absolutely charming." The "studio-reconstitution of the Italian Renaissance" seemed to most other critics to wallow in vulgarity; why is Truffaut being so kind to this film? As with many of his previous notices for slight entertainments, one suspects that he is more than taken with Joan Fontaine and Joan Collins than Fregonese's mise-en-scène.

Decameron Nights (Pages galantes de Bocace)[1953]
American movie by Hugo Fregonese.

These *Decameron Nights* are in pretty Technicolor, and they are entertaining for those spectators who come to watch this movie without having terribly high expectations of their Boccaccio being scrupulously illustrated. The studio-reconstitution of the Italian Renaissance is also rather whimsical, but without any vulgarity. Here is thus an innocent, quick sketch, animated by the always pretty Joan Fontaine, the pleasant Louis Jourdan, and the absolutely charming Joan Collins. (SK)[21]

What's interesting here is that Truffaut does not immediately object to the obvious fraudulence of the studio sets employed in the film, yet at the same time he excoriates filmmakers working within the French studio system for the artificiality of their presentations, as we have seen in his notice on *And God Created Woman*. Perhaps Truffaut's tolerance is a result of his appreciation of the "charming" Joan Collins; perhaps he was in the mood for an undemanding synthetic fantasy when he viewed *Decameron Nights*.

Yet one suspects that cultural displacement is also at work here. Able to appreciate American and British filmmaking as an utterly exterior phenomenon, Truffaut views the studio films of these two countries as constructs in their entirety. This is something he is apparently unable or unwilling to do with studio films made in his own country. An entire system of image substitution is at work here, as Truffaut well knows. Nothing in Fregonese's *Decameron* is real, nor does it pretend to be.

Truffaut's review of Jerry Hopper's *Naked Alibi* (1954) once again demonstrates that Truffaut has a good working knowledge of the American "B" cinema, better, perhaps, than that of many of his contemporaries. Truffaut correctly identifies the sources for many of *Naked Alibi*'s thematic and stylistic structures (see Truffaut's review of *The City Is Dark*, by André de Toth, in chapter one of this volume), and yet, despite the frankly formulaic nature of the film, Truffaut can't bring himself to dislike it. It's too modest a film to put down with full force.

Naked Alibi (L'alibi meurtrier)
American film by Jerry Hopper.

Here is a movie that starts out like *On Dangerous Ground* by Nicholas Ray and continues and ends like *The Big Heat* by Fritz Lang. The entire central part is borrowed from *The City Is Dark* by André de Toth and from *The Racket* by John Cromwell, while the musical score repeats faithfully, and several times, the main theme of *Carousel*. Having given back to Hollywood that which belongs to Hollywood, let us admit that *Naked Alibi* perfectly corresponds to the need for a drug that any lover of American films irresistibly experiences.

Briefly, the movie is about a dismissed policeman who conducts on his own an investigation that ends in the arrest of a murderer who killed another policeman. A classic story, if ever there was one. There is nothing that we like to believe more than that American policeman are sweet, good, calm guys; the actors personifying them immediately gain our sympathy. But was it necessary to sacrifice Gloria Grahame at the end? It is always sad to see her die. (SK)[22]

Truffaut's review of *Naked Alibi* is roughly what the film deserves: he notes the film's many debts, says nothing of Sterling Hayden's performance in the film, and reminds us again of his affection for Gloria Grahame. Of Hopper's mise-en-scène Truffaut says nothing. No doubt this is just. *Naked Alibi* is a patchwork of "borrowings" and retread plot structures, more interesting for what it emulates than what it originates. Truffaut is kind to the film, in part, because he agrees with Hopper's taste in the films he steals from.

Forever Female (1954), however, receives a decidedly less enthusiastic welcome from the young critic. Cobbled together by Irving Rapper to take advantage of the success of Otto Preminger's *The Moon Is Blue* (1953), *Forever Female* is a "failed American comedy," and, as Truffaut notes, "there is nothing worse."

Forever Female (L'Eternel féminin)
American film by Irving Rapper.
A young comedienne (Pat Crowley) manages to convince a "mature" actress (Ginger Rogers) that she has passed the age to play ingenues. The young actress [Crowley] marries William Holden, and Ginger Rogers remarries Paul Douglas. There is nothing worse than a failed American comedy, which is the case here. *Forever Female* also has the drawback of having been overtly undertaken to benefit from the (justified) success of *The Moon Is Blue* [*The Moon Is Blue* also starred William Holden], a movie here clumsily "plagiarized."[23]

Ophüls, Autant-Lara, Ray, and Fellini

The egalitarian spirit that informs Truffaut's criticism is nowhere more evident than in his comments on Max Ophüls's *Lola Montès* (1955), surely one of the most influential and important films of the 1950s, which is reviewed in one of Truffaut's columns in conjunction with Claude Autant-Lara's *Marguerite de la Nuit* (1956), Nicholas Ray's *Rebel without a Cause* (1955), and Robert Hossein's *Les Salauds vont en enfer* (1955). Truffaut likes Hossein's film the least of all, but calls *Lola Montès* "the most exciting film of the year," and cites Ray as "the best current American director." Further, Truffaut states that *Il Bidone* (1955) "may be [Fellini's] best" work to date. The ease of juxtaposition evidenced in these short notices is proof of Truffaut's exhaustive moviegoing, as well as his ability to appreciate a well-made film no matter what its country of origin may be. From our vantage point, the jump from Nicholas Ray to Fellini may not seem that remarkable. Given the time and temper of the period, however, Truffaut's valuation of *Rebel without a Cause* as the near equivalent of *Lola Montès* struck most observers as revolutionary.

If Truffaut now seems more favorably disposed toward *Les Enfants Terribles* (1950), than he did in his review of Melville's *When You Read This Letter*, it is perhaps because the resonance of *Rebel without a Cause* has placed the virtues of the Melville/Cocteau collaboration in sharper relief. "I don't know of another film that deals with adolescence with such clearmindedness," Truffaut says of *Rebel*: yet "one will think of *Les Enfants Terribles* in connection with this work." Both films speak authentically to the grandeur and misery of youth. Did any other critic of the period make this connection? And did any other reviewer have the taste to prefer the refined brutality of *Il Bidone* over the "lopsided" construction of *I Vitelloni* (1953) or the "sentimentality" of *La Strada* (1954)?

Lola Montès—Everything has been said and written about this breathtaking film, the most exciting film of the year. The CinemaScope, the color, the construction of the script, the dialogue here undergoes such a revolutionary treatment that *Lola Montès*'s influence will be visible in many films during the years to come. This delirious film uses as a subject the "calvary" of a star, the very large space taken up by publicity of the worst kind, and stage-managed scandal, made profitable in show business. Cinema needs these fits of madness that are called, according to their time, *Zéro de conduite* [1933; Dir. Jean Vigo], *La règle du jeu* [1939; Dir. Jean Renoir], and *Citizen Kane* [1941; Dir. Orson Welles]. It is also good that artists with as contradictory concerns as Jean Cocteau, Roberto Rossellini, Jean Renoir, Alexandre Astruc, Jules Dassin, Jacques Tati, and Jacques Audiberti act in collusion to organize a systematic defense of this work: when all is said and done, the most enriching and freshest work that I have seen for a long time.

Marguerite de la Nuit—Claude Autant-Lara's *Marguerite de la Nuit* is radically opposed to Max Ophüls's *Lola Montès*. Day and night. *Marguerite de la Nuit* is full of dryness, poor inspiration, intellectual penury, total absence of fancy. Every image remains deliberate, theoretical, always short of the effect aimed at. How many efforts fall between the wall and the bed! Faust, once more, martyrized! This one won't be "My Faust." It's not worthwhile to elaborate on this aberrant enterprise, which conjures up the word "dismaying" and related words.

Les Salauds vont en enfer (The Wicked Go to Hell)—Of all the French films whose ambitious plan led us to expect something of them, *Les Salauds vont en enfer* is the most disappointing, indeed, the worst. Beyond the hopeless script and the poverty of the mise-en-scène, the real intentions pop up, contradictory and sordid, all conspiring to make this the most disagreeable movie possible.

Rebel without a Cause—Nicholas Ray is the best current American director. Nobody can doubt it after seeing *Rebel without a Cause (La Fureur de Vivre)*, a heart-rending film in which James Dean repeats, while expanding upon it, his surprising achievement in *East of Eden (A L'Est d'Eden)*. Exacerbated sensitivity, absolute sincerity: these are the prime virtues of this film, which includes quite a few others. We think of *Les Enfants Terribles* in connection with this work, which shows a nobility and cleverness rarely found in Hollywood. I don't know of another film that deals with adolescence with such clearmindedness.

Il Bidone—Federico Fellini's new film may be his best; the fact remains that one can unveil in this film every quality of *I Vitelloni* and *La Strada* without the lopsided aspect of the first one or the sentimentality of the second. Broderick Crawford, staggering on screen as well as off screen, proves to be, far from his usual California, a wonderful and monstrous actor. (SK)[24]

Truffaut's praise of *Lola Montès* does not, in retrospect, seem hyperbolic.[25] The film was "revolutionary" in its theatrical/cinematic structure, its vertiginous use of CinemaScope framing, and its "delirious" obsession with Lola's "calvary." *Lola Montès* is aptly described as a "fit of madness." The film pushed the limits of color saturation in its sumptuous photography and meticulously upholstered decor. Truffaut is pleased that "artists with as contradictory concerns as Jean Cocteau, Roberto Rossellini,[26] Jean Renoir, Alexandre Astruc [and others] act in collusion to organize a systematic defense of the work." As precise and disciplined as *Lola Montès* seems today, the ferocity of its mise-en-scène and the unrestrained romanticism of the work combined to ensure that the film would receive an initially hostile reception from the critics and the public. The film was severely cut, dubbed, and released in black and white in the United States as *The Sins of Lola Montès*, because its American distributor did not feel that the cost of full-length color prints was justified by the anticipated box office receipts.[27]

Certainly one of the most disturbing aspects of *Lola Montès*'s scenario is its implied censure of both the public and of the critics who shape the desire of the audience. Peter Ustinov, perfect as the oily, opportunistic impresario who masterminds the theatrical recreation of Lola's "lost loves," can be seen as an expert in both presentation and representation ideally in tune with the needs of both his customers and the critics. The matter-of-fact cynicism displayed by Ustinov undercuts the romanticism of the work, grounding the spectacle in the mundane. Ophüls's stylistic splendor—his sweeping pans, his long takes with a constantly moving camera, the formal elegance of his delicately balanced framing—finds in *Lola Montès*'s scenario a perfect match. While the viewer may admire, for example, the opening dolly shot in Ophüls's earlier *La Ronde* (1950), in which Anton Walbrook walks through a series of studio recreations of the various seasons, Ophüls's technique often seems more involved and fully developed than his characters.

Ophüls embraced the studio as the ideal means for the cinematic recreation of past events. His films are patently artificial and linked to the past. "I adore the past," Walbrook states in *La Ronde*. "It is so much more restful than the present, and so much more certain than the future." Ophüls's protagonists live in a dream of a world the director knows has vanished; a world, in fact, that never existed, other than in Ophüls's heart. (Many have pointed out the connection between Lola Montès's "heart condition" in the film and Ophüls's own cardiac complaints.) This studied artificiality finds its fullest expression in *Lola Montès*, and the film, in its direct acknowledgment of both the tradition of theater (as in Renoir's *The Golden Coach* [1952]) and the cinematic apparatus used to simultaneously record and interpret that tradition, seems paradoxically the most realistic and least distanced of Ophüls's later works. While Truffaut does not go into detail on these points, he was no doubt aware of them. "Stage-managed scandal, made profitable in show business arts" is the center of *Lola Montès*. Any work that critiques the process of popular iconography so relentlessly seems certain to find ill-favor with those critics who seek to support that mechanism. If *Lola Montès* is now considered a classic, it is praised as a film made nearly forty years ago, a work often mentioned but seldom revived, particularly in its original CinemaScope format. Thus the criticism within the work is sealed off; the enshrinement of *Lola Montès* has muted the work's intent. Truffaut, along with those he mentions in his review, valued the work upon its initial release, when the force of the film was fresh and immediate.

In contrast, *Marguerite de la Nuit* is indeed "radically opposed to Max Ophüls's *Lola Montès*." The formalism of Autant-Lara's film is "full of dryness, poor inspiration, intellectual penury, total absence of fancy. Every image remains deliberate, theoretical, always short of the effect aimed at." If *Marguerite* found greater initial favor with contemporary critics than *Lola Montès*—and it did—perhaps it is because this "martyrized" *Faust* seeks to achieve less, is safe, dares little. Such a work offers nothing to upset or excite an audience. Both *Lola Montès* and *Marguerite de la Nuit* are studied, carefully composed films. The difference between the two works, as Truffaut notes, is the informing intelligence behind the design of *Lola Montès*. The craft of Autant-Lara is used as a disguise rather than as a medium of expression. Where Ophüls's studio-bound creation seems to burst with energy in every setup, Autant-Lara's embrace of the artificial is a retreat to old mannerisms, empty structures, compositions without clarity or vision. The same can be said for *Les Salauds vont en enfer,* a film that Truffaut dislikes intensely.

Ray's *Rebel without a Cause* and Fellini's *Il Bidone,* used by Truffaut to round out these short notices, both receive far better treatment from the young critic, and they deserve to. The "sincerity" of *Rebel* and the brash energy of Broderick Crawford in *Il Bidone* (for once, other than his work in *All the King's Men* [1949; Dir. Robert Rossen], given a role worthy of his talents) impress Truffaut. Crawford, "staggering on screen as well as off screen [a sly reference to the hard-drinking actor's well-publicized life-style] proves to be, far from his usual California, a wonderful and monstrous actor." *Lola Montès, Rebel without a Cause,* and *Il Bidone* all share one thing in common, despite their differing thematic preoccupations. Each shot in these films is inextricably wedded to the material it presents. There is a "toughness" in the style, an economy, a sparse authority. Nothing is decorative. These films derive their force and impact from the economy of their presentation. Truffaut admires this and appreciates the authority that comes with such distinctive *auteurship. Il Bidone,* as Truffaut notes, is one of the clearest and least "sentimental" films in Fellini's body of work, and the "wonderful and monstrous" Crawford is perfectly cast as the swindling "priest."

The lack of risk that permeates *Marguerite de la Nuit* can also be sensed in Mikhail Romm's *Admiral Ushakov* (1953), a Russian "Hollywood production" that Truffaut compares unfavorably to the film of Cecil B. DeMille. Romm's film, a paean to Russian militarism, is essentially a series of noisy and empty battle sequences, coupled with a nominal romantic subplot. Although "everything happens briskly" in this film, it "is not a great Russian movie," although it can be "watched without regrets."

Admiral Ushakov/Attack from the Sea (L'Amiral Tempête)
Russian movie by Mikhail Romm.

The action takes place in the seventeenth century. Admiral Ushakov ("Tempest" for the ladies) commanded—they say—the pleasure boat of Catherine II, at the time when Russia pushed through to the coast of the Black Sea. Everything happens briskly for these characters with exceptional careers: Ushakov participates in the Russian-Turkish war, and from then on, he is stricken with a never-ending Turko-mania: in 1788, he defeats the Turkish fleet "three times bigger in numbers," etc. He repeats this in 1790 and in 1791. Then follows the campaign of Corfu, the establishment of the Ionian islands, and finally the apotheosis, Sebastopol, in 1800. But Tsar Alexander I keeps an eye on our hero and holds him in semi-disgrace. Whatever, Ushakov-Tempest retires and dies ten years later.

This is the Russian but precise equivalent of a current Hollywood production. Mikhail Romm is very far from being the Soviet. Cecil Blount De Mille [Romm's] rhythm is less secure, the acting less worked out, the technique less effective.

Only the color, offering us some tasteful pastels, can compete. *Admiral Ushakov* is not a great Russian movie, but nevertheless one of those that can be watched without regrets.[28]

Truffaut recognizes that the film owes an enormous stylistic debt to the grandiose productions of De Mille, even if it can only "compete" in its use of color, and falls short in "rhythm . . . acting . . . [and] technique." This is a dubious compliment when one recalls that De Mille was never that accomplished as a director of individual performances. Romm went on to create a second film in 1953, which was designed as a continuation of the Ushakov saga, *The Ships Storm the Bastions*. Though these films are essentially homages to Californian spectacle and lack sincerity because of their politically inspired genesis, Truffaut seems willing to ignore these defects of origin and finds *Admiral Ushakov* lightly diverting. That Truffaut considers the plot of the film less than compelling can be easily discerned from his peremptory summation of the film's narrative: "Whatever, Ushakov-Tempest retires and dies ten years later." The real interest of the film resides in comparing *Admiral Ushakov* to those films it copies. One suspects that audiences lacking this basis for historical comparison would find a great deal less of interest in this film.

In contrast Charles Vidor's *Rhapsody*, a genuine "Hollywood" movie, "is the most boring American movie of the year," lacking even the partially saving grace of a compelling narrative line. That the story is ancient is beyond dispute: Truffaut is not bothered by the fact that *Rhapsody* is a remake of a remake of a remake. What upsets him is the complete "foolishness" of the entire enterprise, the "dullness" of Vidor's direction. Truffaut goes so far as to deny Vidor the authorship of *Gilda* (1946) in this review, preferring to credit cinematographer Rudolph Maté with the success of that production.

If *Gilda* is "pleasant," *Rhapsody* (1954) is torture. Truffaut spends most of this notice detailing the tired, unbelievable plot of the film; notations on camerawork, lighting, and mise-en-scène are totally absent. As with his review of *Houdini*, Truffaut feels obliged to tell his readers that the Technicolor is perfectly acceptable, and he dismissively allows that Elizabeth Taylor is "pretty." Vittorio Gassman seems to have taken his part quite seriously; at least he imparts some energy to his characterization. Nothing is said of John Ericson, or even of Louis Calhern, who lends capable support to this richly appointed yet entirely bankrupt film—a film that Truffaut ridicules with great delight.

Rhapsody (Rhapsodie)
American movie by Charles Vidor in Technicolor.

Louise Durand, a very French girl (Elizabeth Taylor), leaves "her" French Riviera, so dear to her, to follow a violinist with a tormented face (Vittorio Gassman) to Zurich. Jealous because of the time he spends with his bow, Louise brings about his failure in a competition at the music academy. The violinist, who has more than one string to his in-strument, takes a music lover as mistress, and Louise marries an Amer-ican pianist [John Ericson], who, more in love with her than the violinist was, accepts a life of nothing but foolish conduct, idleness, and coquet-tishness. But he suffers from his sacrifice. Louise meets the violinist—who has made it by now—again, and she realizes her selfishness. She encourages her husband-pianist to take up his work again. First concert, first triumph; glory and success unite husband and wife.

This is the most boring American movie of the year. If many viewers are deceived by the foolishness of the script, this silliness will not go unnoticed by the reader. The Technicolor is decent; Elizabeth Taylor is pretty; Vittorio Gassman is an "artist cursed" by the devil and moreover a romantic. The dullness of *Rhapsody* leads one to think that Charles Vidor only gave his signature to the pleasant movie *Gilda* [1946], with cameraman Rudy Maté probably being the real *auteur*.[29]

What interests Truffaut in Pierre Louis's *The Crazy Bus* (1953) is not the film itself but rather Louis's use of the camera, "a very astonishing conception of mise-en-scène." Louis's camera is constantly moving in the film, following the actors without interruption until "subjective vi-sion here melts into objective vision and espouses it." The unrelenting camera movement leaves Truffaut both baffled and ill at ease; he has "a rather painful feeling of absolute inability to move" in watching the film. The result is a left-handed triumph of style over what little content the film possesses. It is safe to say that Truffaut holds little hope for Louis's future as a director, yet Louis is, as an actor, "most likeable," so Truffaut restrains himself from judging the film too harshly.

L'Autocar en folie (The Crazy Bus) (1953)
French film by Pierre Louis.

Pierre Louis is a young French actor who is, all told, most likeable. So he becomes a *metteur-en-scène* and we went to see *The Crazy Bus,* which Jean Nohain and his troupe are putting on. But that's not the interesting part.

Pierre Louis seems to me to have a very astonishing conception of mise-en-scène. Not a character moves without the camera moving with him, creating an identical movement; a girl swings, the camera swings simultaneously and in a parallel fashion. Subjective vision here melts into objective vision and espouses it. The result is that in this film where all is movement—people and machines—a rather painful feeling of absolute inability to move does not abandon us for a second. (RCH)[30]

Jules Dassin

Truffaut was more favorably disposed toward Jules Dassin's *Naked City* (1948). However, in this one instance, it is difficult to agree with his admiration for the film. In an article discussing *Naked City*, *Night and the City* (1950), and the production of *Rififi* (1955), Truffaut traces Dassin's early work as a director, mentioning *The Canterville Ghost* (1944), and states that prior to *Naked City*, Dassin had directed "five" other films. In fact, Dassin's career began with the direction of a series of short films at MGM and, before that, work as an assistant director for RKO. His 1941 short film, *The Tell Tale Heart*, resulted in his assignment to direct the feature *Nazi Agent* (1942). Thus, before the creation of *Naked City*, Dassin had been responsible for the creation of eight feature films and numerous short subjects.

Truffaut praises the "documentary" aspect of the film, a style of recreated reality made fashionable principally through the *March of Time* series of two-reel "docudrama" shorts, produced for Time/Life by Louis de Rochemont from 1935 to 1951.[31] This style, which was also influenced by the postwar Italian neorealists, surfaced most notably in the late '40s films of director Henry Hathaway, including *The House on 92nd Street* (1945), *13 Rue Madeleine* (1946), and *Call Northside 777* (1948). One could therefore argue with some justification that Dassin was building upon a method first developed by Hathaway and de Rochemont. The screenplay for the film, by Albert Maltz and Malvin Wald from a story by Wald, has been published in an edition supervised by Matthew J. Bruccoli; a careful reading of the script, dated May 20, 1947, reveals the inherent theatricality of the production.[32] The most intrusive element is producer Mark Hellinger's gratingly sentimental narration, which intrinsically undercuts the "realism" of the production with a gloss of contrived and forced metaphoric conceits. "Does money ever sleep, I wonder? Does a machine become tired?" Hellinger inquires of the viewer.[33]

This attempt on Hellinger's part to appropriate both the city of New York and the attention of the audience as the center of the film's narrative structure mitigates from the outset of the film. In a sense, what Hellinger is attempting here is very much like the anthropomorphizing of spiders and reptiles in James Algar's *The Living Desert* (1953); Hellinger's presentation of the "naked" city is only effective if he can artificially endow Manhattan with human attributes. Further, in his use of such familiar actors as Barry Fitzgerald, Howard Duff, and Ted De Corsia in key roles, Dassin assures his audience that what we are in fact witnessing is a fictive construct. Hellinger's voice-over further adds to this fabulistic acknowledgment. Thus, while the supporting cast members are, for the most part, unknowns (that is, not immediately recognizable by the average contemporary viewer), the film's hold on "reality" rests safely within the confines of Fitzgerald's brogue and Duff's seedily athletic presence.

To compare this film, then, to *Open City* or *The Bicycle Thief* is both simplistic and incorrect. *Naked City* is more in line with the Rossellini of *General Della Rovere* (1960), a studio recreation of the early days of postwar Italian social commerce. However, in its frank admission of its artificial origins (stock footage in *General Della Rovere* is used in an entirely reflexive manner), *General Della Rovere* is at once more sophisticated and complex, even as it trades upon the ruined visage of Vittorio De Sica as the film's central iconograph. *Naked City* is a shallow film whose "realism" is in fact a set of substituted stylistic conventions. Dassin can be seen to much better advantage in *Brute Force* (1947), *Night and the City* (1950), or even the much later *10:30 PM Summer* (1966). While all these films are indeed creations of the studio, they do not attempt to disguise their origins. *Naked City* attempts to be that which it is not and, as a result, dates badly.

If I have spent considerable time in examining the genesis of *Naked City*, it is because in this instance, as an almost singular exception, Truffaut makes a misstep in his evaluation of the film. The location shooting (and sound recording) is the most compelling aspect of the production; but why does Truffaut refrain from excoriating those structural elements that work against Dassin's naturalism? One can only assume that Truffaut was impressed by the undeniable technical challenge the film represents and, because of this, was willing to overlook the many compromises made in the creation of the finished work.

As Truffaut notes, *Night and the City*, though filmed on the streets of London with a similar "documentary" flavor, is "a more romantic" film, which "shows us Richard Widmark, an adventurer and megalomaniac" in a narrative (significantly, without any framing narration) that is frankly melodramatic. *Naked City* is a police procedural in which the city is elevated to the role of central protagonist; *Night and the City* uses London's poorer neighborhoods as an effective backdrop for Widmark and George Coulouris. Dassin's work in Europe came as a direct result of the House Un-American Activities Committee.[34]

Rififi, generally seen as one of Dassin's best works, was thus created as a "film in exile." Ironically, a number of reviewers began treating Dassin as a European director, despite Dassin's long apprenticeship in Hollywood and the fact that the director was born a United States citizen in Middletown, Connecticut. Truffaut took advantage of the production of *Rififi* to interview Dassin, and this article, a careful (if not always fully accurate) account of Dassin's history and working methods, reveals Truffaut's customary intelligence and tact in dealing with a director not favorably disposed toward journalists.

The release of *Naked City* in Paris in 1947 [actually 1948] introduced us to the name of Jules Dassin. *Naked City* was a gangster film with the features of a documentary, shot almost entirely in real-life decors, and the outside scenes are filmed in the streets of New York. It wasn't the first time a film had been shot in U.S. streets, but now there were no police barriers, no sun-lights, and no crowds gathered. The cameras were hidden in cars that followed the rather unknown actors, who walked in the streets, ran, and in a word, "acted," mixed in with the crowd of passersby. After some research, we found out that Jules Dassin had made other movies, five to be exact, of which only the amusing *The Canterville Ghost* [1944] would be released in France. From *Naked City* on, every new "Dassin" was awaited impatiently, and this waiting period was always rewarded. The movies released were: *Brute Force* about an uprising in a prison; *Thieves' Highway* [1949], about San Francisco truckers; and especially *Night and the City* definitely the best of Dassin's films.

Filmed in London according to the same principles of *Naked City,* but at night and with a more romantic intrigue, *Night and the City* shows us Richard Widmark, an adventurer and megalomaniac, who runs around in the streets of the city looking desperately to set up a "sensational" deal, who fails at the last minute, and who dies shot down by gangsters. The finest idea in the movie was this: that Widmark had lived his whole life at the expense of Gene Tierney; with a price on his head and all hope of escaping the killers in vain, he threw himself in front of them and yelled: "It is she who turned me in," so that the woman who had ruined her life for him would receive the reward. I even remember him saying before he died: "This is the first time that I completed a deal successfully." A true epic inspiration, which was already noticeable at the end of *Naked City* and in some scenes of *Thieves' Highway,* traverses this movie, which was however commercially less successful than the previous ones.

Because of his refusal to "converse" with McCarthy, Jules Dassin found himself unemployed and decided to come to work in France, something that did not happen without difficulty. He was going to direct *Public Enemy Number One,* in which Fernandel and Zsa Zsa Gabor were the stars. In a telegram sent from Hollywood, the American actress refused to be in the movie if Dassin directed it. Fernandel followed suit and the director of *Thieves' Highway* withdrew, giving up his place to Henri Verneuil, who was not at all intimidated by this succession.

At that point we wondered if Jules Dassin would be able to shoot here. A second project, *Rififi,* from a slang novel in the *Grisbi* tradition, did succeed and is nearing completion.

I was told: "You are going to see Dassin? You won't get three words out of him. He is a great film producer, but with regard to journalists, he displays a casualness that borders on coarseness." The press confirmed these words with rather unfriendly remarks. It gives me even greater satisfaction then to be able to affirm that Mr. Jules Dassin is an extremely refined and polite man, instructive and easy to get along with. During my three visits to the studio in Courbevoie and on location in Paris, I was able to exchange a few sentences with him in between two shots in newly minted but respectable "French" mixed with "Grisbi" talk (of course). He assured me that filming in the streets did not pose any more problems in Paris than in London or New York. Yes, he is very satisfied with the scenario that he adapted himself in cooperation with Auguste Le Breton, author of the book. As is the case with *Night and the City,* the action of *Rififi* is very "scraped together": the preparation for a burglary of a jewelry store, the burglary, the theft of the jewelry by a rival gang, the settlement of accounts, corpses "à la Hugo": THE END.

The most amazing scene that I saw being shot took place in the Port-Royal subway station. The traffic was as usual. The camera was put on the station platform, slightly pulled back from the stairs. The trains followed one another as usual, without the passengers who got off being able to notice what was coming off (if I may say so). On the other hand, the travelers arriving on the platform in order to board the subway discovered the camera quickly and looked straight in it—something you shouldn't do.

They did not suspect for one minute that they were only being filmed when the train arrived, at the precise moment when they had to take their eyes off the camera in order not to miss their subway, a luxury no Parisian offers himself anymore. Furthermore, the camera followed the travelers, at the moment the train stopped, with a panning shot. Jean Servais, who climbed the stairs, was thinking, and then came back downstairs to the platform, while the travelers—free extras because they were so involuntarily documented—climbed the stairs in turn.

Some other night scenes were shot in Pigalle, some day scenes in Belleville; in short, scenes were filmed in almost all neighborhoods of Paris.

On the ocean of "noir" films released, being shot, or in preparation, only *Touchez pas au Grisbi* [1954] by Jacques Becker surfaces. Let us hope that the public, if it gets quickly tired of Lemmy Caution [the character played by Eddie Constantine in his many "gangster films"] and his accomplices, will not miss this movie, which is already being dubbed *Rififi* [original French title *Du Rififi chez les hommes*] for short, and which promises to be an unusual thriller. (SK)[35]

Truffaut's admiration for the staging of the subway sequence directly prefigures the early use of actual personages in his first several films. By staring directly into the camera lens, these passersby deconstruct the fourth wall (the camera) of cinema staging and momentarily lock gazes with the

spectators in the audience. This acknowledgment of shared vision paradoxically heightens the verisimilitude of Dassin's mise-en-scène. When
one places a camera in an actual location, those who approach it will
instinctively seek either to avoid it or confront it. Dassin's "extras" confront the camera without knowing it, then turn away, witnesses to the
power of the cinematograph. This intensifies Jean Servais's performance
and centers our attention on him, as he, alone within the frame, pretends
that the camera does not exist. Truffaut would incorporate this technique in *The 400 Blows* (1959), in which Parisians at a fun park, or in
the streets, are pressed into service as part of the world of Antoine Doinel.

Although Truffaut confined himself in most of his critical writings to
discussions of cinema aesthetics, he was well aware of the mechanisms
at work in film production and distribution, particularly as they affected
the work of lesser-known directors. We've already seen Truffaut taking
distributors tangentially to task for inadequate distribution of some films;
in his article *"The Double Crisis of Cinema,"* Truffaut examines the fate
of those French films that will never find an audience.

Truffaut sees one of the problems as the exhibition, in multiple theaters, of imported American films. If every motion picture received "exclusive" distribution (that is, in one theater only), then more theaters
would be available for products. In particular, Truffaut is concerned with
the fate of some sixty-eight unreleased films by directors without a national reputation. Since "Tati's, Cayatte's, Lechanois's, and Duvivier's
[films] won't have any problem being released," that means there are
theaters available for other works. Further, Truffaut asks, "how many
films among these [then being made in France] deserve our interest . . .
once they are completed?" The second half of the "double crisis" Truffaut refers to is a crisis of quality. Audiences do not flock to see French
films, Truffaut feels, because too many of them are inferior to even mediocre American productions. No wonder, then, that "French exhibitors
regret the passing of the postwar 'golden age' when French people, badly
fed, badly heated, and badly housed, used to go the movie theaters to
forget their worries."

Truffaut thus poses a problem for which there is, perhaps, no solution.
The French film industry was then producing too many films of indifferent merit and relying on an inadequate distribution network to present
these films to the public. Except for what Truffaut refers to as "Draconian" measures, involving huge layoffs of industry technicians, only a
greater number of theaters or more strictly controlled distribution patterns offered any real hope for French producers. Otherwise, the industry would continue to lose money (four billion francs in 1955) and make
more films that would never reach an audience. Not only that, but the
cost of film production, Truffaut notices, had doubled in three years,
from 1952 to 1955.

This is a problem the American and French industries, along with the film production units of other countries, still face today, and if anything, the problem has become more severe. However, today producers can rely upon videocassette sales and ancillary rights to offset the rising costs of their films. In 1955, even the television market was still problematic. Nontheatrical distribution was confined to 16mm prints, and videotape was in its infancy. Today's pattern of massive saturation bookings (one film opening in 1,000 to 1,500 theaters nationwide simultaneously) makes the situation Truffaut describes here all the more critical.

The Double Crisis of Cinema

For production: a loss of four billion francs.

For critics: a lack of quality.

People talk a lot about the crisis of French cinema. It is mainly a crisis of overproduction. For the past few years, France, which used to produce less than a hundred films every year, has busied itself producing 100, then over 100.

Every record will be beaten this year [1956] with 130 films.

The cinematographic industry thus works with full employment, and to reduce the number of movies would be equivalent to creating a level of unemployment that the profession hasn't seen for several years.

According to the producers' union, the average cost of a film in 1952 was forty-two million francs; in 1955 it went up to ninety-three, which is to say that it doubled, as did investments. For things to be set in order again, incoming grosses would have to double in turn, which is, alas, not the case—nor did the number of spectators double.

Among the 208 French films made in 1954 and 1955, we are told that sixty-eight are still waiting to be released with exclusive rights [that is, shown in one theater only, rather than booked simultaneously in a number of venues; see Truffaut's remarks in the next paragraph]. First, it would be good to see the list of these sixty-eight films; and then should we deduce, from the quality of these films, that there aren't enough exclusive theaters any more?

These sixty-eight movies, added to this year's excess of production, create a bottleneck, a traffic jam for which it is hard to find a solution. It has been considered, among other possibilities, going back to the "exclusive" notion we had before the war; every movie would be released in one theater only. This would avoid the general releases used by American companies.

Anyway, incoming grosses won't keep up with the rise of investments for all that and, unless we make an unlikely Draconian decision, or unless the audience shows a furious and suddenly increased taste for French films, there is no obvious way to avoid, the four billion franc deficit that threatens the cinematographic industry this year.

First, there is the disenchantment of the audience. Deplored by every exhibitor, it is essentially caused by the current fashion of scooters [as opposed to more expensive automobiles] and the practice of sales on credit (designed to help consumers find apartments and to help with house building in the first place). French exhibitors regret the passing of the postwar "golden age": French people, badly fed, badly heated, and badly housed, used to go to the movie theaters to forget their worries. Since they paid a high price for food (black market), the price of the cinema ticket (higher than today in proportion to the cost of living) didn't scare them away. Having written this, I consulted, out of curiosity, the list of the movies presently being made this week: *La polka des menottes* (Raoul André), *Action immédiate* (Maurice Labro), *Cinq millions comptant* (Berthomieu), *Que les hommes sont bêtes* (Roger Richebé), *Fugue pour clarinette* (Julien Duvivier), *Dimanche nous volerons* (Henri Aisner), *Jusqu'au dernier* (Pierre Billon), *Fric-frac en dentelles* (Guillaume Radot), *Oeil pour oeil* (André Cayatte), *SOS Noronha* (Rouquier), *Mon oncle* (Jacques Tati), *Sylviane de mes nuits* (Marcel Blistène), *Par ici la sortie* (Willy Rozier), *Le Temps de l'amour* (Lacombe), *Sans douleur* (J. Lechanois), *La Passe du diable* (Jacques Dupont), *Les Sorcières de Salem* (R. Rouleau), and *L'Amour descend du ciel* (Maurice Cam).

How many films among those deserve our interest, once they are completed? All the more because Tati's, Cayatte's, Lechanois's, and Duvivier's won't have any problems being released and finding an exclusive theater. As to the others, most of them will go off to amortize their debt in the provinces, which are always hungry for the adventures of Leguignon and other Piédalus. (BFH)[36]

Robert Wise

Truffaut was an admirer of the work of Robert Wise, whose *Born to Kill* (1947) he described as "Bressonian." Truffaut's review of Wise's *Executive Suite* (1954), another "melodrama," is a restatement of the young critic's estimation of Wise's talents as an *auteur* and makes reference to *The Set-Up* (1949), Wise's work with Welles, while acknowledging the importance to the film of John Houseman, producer of the project. As Truffaut recognizes, the triumph of this film, as with *So Big*, resides in its elevation of craft to the realm of art.

Particularly, *Executive Suite* reworks the strategy of the "portrait film," in this instance offering us the portrait of someone who is absent, revealed through the reactions of roughly ten other characters whose existence depends closely on that of the absent person. Wise has "avoided ritual flashbacks" in the construction of the film; rather, "the movie takes place in the present, without interruption." *Executive Suite* is above all a remarkable piece of ensemble acting, and Truffaut credits the large cast with much of the success of the film. Thus it would seem that a good portion of Wise's skills as a creator of mise-en-scène resides in his ability to direct actors rather in than his brilliance as an imagist.

This assumption would seem to be supported by much of Wise's early work: *The Body Snatcher,* for example, derives most of its impact from Henry Daniell's bravura performance in the leading role and the manner in which he plays off Boris Karloff. *Born to Kill* is essentially a struggle for dominance between Claire Trevor and Lawrence Tierney, and it afforded Tierney one of the few roles of dimension in his underappreciated career. Wise is clearly sympathetic to actors, and "the jury in Venice" that Truffaut alludes to near the end of his notice is unquestionably correct in assigning to William Holden, Barbara Stanwyck, June Allyson, and the other cast members a key share in the qualities of *Executive Suite.*

Executive Suite (La Tour des Ambitieux)
(Great Style)

A furniture magnate and swindler dies suddenly in the street. Five vice-presidents engage in a bitter dispute concerning his succession. The most qualified one of the five—who is at the same time the only likeable one—is elected.

Executive Suite is one of those movies in which the producer counts as much as the director; John Houseman was not long ago the shrewd producer of *Citizen Kane* and just recently of *The Bad and the Beautiful. Executive Suite* borrows the essential elements from these two films' scenarios: the portrait of someone who is absent, revealed through the reactions of roughly ten other characters whose existence depends closely on that of the absent person.

The novelty here lies in having avoided ritual flashbacks: the movie takes place in the present, without interruption. Extremely skillful construction of the film thoroughly informs us about the characters in a minimum of scenes, without cutting up the action in sketches. If the film is rather literary, indeed theatrical, *Executive Suite* succeeds as an excellent piece of cinema thanks to the work of Robert Wise.

We are familiar with the name of this director since the release of *The Set-Up.* Having been the chief editor for Orson Welles previously, Robert Wise makes subtle use of the camera, which no longer holds any secrets for him. Each shot's reliability, sureness, its length and density, contributes to the creation of a style essentially characterized by efficiency.

For an hour and forty-five minutes, we live at the top of this famous tower in a closed universe; and the actors succeed in making us believe in the considerable importance of a character we have not even glimpsed: the election of a new president for this furniture factory seems to be as serious as an election at the White House. The success of such a film is closely related to its cast of characters. The jury at Venice crowned them unanimously—and deservedly: William Holden, Barbara Stanwyck, June

Allyson, Walter Pidgeon, Louis Calhern, Frederic March, Nina Foch, and Shelley Winters. (BFH)[37]

The festival jury may well have been correct in their praise of the actors in *Executive Suite* and of Wise's direction of these actors. But what of Wise's visual sensibility? This is the problem that militates against Wise's full success as an *auteur* of the first rank.

Much of the effectiveness in the compositions of *Born to Kill* can be traced to the RKO house-style of lighting, as evidenced in other RKO productions of the period, such as *Murder, My Sweet* (1944; Dir. Edward Dmytryk) or *Step by Step* (1946; Dir. Phil Rosen). Once Wise left RKO, the quality of his work became less and less individual. This reached an apotheosis of sorts in *The Sound of Music* (1965) and continues up to Wise's most recent production, *Rooftops* (1989). *Executive Suite* may be slick, well mounted, and impeccably assembled, but it lacks the uniqueness of approach one associates with Bresson or Tourneur.

Robert Aldrich

During the early 1950s, Robert Aldrich was another young "director to watch." Already established abroad (though not in the United States) with his direction of *Kiss Me Deadly* (1955), *The Big Knife* (1955), and *Vera Cruz* (1954), Aldrich was at the high point of his early career when he made *Autumn Leaves* in 1956, with Joan Crawford and Cliff Robertson. Truffaut's assertion to the contrary, however, *Autumn Leaves* was not made to order for Columbia but was rather "Aldrich's second indo pendent production,"[38] distributed by Columbia on a negative pickup deal. *Autumn Leaves* and *The Big Knife* were both produced by The Associates and Aldrich, Aldrich's own production company. Truffaut makes several references to *The Big Knife* in his review of *Autumn Leaves*; what made *The Big Knife* especially popular with foreign audiences was its cynical, downbeat portrayal of the Hollywood studio system. This view can certainly be seen as emblematic of Aldrich's own feelings on the matter. For most of his career, Aldrich would struggle to work outside of the major studios; he even went so far as to set up his own studio in 1968, though it went under in 1971.

Aldrich was a man at odds with himself and with the industry he is nominally associated with. Driven to create individual projects, yet very much dependent on the studios to distribute his films, Aldrich vacillated between personal works and work-for-hire for his entire working life. *Autumn Leaves*, though possessing certain elements (such as the presence of Joan Crawford) designed to ensure audience receptivity, was very much a film that Aldrich wanted to do, not one that was thrust upon him. Of *Autumn Leaves*, Aldrich commented that "I thought it was time that I did a soap-opera—firstly, because I wanted to do one anyway, and secondly, because this seemed a pretty good one."[39] Aldrich signed Joan Crawford in September of 1954, after having bought the rights to Jean Rouverol's story "The Way We Are" in July of that same year.[40] After the release of *Autumn Leaves,* Aldrich told Truffaut in a separate interview that "of all my films it's probably the best acted."[41] Thus *Autumn Leaves* is a personal statement disguised as entertainment in the tradition of Sirk and Ophüls.

Truffaut is something of a prognosticator in his identification of the "Grand Guignol" aspect of the work. Aldrich would shortly go on to the greatest commercial success of his career with *Whatever Happened to Baby Jane?* (1962). *Autumn Leaves* does not lack faults. Truffaut writes that there are "too many endless scenes of dialogue, which Aldrich probably filmed without passion." Yet *Autumn Leaves* is, despite the commercial trappings, a project Aldrich believed in and executed with style and intelligence.

Autumn Leaves (Feuilles d'automne) "Frantic Love"

To make *The Big Knife,* Robert Aldrich created his own production company: "Robert Aldrich and Associates." The movie cost him $458,000 and, in spite of the Grand Prize for mise-en-scène that it won in the Biennial Festival in Venice, it brought in only $300,000. Dead loss of $158,000 then, in this anti-Hollywoodian movie, a loss that the very big success in America of *Attack!* [1956] will, I think, highly make up for.

All the same, after *The Big Knife,* Robert Aldrich, who needed to regain the financiers' trust, accepted a contract to film for Columbia, in forty days, a sentimental melodrama made-to-measure for Joan Crawford, *The Way We Are,* which became *Autumn Leaves*—which is also the American title of the too-famous song by Prévert and Kosma, *Les feuilles mortes* [*Autumn Leaves*]. Pitifully scored in six different ways by The Nat King Cole Trio, this song is used as a leitmotif for the film.

The fact that it is thanks to the money he made with *Autumn Leaves* that Aldrich was able to produce and make *Attack!* mustn't make us lenient. Besides, does Robert Aldrich, who is the embodiment of lucidity, need our leniency? Certainly not. With *Autumn Leaves,* he made the film on order, and then he did his best to "save something from the wreck" as honestly as he could. From this point of view, the film is quite a success and is worth seeing.

A woman (back again, hotheaded, menopausal—Joan Crawford), who is about forty, has remained single up to now against her will. One nice evening, a young boy, who could be, in a pinch, her son, starts an eager courtship, which quite quickly leads them to marriage.

At that moment, the center of interest of the movie is shifted, and the character of the boy (Cliff Robertson) becomes the dominant one. Is he just a liar, a thief, a mythomaniac, or a neurotic hungry for affection, a sick man who needs to be cured?

His drama? An unhappy childhood, a first and disastrous marriage (his wife, Vera Miles, became the mistress of his own father). After narrowly avoiding a typewriter that her young spouse throws at her head, Joan Crawford decides to have him committed.

An ending that looks a lot like sidestepping shows him both cured of his neurosis and still in love with Joan Crawford.

There are several ways of dealing with this important subject of a woman's solitude and of distressed adolescence; I prefer Aldrich's way—taking into account the fact that it was an assigned project—making a large allowance to Grand Guignol, to the way of Bardem, falsely serious in *Main Street,* or to the way *Summertime* [1955; Dir. David Lean] is made: purely sentimental.

Here, at least, in spite of conventions, the carnal, epidermal, physical aspect of this marriage is not conjured away; the scene where, in the cabana, Joan Crawford, anxious, climbs onto a small table to stretch her bathing suit in front of the mirror, before showing her body for the first time to Cliff Robertson, who's waiting for her on the beach, whistling to himself, is, in this respect, wonderful in its reality, intelligence, and beauty. We must only regret that the film doesn't keep this tone till the end; too many endless scenes of dialogue, which Aldrich probably filmed without passion, link the good moments together.

What we ought to admire here is essentially the precision of the direction of the actors; the strength and quiet confidence of that direction; Joan Crawford, raw and at fever pitch as never before, stroking Cliff Robertson, a frail and mischievous youngster—this alone is worth the price of the ticket.

(Finally, let us deplore the appalling state of the American print, which harms the movie by repeatedly switching from blackish-brown to purple.) (SK)[42]

In the final lines of this review, Truffaut reminds us that, as a director, one has above all a responsibility to one's actors. The "strength and quiet confidence" that Crawford presents in *Autumn Leaves* can be seen as a direct result of Aldrich's assured direction, and Aldrich was sufficiently comfortable with Crawford to direct her later in *Baby Jane.* (Aldrich started *Hush, Hush Sweet Charlotte* [1964] with Crawford and Bette Davis, but the two actresses proved, finally, that they could not coexist within the confines of a single film, and Crawford was replaced by Olivia de Havilland.)

Truffaut admired Aldrich and shared Aldrich's distrust of the major studios; and Aldrich and Truffaut were united in one common precept: respect for performers. If Aldrich's later films, no matter how well rehearsed they were, failed to ignite either critically or commercially, it is perhaps because Truffaut, as a director, was far more daring and innovative in his use of the camera than Aldrich. In this, Aldrich shared the

142   The Early Film Criticism of François Truffaut

same birthright, with the same limitations, as did Robert Wise. Such interesting late Aldrich films as *The Legend of Lylah Clare* (1968) or *The Longest Yard* (1974) would have been even more successful if executed with a more flexible mise-en-scène. Even in his own studio, completely in charge of all aspects of his films, Aldrich never strayed far from the Mitchell camera mounted on a Crab Dolly. Truffaut, with his hand-held Eclair, lived and worked with his actors, yet he also gave them a frame that permitted both his compositions and his protagonists to breathe.

Edward Dmytryk

Truffaut's estimation of Wise is made all the more problematic by his lack of respect for the works of Edward Dmytryk, another executor of '40s studio style. The stolid solidity of Wise's mise-en-scène is one aspect of classical Hollywood narrative; Dmytryk's pyrotechnical flash is the opposing vision. In his review of Dmytryk's *The Caine Mutiny*, Truffaut takes the opportunity to examine Dmytryk's career as a whole, and even to indulge in a bit of biography.

Truffaut compares Dmytryk to André Cayatte, stating that both "directors share the same flaws: lack of taste, lack of technical skill, and lack of sensitivity; the direction of the actors is left, at random, to their talent." There is some truth in these charges, as well as some oversimplification. Cayatte, who gave up the practice of law to write essays and novels, saw film as a medium of instruction and a catalyst for reform. As a stylist, Cayatte's work is unremarkable. Nevertheless, particularly during the early part of his career, Cayatte was showered with honors (precisely because, one suspects, of the transparency of his intent). Up until the early 1960s, Cayatte functioned as the predecessor of Costa-Gavras and the equivalent of a number of American directors who openly espoused liberal concerns.

Dmytryk was one of these directors. Truffaut briefly traces Dmytryk's early career; among the high points of Dmytryk's early work is his editing of *Ruggles of Red Gap* (1935; Dir. Leo McCarey).

Truffaut has distinct reservations concerning Dmytryk's films. One might accuse Dmytryk of a "lack of taste," in that his most personal films are almost naked in the social and political agendas; the weakest aspect of Dmytryk as a director is his primitive "social conscience." Direction of actors is also not Dmytryk's strong suit, but as his early films indicate, Dmytryk is more interested in the force and drive of his narrative than in taking time to develop his characters. The "lack of technical skill," however, is hard to credit. Dmytryk may be a traditionalist, tied to the big-studio "look" and to its stylistic ethos of working within the boundaries imposed by the system. But his camera work, though never extraordinary, is more than competent, and as a stylist, along with Anthony Mann, Boris Ingster, Fritz Lang, and others, Dmytryk helped to shape and define the hard-bitten '40s style that later became known as "film noir." The career of Dmytryk is also curious in that no sooner had he hit his real stride than he ran afoul of the House Un-American Activities Committee (HUAC) for his past political affiliations. Dmytryk's work is unquestionably only a fragment of what it might have been.

The Caine Mutiny (1954) is not top-drawer Dmytryk, and it seems unfair to judge his work in the light of that film's many defects, even though the film was highly praised when first released. As for Truffaut's charge that Dmytryk leaves the direction of his actors "at random, to their talent," Humphrey Bogart is superb in Mutiny, which should be no surprise, but Fred MacMurray is weak and unfocused. Dmytryk favors Bogart with tight close-ups at key points in the narrative (particularly in the final sequence during the court martial, when Bogart breaks down on the stand), allowing the actor to dominate the proceedings and to use all of his considerable skill as the creator of a cinematic presence. MacMurray, whose best work can arguably be seen in Billy Wilder's Double Indemnity (1944), needs closer handling, and this Dmytryk cannot provide. Nevertheless, Truffaut is too harsh in his complete dismissal of Dmytryk as an auteur. If Robert Wise can achieve brilliance as an auteur through his dedication to the studio mechanism, despite his lack of a visual signature, then certainly Dmytryk, despite his acknowledged defects, is a filmmaker of style, taste, and sensibility, at his best when he does not feel compelled to reorient the political beliefs of his audience.

The Caine Mutiny (Ouragan sur le Caine)

The action takes place on the ship Caine during World War II. Through several incidents, the commander of the boat displays all the symptoms of extreme paranoia, if not of madness. The officers, and then the crew, soon become convinced of their commander's mental irresponsibility. During a storm, when the commander orders a manoeuver that endangers the ship, the second officer takes over command according to article 184 of the Marine Officer's Code, and brings the ship home safely.

When the commander of the Caine has been declared sane by a psychiatric commission, his second officer is considered a mutineer and is impeached before a war committee. His cause seems lost up until the moment when the commander, who has to testify, betrays himself. His manner of persecuting his men, his anxiety, his need to dominate, and his neurosis become clear behind all of his remarks. He is dismissed from the service, and the second officer is acquitted.

Some compare, with good reason, Edward Dmytryk to André Cayatte. Indeed, the director of Crossfire [1947] and the director of Avant le Déluge [1954] reveal the same ambition: to make didactic movies. The two directors share the same flaws: lack of taste, lack of technical skill, and lack of sensitivity; the direction of the actors is left, at random, to their own talent. Nevertheless, The Caine Mutiny, which came back from

Venice bestowed with many honors, might be the best film of Dmytryk insofar as the scenario is superior to that of *Crossfire, Give Us This Day* [1949], *Murder, My Sweet* etc.

We do not want to forget to mention *From Here to Eternity* [1953] in relation to *The Caine Mutiny*. In both, one recognizes the naive desire of Hollywood to gain access to intellectual cinema by means of the best-seller of the year. But if Dmytryk's movie seems more interesting than Zinnemann's, it is because it has a more original scenario and because the good scenes are better, despite the bad ones being worse. Probably the pleasure of watching *The Caine Mutiny* stems from the directors' vagueness about what they're trying to convey.

Our sympathy as spectators, oscillating between different characters in this drama, ends on the side of the one who seems to be in a bad plight, which keeps changing. At the end of the movie, we don't know what to think about this commander, so well played by Humphrey Bogart: whether he is crazy or whether we made the same mistake as the "second" to believe he is. The color is barely acceptable, and the casting is uneven. The stars, who are very good at what they are doing, are excellent: José Ferrer, Bogart, Fred MacMurray, and Van Johnson are less so. As for the young officer and his fiancee, of whom we learn in the credits that this is their film debut, they are pretty awful.

Thanks to two purple passages—the storm and the testimony of the commander—*The Caine Mutiny* can be watched without regrets. Edward Dmytryk was born in 1908 in Canada to Ukrainian parents. He first ran errands at Paramount Studios and later became head editor until 1939. Afterward he made short films, and then "B" films. His first big success was *Murder, My Sweet* with Dick Powell, a detective film in the style of the "noir" series (1944); then came *Crossfire*, a film with a message in the fashion of *Cayatte* (1947).

Later, Dmytryk ran into difficulties with the famous "Committee for Un-American Activities" [HUAC]. He first refused to answer the questions of the committee, which cost him a stay in prison and made it impossible for him to work in the United States. He exiled himself and made *Obsession* (1948) and *Give Us This Day* (1949) in London.

When he came back to the U.S., he underwent a second questioning session of the McCarthy committee; this time he gave answers. Apparently, the committee obtained "confessions" from him, and he "gave" the police the names of numerous *cinéastes* accused of "communism." At this price he was allowed to work again, and he directed *The Sniper* [1952] for Stanley Kramer, *The Juggler* [1953], and finally *The Caine Mutiny*. He is now working on a movie based on a novel of Graham Greene [which became *The End of the Affair*, shot in England by Dmytryk in 1954]. (SK)[43]

Minor Auteurs

In the final pages of this volume, I'd like to consider some less well-known directors whom Truffaut favored with critical analysis, including Abner Biberman, Clarence Brown, Delmer Daves, Jean Négulesco, and Mark Robson. Abner Biberman, who is not to be confused with Herbert J. Biberman, never aspired to greatness. As an actor, Abner Biberman appeared in character parts in *Gunga Din* (1939; Dir. George Stevens), *The Roaring Twenties* (1939; Dir. Raoul Walsh), *The Leopard Man* (1943; Dir. Jacques Tourneur), and other films. As a director, Abner Biberman directed *The Looters* (1955), *Running Wild* (1955), *The Price of Fear* (1956), and three other features before making his last feature film as a director, *Flood Tide* (1958). Abner Biberman then went over to television, where he worked as director on numerous television programs, including *Ironside*, *Ben Casey*, and *The Virginian*. Truffaut finds *The Price of Fear* devoid of interest and ambition: the film "doesn't justify the price you have to pay for your seat."

The Price of Fear (Le Prix de la Peur) by Abner Biberman.

American cinema this year counts a bit too much on the known fact that the sun (even though it is a rotten summer sun) invites indulgence, prompting the studios to release their old chestnuts that are bound to flop. Everything looks as if we are being forcibly pushed out of the theaters toward the swimming pools or even the countryside.

The Price of Fear isn't worth the price you have to pay for your seat, and if it makes you laugh, it's without meaning to. This Biberman would gain by appearing before the Un-Cinematic Activities Commission [Truffaut's apocryphal cultural police]. Too much ingenuity to start with is often prejudicial, especially when the threads of the plot, instead of getting nicely untied, get entangled into an inextricable knot. The thick-set Lex Barker, anointed Tarzan of Hollywood, though dressed here, looks naked and seems to feel naked, not knowing what to do with his hands, planted in front of the camera as he would be in front of a medical board examining recruits, and is completely innocent of everything he is accused of. He did not shoot "So-and-so," and kill him with a shotgun, although he did threaten to kill him an hour before. Incidentally, when the crime was committed, he was on the road driving a car he had "borrowed" in the street ten minutes after the very same jalopy had run over an old man. Tarzan is in a fine mess, and in Merle Oberon's bed— Merle Oberon who, when we see her, doesn't make us feel much younger, especially when we think of the *Wuthering Heights* [1939; Dir. William Wyler] of the day before yesterday. The old man run over by the car had a daughter to marry off, who falls in love with the one she mistakes for the hit-and-run driver: Tarzan again. When she learns that he is innocent, oh! paradox, she loves him even more.

Had Rodrigue's innocence been revealed in the last act of *Le Cid,* would Chimène's love have increased? That kind of reflection, and others even more preposterous, comes to mind as you sit stargazing while watching *The Price of Fear,* which gets first prize for the most frightfully boring film of the week. (BFH)[44]

Clarence Brown fares somewhat better; but then his work is a good deal more distinguished than Abner Biberman's. Starting as a director in 1923 with *Don't Marry for Money,* Brown went on to direct Rudolph Valentino in *The Eagle* for Universal in 1925. It is this film more than any other of his early works that firmly established his reputation. When talkies arrived, Brown made the transition with little difficulty. He directed his first sound film in 1929 for MGM, *The Trial of '98.* Thereafter, Clarence Brown would work exclusively for MGM. In 1930, Brown directed Greta Garbo in her first talking film, *Anna Christie,* a film that has since attained the status of a classic. The film has numerous structural defects, most of them arising out of the inherent clumsiness of early sound-recording apparatus, yet Brown's handling of Garbo is diligent and assured. Garbo went on to make *Anna Karenina* (1935) and *Conquest* (1937) for Brown, and it was during this period of his career that the director created his most successful and fully realized works.

However, Brown was moving in a different direction by the end of the 1930s, and the following decade would find him immersed in a series of generally undistinguished sagas and spectacles, particularly *The Rains Came* (1939) and *The White Cliffs of Dover* (1944). Brown's methodical direction, exacerbated by the crushing gloss of the typical MGM production, became more and more tedious. Beginning in 1946, Clarence Brown also served as producer on all his films.

While many viewers remember *National Velvet* (1944) and *The Yearling* (1946) with great fondness, Brown's other work during this era included *Edison, The Man* (1940), *Song of Love* (1947), and *To Please a Lady* (1950), all films that lack anything approaching a personal or individual style. Clarence Brown had become a house director, committed to schedule and budget but nothing more. *Plymouth Adventure* (1952), reviewed by Truffaut shortly after its initial release, was Brown's last film as a director. One is forced to agree with Truffaut's assessment of Brown as a "boring and grave" director, a "storyteller who does not want to make any concessions," who requires his viewers "always to take the first step." Yet for all these reservations, and the fact that Truffaut finds *Plymouth Adventure* "as boring as rain, or as fascinating as a 'thriller,' depending on the goodwill of the viewer," "the attention that one is willing to bring [to the film] from the beginning is well rewarded." Truffaut's analysis of the film, particularly in the second paragraph of his review, reveals the essential paradox of Brown's approach to his material. For an *auteur* whose films are "exclusively psychologically developed, without any recourse to sudden change," Brown is nevertheless seduced by the physical production afforded by his home studio. *Plymouth Adventure,* Truffaut feels, is "sober and carefully done, but lightly insufficient."

This external substantiality, coupled with an emphasis on interior motivation, makes Clarence Brown one of the more curious Hollywood contract directors. There is certainly an individual vision in Brown's work, yet Brown willingly allows it to be submerged within the MGM machine; indeed, he seems to welcome the respite from responsibility that surrender to the system brings. Brown is ultimately anonymous, even as he maintains a firm hand on the physical aspects of his projects (as exemplified by his interest in production). *Plymouth Adventure* seems sincere yet stillborn. Clarence Brown is present everywhere within this work. Though his mise-en-scène remains firmly anchored within the narrative, and he is certainly not a visual director, despite his love of spectacle, Clarence Brown manages to serve several masters; he is faithful to his concerns, yet he never neglects his responsibility to his audience, or his obligation to those who finance and distribute his works.

Plymouth Adventure (Captaine sans loi)
American movie by Clarence Brown.

The story takes place a century ago. Captain Jones (Spencer Tracy) betrays the navigation company that employs him by taking about a hundred emigrants (who come from England) to uninhabited territory in North Virginia. During the crossing, the captain falls in love with a colonist's wife (Gene Tierney), who, divided between duty and love, commits suicide. Faithful to his promise to this marvelous woman, Jones will not set sail before making sure that the colonists are well settled and have everything they need.

Clarence Brown is quite a curious man. Let us bring back to mind some films directed by him: *Of Human Hearts* [1938], *The White Cliffs of Dover* [1944], and *Intruder in the Dust* [1950] from Faulkner's work. All of Brown's movies resemble each other and possess the same characteristics; they are at the same time boring and serious, popular but with integrity, austere and attractive. Brown is a storyteller who does not want to make any concessions—or maybe he doesn't know the rules of the genre. His films do not contain any comic relief, no gags, no secondary funny role. The action is exclusively psychologically developed, without any recourse to twists in the plot. The interpretation of the actors is sober and carefully done, but slightly insufficient. The vigor is completely internal. *Plymouth Adventure* constitutes a film as boring as rain, or as fascinating as a "thriller," depending on the goodwill of the viewer.

With Clarence Brown, the viewer has to make the first move. The attention that one is willing to bring to it from the beginning is always well rewarded.[45]

Delmer Daves began as a writer and later moved to direction. His very first job in films was on *The Covered Wagon* (1923; Dir. James Cruze); Daves served as a prop boy on that production. Various bit parts as an actor followed, and then work as a scenarist and story writer on such films as *Flirtation Walk* (1935; Dir. Frank Borzage) and *Love Affair* (1939; Dir. Leo McCarey). In 1943, Daves directed *Destination Tokyo*, then going on to direct more than twenty-five films, working for Warner Brothers, Columbia, 20th Century-Fox, MGM, and United Artists. Starting with *A Summer Place* in 1959, Daves functioned as the producer and scenarist of all his works, with the sole exception of his last film, *The Battle of Villa Fiorita* (1965).

Daves is not without interest as a director, but *Never Let Me Go* (1953) must qualify as perhaps the least interesting of his efforts. Most cinéastes remember *The Red House* (1947), Daves's bizarre and generally overlooked Gothic suspense film, with Edward G. Robinson; or *Dark Passage* (1947), starring Humphrey Bogart and Lauren Bacall, a film notable for its extensive use of first-person camera work. Later in his career, Daves became a specialist in formulaic melodrama with *A Summer Place* (1959), *Parrish* (1961), *Susan Slade* (1961), and *Youngblood Hawke* (1964). In all his films, Daves seems most involved in the narrative line of his works, and he leaves the performers pretty much on their own. Daves is also fond of complicated visual embellishments, particularly sweeping crane shots. His visual compositions are usually exaggerated and extreme. Daves is ultimately a director of effects and accents who documents the exterior of events rather than entering into the world of his characters. For all his fascination with narrative twists (and *Dark Passage*, particularly, is a film that depends upon a complex and ever-changing plot line), Daves is more an illustrator than a *metteur-en-scène*.

Truffaut follows his remarks on *Never Let Me Go* with brief paragraphs on two minor films, *Lure of the Wilderness* (1952), by Jean Négulesco, and *Return to Paradise* (1953), directed by Mark Robson. Négulesco's other memorable films of the 1950s include *Three Coins in the Fountain* (1954), *Daddy Long Legs* (1955), and *The Best of Everything* (1959).

Mark Robson directed *Champion* (1949), a film that Truffaut feels was "praised too highly." *Return to Paradise* (1953) is primarily of interest to Truffaut because of the air of general malaise that is attached to the production. "Gary Cooper walks through it, worn out, stupefied, disillusioned."

Never Let Me Go (Ne me quitte jamais)
American film by Delmer Daves.

Jargon is like spit flying through the air: you're in danger of having it fall on your own head. The scholarly expression "auto-demystification" seems to impose itself as soon as one talks about a Russian film. We'll come back to that.

The American film *Never Let Me Go,* portraying the honeymoon of an American (Clark Gable) and a Russian (Gene Tierney) in Russia, will provoke smiles. Gable, a freelance journalist, is talked into writing a series of articles about the cold war; these articles offend the Russian government. He is given notice of his expulsion: "U.S. go home!" After encountering all possible difficulties in securing a visa for his Russian wife, he obtains it. The day of the flight, he boards the plane, thinking his wife is following directly behind him; unfortunately, as the engine buzzes and the propellers turn, she is retained on the ground. He wants to get off, but he's pulled back. The plane takes off and he yells: "I'll come back!" The only thing left for Gene Tierney to do is to run after the airplane, for the sake of poetic form. Clark has not said his last word; he comes back illegally by boat and takes his wife away under the very nose of 1,000 officers of the Russian army, in the best "Sabotage in Berlin" tradition.

If it could ever be wrong to have smiled, this would be the time; the *auteur* of *Dark Passage* is that clever about moving us. In spite of the scoffers, I don't see anything very extravagant here, nor anything you don't already know if you've already watched a few Russian films. *The Cossacks of Kouban,* for example, showed us what a to-do it was for a girl from over there to marry a guy from the next kolkhoz. All the more if it's an American!

Gene Tierney, as Russian as the whole Pitoeff family put together, makes us want to look for our future wives on Russian soil, but only if we could be sure, like Gable, of getting them home.

Besides, isn't Gene a Brooklyn native?

Lure of the Wilderness (Prisonniers du Marais)
American film in Technicolor by Jean Négulesco.

I am writing this note as Gide writes his books: to "warn." To warn the reader that *Lure of the Wilderness* is, above all, a film to avoid. It is a less-than-pale remake of the very beautiful *Swamp Water* [1941], shot by Jean Renoir in Georgia (U.S.A.). The potential of pretty Jean Peters is not utilized, the Technicolor is nothing more than adequate, and the whole is extremely boring.

Return to Paradise (Retour au paradis)
American movie by Mark Robson.

A curious film that attaches itself to the viewer and is also baffling, one that we wish we could like more. Gary Cooper walks through it, worn out, knocked out, disillusioned. Lots of sunny days outdoors, in

proper Technicolor. The island girls are pretty but we don't see enough
of them. Robson, whose *Champion* [1949] was praised too highly, never
breaks out from adequate quality. (SK)[46]

Truffaut admired Henry Hathaway's *Niagara* because of the presence
of Marilyn Monroe in that film. With Hathaway's other efforts, he was
less charitable, as seen in Truffaut's review of *Garden of Evil* (1954). In
his review of *Niagara*, Truffaut spent next to no time discussing Hathaway's directional style and acknowledged that his analysis of the film
was, to say the least, eccentric. Discussing *Garden of Evil*, Truffaut finds
that Hathaway's style has deteriorated with the implementation of the
CinemaScope process in his work.

Niagara, a film Truffaut had heretofore dismissed, is now seen as a
work of "admirable surety." Nevertheless, Truffaut feels that *Garden of
Evil* "is the best CinemaScope film released this year . . . after *River of
No Return*." Shot entirely outdoors, *Garden of Evil* stars an aging Gary
Cooper, who appears "exhausted and tired" before the camera. Hathaway's mise-en-scène, in Truffaut's view, resorts to the use of "stage tricks
. . . as coarse as they are worn out." Susan Hayward "will end up tiring
us, by refusing time after time to revitalize the character she plays." The
overall impression one gets from the film is fatigue, a sense of compromised execution.

Garden of Evil (Jardin du Diable)
American film in CinemaScope by Henry Hathaway.

Except for *River of No Return,* which could be recommended without
reserve, no CinemaScope film released in France up until now has been
totally satisfactory. This imperfection stems less from the process or from
the directors than from the uses of this process and from the general
directions given by the CinemaScope technicians to directors.

In any case, after *River of No Return, Garden of Evil* is the best
CinemaScope film released this year. At the time of the gold rush, a
woman and five adventurers are trapped by Indians in a desolate Mexican region. So, here again, we have a movie shot outside from beginning to end. The scenario is too ambiguous at the film's start to remain
that way: indeed, halfway through the movie the "stage-tricks" appear,
as coarse as they are worn out. But the art lies rather in the manner of
the execution. . . . Susan Hayward will end up tiring us, by refusing
time after time to breathe any life into her character, who is without any
glamour today: someone like Ava Gardner would have suited us better.
Gary Cooper seems exhausted and tired of an already long career. He
does not take off his hat once in the course of the movie, and it is easy
to guess why; the wrinkles covering his face do not alter the look in his
eyes, which is always marked by an astonishing bluishness. He still makes
subtle use of a native clumsiness that became—thanks to Capra—a very

effective acting style. Because of his looks, Cooper can kill with a face expressing complete goodness. Richard Widmark sneers, as his contract must ordain, but he does so without conviction. As far as Hathaway is concerned, we regret not being able to find in his Scope films the same admirable surety of his last "flat" [standard aspect ratio] films (cf. *Niagara* [1953]). Four big names that don't come up to their usual standards nevertheless justify our pleasure; and they are probably worth more than four mediocre names who would surpass themselves. The lover of American movies ought to see *Garden of Evil.* (BFH)[47]

Truffaut's First Films as Director

. By 1956, Truffaut was becoming increasingly impatient with merely criticizing the work of others. He longed to do his own work, and in 1957, he decisively took the plunge with his direction of *Les Mistons*, a twenty-three minute film. It therefore seems appropriate to conclude this volume with Truffaut's thoughts on the films made in France during 1956, his last year as a full-time critic.

We may easily recognize the style of Truffaut, the critic and moralist, in this ranking of films. The best film of the year, in Truffaut's view, is unquestionably Alain Resnais's *Nuit et brouillard (Night and Fog)* which "makes every other film look trivial." This short film, only thirty minutes in length, manages to eclipse every other film of 1956. The "terrible sweetness" of *Night and Fog*, "an interrogative meditation about the Nazis' concentration camps," gives proof of the fact that "a torturer, a deporter, lies dormant within each of us." Aside from the epigrammatic intensity of *Night and Fog*, what makes the inclusion of the film unusual is that it is the only short film on Truffaut's list. In judging *Night and Fog* against its feature-length competition, Truffaut refuses to recognize arbitrary categories of length in evaluating a film. As always, it is the ambition of a film that matters most to him, and the terrible moral urgency of *Night and Fog* makes even Robert Bresson's austere *A Man Escaped* look "like some kind of entertainment."

Along with *Night and Fog*, Truffaut finds Bresson's *Un Condamné à mort s'est éschappé (A Man Escaped)*, Renoir's *Eléna et les hommes (Elena and Her Men)*, Claude Autant-Lara's *La Traversée de Paris (Four Bags Full)*, and Vadim's *Et Dieu créa la femme (And God Created Woman)* to be the best feature films made in France during the year. To those films, he adds Agnès Varda's first feature, *La Point courte*, a film actually made in 1954 and edited by Alian Resnais. *And God Created Woman* has already been discussed in these pages; *Elena and Her Men* seems, in retrospect, a minor *divertissement* of the great director. *A Man Escaped*, a precisely formalist examination of the mechanics of guilt, punishment, and society's role in defining the limits of individual action, has taken its rightful place within the canon of Bresson's fiercely individual works.

La Traversée de Paris, released in the United States as *Four Bags Full*, has receded into memory as a pleasant but relatively undistinguished film; it is difficult to credit its inclusion in Truffaut's list.

As always, Truffaut brings much of himself to his evaluations. His categories (*The Bad Films, A Few Respectable Failures, Not Very Respectable Failures, Good "B" Films*) are opinionated and idiosyncratic. Not surprisingly, Truffaut expresses admiration for those "young filmmakers who are still unpretentious enough to shoot average-budget films," or "B" movies. "As a general rule," Truffaut observes, "the more expensive a film is, the more chances it has to be stupid." The other great discovery of 1956 is that "cinema can do without scriptwriters," an assumption based on the success of Vadim's film, "personal notations take precedence over outdated plot devices" in *And God Created Woman*; "it will be difficult, from now on, if you want to make intelligent movies, to repeat indefinitely old tricks: a gentlemen meets a lady, etc." The future of cinema will belong to those films that will be "more intelligent, more sincere, and more personal" than the precisely plotted narratives of the past. Truffaut sees each film as an opportunity for personal expression, even when one creates a commercial entertainment. To do less is unforgivable.

Finally, it is worth noticing that Truffaut places Bunuel's *Cela s'appelle l'aurore* and *La Mort en ce jardin (Death in the Garden)* in his list of *"A Few Respectable Failures."* While Truffaut values Bunuel as an *auteur* highly, he recognizes that those two films, while interesting, do not represent Bunuel at his most accomplished. Most would agree with this view.

Despite the fact that most of Truffaut's judgments seem valid today, one can imagine the furor this list created when it first appeared. In his first category of consideration, *The Bad Films*, Truffaut dismisses (without even naming them!) films by Hunebelle, Lacombe, Kirsanoff, and others in a single sentence. "We will review only the movies that show a minimum of ambition," Truffaut vows, stating further that "critics are not concerned with productions" signed by these *auteurs*. It's both sad and ironic to see the final work of Dimitri Kirsanoff lumped into a category of films without "a minimum of ambition." Kirsanoff's *Ménilmontant* (1926) was a ground-breaking film of the first French cinema avant-garde. The director's last films, however, including *Le Crâneur* (1955), *Ce soir les jupons volent* (1956), and the aptly named *Miss Catastrophe* (1956), are all rather ordinary. The directors listed as makers of "bad" films were the most successful popular *auteurs* of the day; time has proven Truffaut's evaluation correct, however, as almost none of these directors, or their films, are remembered or discussed today.

In 1956, Five Great Films, Seven Good Ones, An Event: It Is Proved That Cinema Can Do Without Scriptwriters.

A simple comparative look at the list of French films released in 1955 and at the list of French films released in 1956 is enough to prove it: the year that is drawing to a close has been an excellent one, superior in any case to the preceding ones.

In 1955, France barely gave us four good films: *Lola Montès,* by Max Ophüls; *French Cancan,* by Jean Renoir; *Les mauvaises rencontres,* by Alexandre Astruc; and *Rififi,* by Jules Dassin. To these four titles we could add *Les Diaboliques* by H. G. Clouzot and *Les grandes manoeuvres* by René Clair, to get half a dozen.

The improvement in French production for 1956 essentially concerns the movies that, in Hollywood, would be labeled as "B-category films," notes Mr. Jacques Flaud, who judiciously expressed last year the wish to see more average-budget films produced. The wonderful and very eloquent statistics published this week in *Le Film français* indeed disclose a decrease in high-grossing films.

The Bad Films

Since critics are not concerned with productions signed Hunebelle, Laviron, Berthomieu, Lepage, Boyer, Chevalier, Lacombe, Decoin, Gaspard Huit, Kirsanoff, Gourguet, etc., we will review only the movies that show a minimum of ambition.

A Few Respectable Failures

Claude Autant-Lara was bound to fail with *Marguerite de la nuit,* a movie strictly opposed to his temperament; the director of *La traversée de Paris [Four Bags Full],* whose qualities are those of a ferocious and disheveled satirist, didn't have enough intuition, fantasy, taste, poetry, and sensitivity to save such a delicate enterprise.

Cela s'appelle l'aurore was too sentimental and too rudimentary a subject for Luis Bunuel, who, with *Death in the Garden* didn't exactly succeed in satisfying the two kinds of audiences: those who came to see a film of his, and those who expected an adventure film; nevertheless, *Death in the Garden* is a half-success rather than a half-failure. Bunuel would be infinitely more commercial if the producers who want him would put complete faith in him, instead of distrusting him.

Le pays d'où je viens is a lame enterprise: Bécaud being the idol of young people, why make a film for old people?

La meilleure part, like *Oasis,* proves that Yves Allégret doesn't have the necessary "punch" to rescue too weak a script.

Not Very Respectable Failures

Crime et châtiment, Le sang à la tête, Club de femmes, and *L'homme aux clés d'or* show well that the "scriptwriter king" season is finished and that a movie cannot possibly be a success when the director only half understands what he films; it's also from an incredible lack of lucidity that *Till l'espiègle, Pardonnez nos offenses, Soeur Angèle,* and so many others not worth mentioning, suffer.

Good "B" Films

Most of these are made by young filmmakers who are still unpretentious enough to shoot average-budget films, which ensures them a kind of freedom. (As a general rule, the more expensive a film is, the more likely it is to be stupid.)

From film to film, Henri Verneuil improves; he knows how to tell a story using its smallest details to best advantage, and since he isn't a film *auteur,* it's in his interest to choose the best scriptwriters. *Des gens sans importance,* an attractive film, suffers from the 1936 aspect of the script, whereas *Paris-Palace-Hotel,* nimbly constructed, tells a story that is just as old-fashioned but straightforwardly vulgar.

An interesting first film is Claude Boissol's *Toute la ville accuse,* influenced by Capra: we hope that Boissol won't stop at that.

Even though Julien Duvivier isn't a young filmmaker, *Le temps des assassins,* made with an exemplary probity and a touching love for well-done work, is attractive, naive, falsely gloomy, and, all in all, an enterprise generous in spirit.

Michel Boisrond, with *Cette sacrée gamine* and *Aux environs d'Aden* (provided we forget about *Lorsque l'enfant paraît,* which is a chore), brings to French cinema a little of this Hollywoodian "skill": the solidity one finds in "square" movies, qualities that won't become a sheer habit if Boisrond, in his next films, manages to get closer to his characters, and to be moved a little bit more by a story.

Bob le flambeur is difficult to recommend insofar as its charm comes from its imperfections and the amateurish side of the undertaking; Henri Decae's wonderful photography and Isabelle Corey's dynamic posing play no small part in our pleasure. Script, mise-en-scène, intentions, all this remains vague, but what is filmed, Pigalle at daybreak, rings truer than usual, and more poetic, too.

The Great Films

The year has been dominated by Alain Resnais's movie *Nuit et brouillard (Night and Fog),* an interrogative meditation about the Nazis' concentration camps. Not only because of the importance of the subject does this movie deserve to come first, but also because of Resnais's style and the tone he managed to give to the film: a "terrible sweetness." By relieving the subject of its immediate pathetic aspect, Resnais forces us to receive the movie through our brains rather than through our stomachs, which, instead of making us feel sorry, makes us leave the theater ashamed and not very happy with ourselves: all of us are liable to be deported some day, that goes without saying, but the main thing is the fact that a torturer, a deporter, lies dormant within each of us.

Night and Fog makes every other film look trivial, beginning with *A Man Escaped,* which looks like some kind of entertainment by comparison.

Finally, I'd like to show what the four best French films of the year (*A Man Escaped, Elena and Her Men, Four Bags Full,* and *And God Created Woman*) may have in common, adding to them Agnès Varda's *La Pointe courte,* an unusual and attractive enterprise.

These five movies, independently of their intrinsic value, have the advantage of being based on scripts devised in a new way.

As far as the excellent *Four Bags Full* is concerned, I regret that Autant-Lara should be the exception that proves the rule of the *auteurs'* policy, since, working on a screenplay written by Aurenche and Bost, he does a better job than when he is his own screenwriter (see *Marguerite de la nuit*). This year, Aurenche and Bost prove themselves indispensable with *Four Bags Full,* which they wanted to be clever and new, as well as with *Gervaise,* which they wanted academic and conventional; according to what you want, they will "wrap it up" very neatly.

If *Elena and Her Men* were only the most contemptuous movie ever made about politicians, it would already be capital, but it is much more; Jean Renoir again took up his favorite theme, the theme of false vocation, insisting so much on extremes—the bitterness of happy times, the buffoonery of sad times—that the audience is left behind during the film; like *The Golden Coach, Eléna* confuses you when you see it for the first time, but it becomes strictly logical when you see it again.

A Man Escaped is a film made against cinema, and it is so remarkably designed that, by means that have never been seen before, it manages to create a new and faultlessly pure emotion.

Roger Vadim's *And God Created Woman* opens the way to a new kind of screenplay, in which personal touches take precedence over outdated plot devices. From now on it will be difficult, if you want to make intelligent movies, to repeat old tricks *ad infinitum:* a gentleman meets a lady, etc. . . .

The year 1956 has seen French cinema start a most beneficial turn thanks to the explosion of a myth: the script done away with, tomorrow's good films will be more different from one another, more intelligent, more sincere, and more personal. (SK)[48]

As Truffaut began his career as a director, his interest in criticism receded. He still wrote for *Cahiers du Cinéma* and *Arts,* but more and more of his energy went into his own films, as director or scenarist. Still, as he told Anne de Gaspéri in an interview in May of 1975, "I can't get away from writing . . . the taste for writing has been pursuing me ever since I concerned myself as a critic with the form of the screenplay. I didn't think I would become a filmmaker but, rather, a scriptwriter."[49]

Signaling a new direction in film study, many recent critical theorists extend careful consideration to all films and television programs regardless of their commercial origins, viewing these works as cultural artifacts of their respective periods of production. Perhaps what really interests us in film criticism and theory are the intricate series of latent behavioral codes woven into all films, rather than the themes that the films themselves choose to address.

Truffaut is more romantic: he views a successful film primarily as an individual creative act, as poetry. His work on the American genre film is some of the first writing that seriously considers these works and their makers. Truffaut sought to establish his own voice—and that of his colleagues—as a locus of authority in film criticism. Though his early writings now seem comparatively primitive, and are embarrassingly sexist and objectivist in their view of women, Truffaut still had the prescience to develop a critical style that was unprecedented for the period, a style that considered "entertainments" as works for serious study.

If we will follow Truffaut's lead in this area (granting his work a double resonance because of his later brilliance as a director), cinema history will open up a whole new body of important, engaging, and enlightening work that has been ignored for too long because, as Truffaut states in his review of South Sea Sinner, "no critic saw fit to take the trouble." Truffaut has seen fit to take that trouble. If his writing on those films that have been previously marginalized by "mainstream" criticism opens up the existing canon to further research, he will have discharged his critical mission with great distinction.

Notes

1. The Boundaries of Canon

1. Jim Hillier, ed., *Cahiers du Cinéma: The 1950s; Neo-Realism, Hollywood, New Wave* (Cambridge, MA: Harvard UP, 1985); *Cahiers du Cinéma: The 1960s; New Wave, New Cinema, Reevaluating Hollywood* (Cambridge, MA: Harvard UP, 1986).

2. Andrew Sarris published a first draft of his book *The American Cinema* in the spring 1963 issue of *Film Culture* (28). Sarris subsequently revised the text into *The American Cinema: Directors and Directions, 1929–1968* (New York: E. P. Dutton, 1968).

3. Jean-Luc Godard, often writing as Hans Lucas, also wrote frequently and persuasively for *Cahiers du Cinéma*. Some of his writings have been translated in *Godard on Godard: Critical Writings by Jean-Luc Godard* (edited by Jean Narboni and Tom Milner, with an introduction by Richard Roud; London: Secker and Warburg; New York: Viking Press, 1972) (Cinema Two Series); originally published as *Jean Luc-Godard par Jean-Luc Godard* (Paris: Editions Pierre Belfond, 1968). However, a good deal of Godard's work on the American "B" film has yet to be translated into English. Future scholarly work on Godard's criticism might profitably examine these writings.

4. François Truffaut, "Une Certaine Tendance du cinéma français," *Cahiers du Cinéma* 6.32 (January 1954), 15–29. Translated as "A Certain Tendency of the French Cinema," *Cahiers du Cinéma In English* 1 (January 1966), 31–41. Also translated in Bill Nichols, ed., *Movies and Methods* (Berkeley: U of California P, 1976), 224–37.

5. François Truffaut and Jacques Rivette, "Entretien avec Jean Renoir," *Cahiers du Cinéma* 5.34 (April 1954), 3–22. Translated as *Renoir in America*, in *Sight and Sound* 24.1 (New Quarterly Series) (July–September 1954), 12–17.

6. François Truffaut, "Notes sur d'autres films: Dr. Cyclops," *Cahiers du Cinéma* 5.25 (July 1953), 58. Translated as "Dr. Cyclops" in William Johnson, ed., *Focus on the Science Fiction Film* (Englewood Cliffs, NJ: Prentice-Hall, 1972), 48–49.

7. François Truffaut, "Aimer Fritz Lang," *Cahiers du Cinéma* 6.31 (January 1954), 52–54. Translated as *Loving Fritz Lang* in Leo Braudy and Morris Dickstein, *Great Film Directors* (New York: Oxford UP, 1978), 607–10. The translation in the Braudy/Dickstein volume is by Sallie Iannotti.

8. François Truffaut, "Prisonnière du désert," *Arts* 581 (August 22–28, 1956), 3.

9. François Truffaut, "About John Ford," *Action* 8.6 (November–December 1973), 11. Truffaut reprinted the essay under the even more unequivocal title "God Bless John Ford" in his collection of essays *The Films in My Life*, trans. Leonard Mayhew (New York: Simon and Schuster, 1978; London: Allen Lane, 1980); originally published as *Les Films de ma vie* (Paris: Flammarion, 1975), 63. In *François Truffaut: A Guide to References and Resources* (Boston: G. K. Hall, 1982), critic and researcher Eugene P. Walz notes that when Truffaut reprinted the essay in *The Films in My Life*, the piece was "trimmed slightly" (240); Truffaut also misdates the essay as being written in "1974" (63).

10. As noted in Wheeler W. Dixon, "Cinema History and the 'B' Tradition," *New Orleans Review* 14.2 (Summer 1987), 65–71.

11. François Truffaut and Jacques Rivette, "Entretien avec Jean Renoir," *Cahiers du Cinéma* 6.34 (April 1954), 3–22. Translated as *Renoir in America* in *Sight and Sound* 24.1 (New Quarterly Series) (July–September 1954), 12–17. The translation here is by Ruth Cassel Hoffman.

12. It should be noted here that *The Films in My Life* lacks precise attribution on the works it includes. Generally, the year in which the work originally appeared is given, but never the journal, issue number, page number, or any other data to assist the researcher. In some instances, Truffaut combines a number of reviews into a new, "composite" article. This makes Walz's book all the more indispensable.

13. See Wheeler W. Dixon, *The B Directors: A Biographical Directory* (Metuchen, NJ: Scarecrow Press, 1985), 39–45, for an overview of Beaudine's long career.

14. Truffaut here refers to the cutback in Hollywood production in the early 1950s due to the inroads of the early days of television.

15. François Truffaut, "Notes sur d'autres films," *Cahiers du Cinéma* 5.29 (December 1953), 59, signed "R.L."

16. See Walz, *François Truffaut*, 2.

17. See Walz, *François Truffaut*, 153–247.

18. *Motion Picture Production Encyclopedia, 1950 Edition* (1945–1949), ed. Audrey Kearns (Hollywood: The Hollywood Reporter Press, 1950), 490.

19. Other than Truffaut's review, the most perceptive analysis of the film appears in *The Hollywood Reporter*, in their issue of March 10, 1949.

20. François Truffaut, "Les Dessous du Niagara," *Cahiers du Cinéma* 5.28 (November 1953), 60–61, signed "Robert Lachenay."

21. See Tania Modleski's "Film Theory's Detour," *Screen* 23.4 (November–December 1982), 72–79. This excerpt is on page 76. The quote from Melanie Klein is from "The Emotional Life of the Infant," in *Envy and Gratitude and Other Works, 1946–1963* (London: The Hogarth Press and the Institute of Psycho-Analysis, 1975), 64.

22. See Dixon, *B Directors*, 235.

23. François Truffaut, "Présence de Marilyn Monroe," *Arts* 582 (August 29–September 4, 1956), 3, signed "R.L."

24. See Ephraim Katz, *The Film Encyclopedia* (New York: Thomas Y. Crowell, 1979), 819–21, for a brief but thorough view of Marilyn Monroe's life and work.

25. See Laurence Olivier, *Confessions of an Actor: An Autobiography* (New York: Simon and Schuster, 1982), 205–13, for Olivier's remembrances of his association with Monroe. Olivier asserts that he "refused to treat Marilyn as a special case—I had too much pride in my trade" and tells the reader that his working method included long and detailed explanations of motivation and character analysis directly before each take. Monroe understandably grew impatient with this approach; she trusted her instincts.

26. See Walz, *François Truffaut*, 163.

27. François Truffaut, "Les Extrêmes me touchent," *Cahiers du Cinéma* 4.21 (March 1953), 61–65.

28. François Truffaut, "De A jusqu'à Z," *Cahiers du Cinéma* 4.24 (June 1953), 53–55.

29. See Dixon, *B Directors*, 1–14; see also Dixon, "Cinema History and the 'B' Tradition," 65–71.

30. Modleski, "Detour," 72.

31. François Truffaut, "Girls in the Night," *Cahiers du Cinéma* 6.32 (February 1954), 51–52, signed "R.L."

32. François Truffaut, "Dead Line," Cahiers du Cinéma 4.23 (May 1953), 63.

33. Ephraim Katz, Film Encyclopedia, 239.

34. Fritz Lang plays himself in Godard's Le Mépris (1963). The quoted remark comes early in the film, during a sequence in a screening room.

35. See particularly Richard Kohler and Walter Lassaly, "The Big Screens," Sight and Sound 24.3 (January–March 1955), 120–26.

36. It is important to remember that Truffaut shot his first three films (The 400 Blows [1959]; Shoot the Piano Player [1960]; and Jules and Jim [1961]) in Franscope, the French equivalent of CinemaScope. Existing "flat" prints offer only an approximation of the visual richness these films have to offer.

37. See Katz, Film Encyclopedia, 240–41, for a discussion of Cinerama, developed by Fred Waller and, according to Katz, "first introduced at New York's 1939 World's Fair as Vitarama. . . . [A]t that time, the process involved 11 projectors," rather than the three machines which later became commonplace in the 1950s. Katz also notes that Cinerama was preceded by other multi-screen processes, dating back to an 1896 process of inventor Raoul Gromoin-Sanson using ten projectors, which Sanson dubbed "Cineorama." In an interesting promotional hardcover pamphlet prepared by MGM and Cinerama for the production of How the West Was Won (Anonymous; New York: Random House, 1963, unpaginated), the two companies offer this explanation of how the process works: "Cinerama is a process of filming by three synchronized cameras. These cameras [each with a 27mm lens] are pointed at different angles to encompass 146 degrees of horizontal planes and 55 degrees of vertical planes. This approximates the full breath of human vision. . . . Cinerama employs seven channels of stereophonic sound. There are five points of sound dispersed behind the screen. These are side right and left of the audience, as well as speakers behind the audience for a 'total surround' sensation. The sound system is provided for by 35mm magnetic film which runs on an electronic reproducer, which interlocks with the projectors. The screen surface is a series of louvers on a curved panel." However, the pamphlet also claims that "old problems [with the process] have been solved with addition of new devices until there are no longer discernable defects." This, unfortunately, was not true, and it is these technical defects that led to the discontinuation of Cinerama. The three interlocked projectors produced irritating seams in the middle of the picture, and the different color stocks for the three individual films were sometimes not properly balanced, creating a jarring, multi-panel effect that distracted the viewer. After How the West Was Won, the process was abandoned in favor of "seamless" Ultra-Panavision, first introduced in It's a Mad, Mad, Mad, Mad World (1963); however, this process produced no illusion of depth at all and was basically indistinguishable from CinemaScope, Panavision, and other anamorphic wide-screen processes.

38. François Truffaut, "Petit lexique des formats nouveaux," Arts 487 (October 27–November 2, 1954), 3, signed "F. T."

39. See Dixon, B Directors, 142–44, for a brief discussion of the peculiar circumstances surrounding this production; de Toth was one of the very few Hollywood directors then working (Raoul Walsh also comes to mind) who was blind in one eye.

40. François Truffaut, "En avoir plein la vue," Cahiers du Cinéma 5.25 (July 1953), 22–23.

41. François Truffaut, "Man in the Dark," Cahiers du Cinéma 5.25 (July 1953), 59.

42. See Dixon, B Directors, 298–303, for a discussion of Landers's life and work.

43. François Truffaut, "Cinerama Holiday," Arts 603 (January 23–29, 1957), 3.

44. Robert Bresson, Notes on Cinematography, trans. Jonathan Griffin (New

York: Urizen Books, 1977). Originally published by Editions Gallimard, Paris, 1975.

45. François Truffaut, "La Chasse au gang (City Is Dark)," *Cahiers du Cinéma* 7.38 (August–September 1954), 55, signed "R. L."

46. See Dixon, *B Directors*, 96.

47. See Walz, *François Truffaut*, 164.

48. François Truffaut, "The Mummy's Hand," *Cahiers du Cinéma* 5.25 (July 1953), 59.

49. François Truffaut, "Notes sur d'autres films," *Cahiers du Cinéma* 5.29 (December 1953), 58–59, signed "R.L."

50. François Truffaut, "Notes sur d'autres films," *Cahiers du Cinéma* 5.29 (December 1953), 59.

51. François Truffaut, "Notes sur d'autres films," *Cahiers du Cinéma* 5.29 (December 1953), 59, signed "R. L."

52. François Truffaut, "Notes sur d'autres films," *Cahiers du Cinéma* 5.26 (August/September 1953), 59. Signed "F. de M." . . . "François de Monferrand."

53. Truffaut here is making a joke based on *Kansas City Confidential*'s French release title, *The Fourth Man*, in reference to Carol Reed's earlier film, *The Third Man* (1949), though what connection Orson Welles has with *The Fourth Man* (if any) is unclear. To further complicate matters, *Kansas City Confidential* was also released in the U.S. and Britain as *The Secret Four*, and the French release title refers to this alternative billing.

54. François Truffaut, "Le Quatrième Homme," *Cahiers du Cinéma* 5.25 (July 1953), 58.

55. François Truffaut, "Notes sur d'autres films," *Cahiers du Cinéma* 5.26 (August/September 1953), 59. Signed "F. de M" . . . "François de Monferrand."

56. See Dixon, *B Directors*, 390–93.

57. François Truffaut, "Autres films," *Arts* 486 (October 20–26, 1954), 3.

58. François Truffaut, "Autres films," *Arts* 491 (November 24–30, 1954), 5.

59. François Truffaut, "Terre année zéro," *Cahiers du Cinéma* 5.25 (July 1953), 55–56.

2. A Private Pantheon

1. Peter Bogdanovich, *Fritz Lang in America* (New York: Praeger, 1967), 102–108.

2. Bogdanovich, *Fritz Lang*, 116.

3. François Truffaut, "La Cinquième Victime," *Arts* 581 (August 22–28, 1956), 3. Portions of this article (not translated here) appeared in Truffaut's article "Fritz Lang in America" in *The Films in My Life*, trans. Leonard Mayhew (New York: Simon and Schuster, 1978; London: Allen Lane, 1980), 64–68.

4. In *Le Mépris* (1963), as previously noted, Lang, as the director of film-within-the-film, must cope with the obnoxious and uncomprehending Jack Palance as his producer, as well as the "off-screen" deterioration of the marriage between the scenarist forced upon him by Palance (Michel Piccoli) and the scenarists' wife (Brigitte Bardot), while still trying to get his version of the *Odyssey* finished on time and on budget. Significantly, even the death of Palance and Bardot fails to prevent Lang from completing the production of the film: the last shot of *Le Mépris* is also the last shot of "Lang's" *Odyssey*.

5. Tag Gallagher, *John Ford* (Berkeley, CA: U of California P, 1986).

6. François Truffaut, "La Charge des Tuniques bleues," *Arts* 581 (August 22–28, 1956), 3.

7. François Truffaut, "Prisonnière du Désert," *Arts* 581 (August 22–28, 1956), 3.

8. Truffaut, *The Films in My Life*, 63.

9. See Roy Armes, *French Cinema* (New York: Oxford UP, 1985), 230–31, for a brief discussion of Truffaut's later, less intense work as a director. Armes, however, seems to vacillate in his view on Truffaut's films of the 1970s, as seen on pages 254–57 of the same text.

10. Eugene P. Walz, *François Truffaut: A Guide to References and Resources* (Boston: G. K. Hall, 1982), 166.

11. François Truffaut, "Autres films," *Arts* 485 (October 13–19, 1954), 3.

12. Walz, *François Truffaut*, 180.

13. Walz, *François Truffaut*, 187.

14. The diary entry credited to Lachenay may be found in *Cahiers du Cinéma* 7.41 (December 1954), 10–15.

15. A reference to the newspaper campaign designed to ruin Rossellini and Ingrid Bergman, after Bergman left her husband to live and work with Rossellini in Italy.

16. Rohmer would return to 16mm after working in 35mm during the late 1960s and early 1970s, preferring the flexibility and economy of the smaller-format medium, which allowed him to make films without undue interference from his backers.

17. François Truffaut, "Petit Journal intime du cinéma," *Cahiers du Cinéma* 7.37 (July 1954), 34–38.

18. François Truffaut, "L'Affaire de Trinidad," *Cahiers du Cinéma* 4.22 (April 1953), 57–58.

19. François Truffaut, "Autres films," *Arts* 484 (October 6–12, 1954), 3.

20. Truffaut, "Autres films," *Arts* 484 (October 6–12, 1954), 3.

21. Truffaut, "Autre films," *Arts* 484 (October 6–12, 1954), 3.

22. François Truffaut, "Drôle de meurtre," *Cahiers du Cinéma* 7.37 (July 1954), 63, signed "R. L."

23. François Truffaut, "Les Frontières de la vie," *Cahiers du Cinéma* 7.38 (August–September 1954), 54, signed "R. L."

24. Ephraim Katz, *The Film Encyclopedia* (New York: Thomas Y. Crowell, 1979), 669–70.

25. François Truffaut, "La Fille de l'Ambassadeur," *Arts* 581 (August 22–28, 1956), 3.

26. See Wheeler W. Dixon, *B Directors: A Biographical Directory* (Metuchen, NJ: Scarecrow Press, 1985), 494, for a brief look at Webb's work as a feature film director.

27. See Wheeler Winston Dixon, "The Camera Vision: Narrativity and Film," *New Orleans Quarterly Review* 12.2 (Summer 1985), 57, in which I quote Bordwell and Thompson's citation of Graham's summary of Truffaut's claim that "we identify with a character not when we look with the character [as a POV shot], but when the character looks at us. A subjective camera is the negation of subjective cinema. When it replaces a character, one cannot identity oneself with him. The camera becomes subjective when the actor's gaze meets that of the audience."

28. François Truffaut, "La Peau d'Un Autre," *Arts* 576 (July 11–17, 1956), 5.

29. François Truffaut, "Un Homme Traqué," *Arts* 576 (July 11–17, 1956), 5.

30. François Truffaut, "Autres films," *Arts* 485 (October 13–19, 1954), 3.

31. François Truffaut, "Un Pitre au pensionnat," *Arts* 601 (January 9–15, 1957), 3.

32. François Truffaut, "Notes sur d'autres films," *Cahiers du Cinéma* 5.26 (August–September 1953), 58. Signed "F. de M." . . . "François de Monferrand."

33. Katz, *Film Encyclopedia*, 718.

34. François Truffaut, "Autres films," *Arts* 491 (November 24–30, 1954), 5.

35. This is not precisely true, as *Le Petit Chaperon Rouge* was presented without incident to the public on May 14, 1930, at the Tribune Libre de Cinéma. But it certainly is true that both this film and *Charleston* are uninhibited examples (and thus revealingly self-reflexive unconscious instances of cinematic practice) of the female body displayed within the confining locus of the male spectatorial gaze, by one of the central figures of the patriarchal narrative cinema.

36. François Truffaut, "B.B. est victime d'une cabale," *Arts* 597 (December 12–18, 1956), 3.

37. In his book *Bardot Deneuve Fonda* (New York: Simon and Schuster, 1986; trans. Melinda Camber Porter), Vadim acknowledges Truffaut's review as one of the few favorable notices the film received (111). Vadim discusses the making of *And God Created Woman* on pages 67–116 of the book.

3. A Passion for the Cinema

1. See Ephraim Katz, *The Film Encyclopedia* (New York: Thomas Y. Crowell, 1979), 1132.

2. François Truffaut, "Autres films," *Arts* 493 (December 8–14, 1954), 5.

3. *The Quatermass Xperiment* (so titled because of the "X" British Film Censor's Certificate the film received upon initial release) was an early effort by Hammer Studios, which would become, with such later films as *Curse of Frankenstein* (1957) and *Dracula* (1958; U.S. release title *Horror of Dracula*), the preeminent Gothic horror film studio between 1957 and 1968. *The Quatermass Xperiment* as released in the United States as *The Creeping Unknown*.

4. *The Thing from Another World* was, in fact, directed by Christian Nyby, with a hefty uncredited assist from Hawks, who served as the film's producer. Rumors also persist to this day that Orson Welles directed portions of the project; though these rumors have never been substantiated, they have also never been conclusively disproved.

5. François Truffaut, "Le Monstre," *Arts* 615 (April 17–23, 1957), 3.

6. François Truffaut, "La Revue des revues," *Cahiers du Cinéma* 4.24 (June 1953), 59–60.

7. As quoted in Dominique Rabourdin, *Truffaut by Truffaut* (texts and documents compiled by Dominique Rabourdin, translated from the French by Robert Erich Wolf; New York: Abrams, 1987), 45. First published as *Truffaut par Truffaut* (Paris: Sté Nlle des Éditions du Chêne, 1985). This volume is an excellent compilation of Truffaut's public pronouncements over the years.

8. An excellent and generally overlooked account of the "battle for the Cinémathèque" can be found in Richard Roud's biography of Henri Langlois, *A Passion for Films* (London: Secker and Warburg, 1983), 148–60. Truffaut contributes a brief but illuminating introduction to the volume, xxiii–xxviii.

9. François Truffaut, *Letters*, edited by Gilles Jacob and Claude de Givray, translated and edited by Gilbert Adair, foreword by Jean-Luc Godard (London: Faber and Faber, 1989), 422–23. Originally published as *François Truffaut Correspondance* (Rennes: Hatier, 1988). See Katz, *Film Encyclopedia*, 719, for a brief review of L'Herbier's body of work.

10. Truffaut, *Letters*, 461–64.

11. Truffaut, *Letters*, 423–28.

12. Truffaut, *Letters*, 462.

13. François Truffaut, "Giant," *Arts* 611 (March 20–26, 1957), 3.

14. François Truffaut, "Une Femme diabolique," *Arts* 577 (July 18–24, 1956), 5.

15. See Katz, *Film Encyclopedia*, 752, for a paragraph on MacDougall's work.

16. François Truffaut, with the collaboration of Helen G. Scott, *Hitchcock* (New York: Simon and Schuster, 1967). Originally published as *Le Cinéma selon Hitchcock* (Paris: Robert Laffont, 1966).

17. Truffaut, *Hitchcock*, 7–8. Portions of this aborted interview were used in the composition of *La Main au collet* (*Arts* 548, December 28–January 3, 1955), 5.

18. The genesis and reception of the Hitchcock project can be traced in François Truffaut, *Letters*, 177, 199, 283, 289, 299, 309, 317, and 324.

19. Walz, *François Truffaut: A Guide to References and Resources* (Boston: G. K. Hall, 1982), 317–19.

20. François Truffaut, "Autres films," *Arts* 495 (December 22–28, 1954), 5.

21. See Truffaut, *Hitchcock*, 95, for Hitchcock's comments on this. See also Donald Spoto, *The Dark Side of Genius: Life of Alfred Hitchcock* (Boston: Little, Brown, 1983), 499, for an account of Hitchcock's treatment at the hands of the academy in later years.

22. See Spoto, *Genius*, 406, for one of many discussions of this aspect of Hitchcock's career as a director.

23. Walz, *François Truffaut*, 201.

24. François Truffaut, "*Lifeboat* d'Alfred Hitchcock," *Arts* 571 (June 6–12, 1956), 5.

25. François Truffaut, "Quelques films récents," *La Parisienne* 33 (May 1956), 114.

26. Spoto, *Genius*, 376.

27. Truffaut, *Hitchcock*, 168.

28. Truffaut, *Hitchcock*, 169.

29. Spoto, *Genius*, 354.

30. Spoto, *Genius*, 354.

31. Truffaut, *Hitchcock*, 170.

32. As noted in the text, the actual budget was one million dollars. The film simply *looks* modest, when in fact the circumstances of its production were quite generous for the period.

33. François Truffaut, "Qui a tué Harry?" *Arts* 560 (March 21–27, 1956), 5.

34. Spoto, *Genius*, 354–55.

35. Spoto, *Genius*, 355.

36. It is perhaps significant that Huston has never been the subject of a carefully considered critical study. Ephraim Katz discusses Huston's work in his *Film Encyclopedia* on pages 591–92; other books about the director include Gerald Pratley, *The Cinema of John Huston* (New York: A. S. Barnes; London: The Tantiny Press, 1977); William F. Nolan, *John Huston, King Rebel* (Los Angeles: Sherbourne, 1965); Axel Madsen, *John Huston* (Garden City, NY: Doubleday, 1978); Robert Benayoun, *John Huston* (Paris: Editions Seghers, 1966); Stuart Kaminsky, *John Huston: Maker of Magic* (Boston: Houghton, 1978). Benayoun's volume is perhaps the most incisive study of Huston's work, despite its age, with telling contributions from other *Cahiers* critics, including Eric Rohmer.

37. It is only fair to note that cinematographer Freddie Francis was, in fact, responsible for much of the impact of these scenes in *Moby Dick*, serving as second unit director, photographer, and special-effects coordinator on the film often in an uncredited capacity. See Wheeler Dixon, *The Films of Freddie Francis* (Metuchen, NJ: Scarecrow, 1991), 26–27, for the details of Francis's working relationship with Huston.

38. François Truffaut, "John Huston ne sera-t-il toujours qu'un amateur?" *Arts* 593 (November 14–20, 1956), 3, signed "Robert Lachenay."

39. As recounted by Ted Newsom in "Deputy Seraph: The Marx Brothers Lost Sitcom" in *Filmfax* 14 (March–April, 1989), 52–55, 84.

40. François Truffaut, "*Animal Crackers:* Reprise d'un classique," *Arts* 465 (May 26–June 1, 1954), 3, unsigned.

41. Parenthetically, it seems interesting to me that one of the most iconoclastic American comedians, W. C. Fields, gets such short shift in Truffaut's critical writings.

42. Recent research indicates that Alice Guy Blaché's *La Fée Aux Choux (The Cabbage Fairy)*, made in 1896 for Gaumont, is another film that lays claim to the title of "the first film with a scenario."

43. François Truffaut, "La Comédie américaine," *Arts* 480 (September 8–14, 1954), 3.

44. Truffaut wrote two reviews of *It Should Happen to You.* The first appeared in *Arts* 458 (April 7–13, 1954), 3; the second in *Cahiers du Cinéma* 6.35 (May 1954), 50–52. The *Cahiers* review is reprinted in *The Films in My Life.*

45. François Truffaut, "Western et comédie," *Arts* 481 (September 15–21, 1954), 3.

4. The Egalitarian Spirit

1. François Truffaut, "Autres films," *Arts* 490 (November 17–23, 1954), 5.

2. Mann's career is extraordinary, beginning with early work for Eagle Lion Studios (*Railroaded* [1947], *T-Men* [1947]) and Republic (*Strange Impersonation* [1946], *The Great Flamarion* [1945]) and concluding with some rather indifferent biblical spectacles for Samuel Bronston in the 1960s. See Wheeler Winston Dixon, *The B Directors: A Biographical Dictionary* (Metuchen: NJ: Scarecrow Press, 1985), 338–39.

3. François Truffaut, "Autres films," *Arts* 486 (October 20–26, 1954), 3.

4. See Ephraim Katz, *The Film Encyclopedia* (New York: Thomas Y. Crowell, 1979), 403; and Dixon, *B Directors*, 167–70.

5. François Truffaut, "Autres films," *Arts* 495 (December 22–28, 1954), 5.

6. See Katz, *Film Encyclopedia*, 265–66, for more information on Eddie Constantine's career.

7. François Truffaut, "Le Grand Bluff," *Arts* 624 (June 19–25, 1957), 5.

8. See James Naremore, *The Magic World of Orson Welles* (Oxford: Oxford UP, 1978), 321.

9. Interview with Edgar G. Ulmer in Todd McCarthy and Charles Elynn's *Kings of the Bs: Working within the Hollywood System: An Anthology of Film History and Criticism* (New York: E. P. Dutton, 1975), 402–403. Working from an outline, Ulmer created the "script" for *Club Havana* as shooting progressed, on a page-by-page basis.

10. Ironically, in 1960, Truffaut worked on the screenplay of an Eddie Constantine film, *Me faire ça à moi*, as a favor to the film's producer/director, Pierre Grimblat. See Truffaut, *Letters* (London: Faber and Faber, 1989), 149.

11. Cocteau wrote the screenplay for *Les Enfants Terribles*, as well as serving as narrator for the film. He also directed one exterior sequence when Melville fell ill.

12. Katz, *Film Encyclopedia*, 798.

13. François Truffaut, "Notes sur d'autres films," *Cahiers du Cinéma* 5.29 (December 1953), 59–60, signed "R.L."

14. François Truffaut, "Autres films," *Arts* 493 (December 8–14, 1954), 5.

15. François Truffaut, "Écrit dans le ciel," *Arts* 488 (November 3–9, 1954), 3.

16. See Dixon, *B Directors*, 194–97 (on Fuller); 144–45 (on Maury Dexter); and 184–85 (on Gene Fowler, Jr.), to see how these disparate directors used these preconditions to their stylistic advantage.

17. See Phil Hardy's *Samuel Fuller* (New York: Praeger, 1970), 122–28, for an interesting discussion of *Forty Guns*.

18. François Truffaut, "Autres films," *Arts* 494 (December 15–21, 1954), 5.

19. François Truffaut, "Autres films," *Arts* 483 (September 29–October 5, 1954), 3.

20. François Truffaut, "Autres films," *Arts* 483 (September 29–October 5, 1954), 3.

21. François Truffaut, "Autres films," *Arts* 489 (November 10–16, 1954), 5.

22. François Truffaut, "Autres films," *Arts* 489 (November 10–16, 1954), 5.

23. François Truffaut, "Autres films," *Arts* 493 (December 8–14, 1954), 5.

24. François Truffaut, "Quelques films récents," *La Parisienne* 33 (May 1956), 113–14.

25. Truffaut wrote several other notices on *Lola Montès*, including one in *Arts* 548 (December 28–January 3, 1955), 5, and another in *Cahiers du Cinéma* 10.55 (January 1956), 28–31. These two reviews were later combined by Truffaut into one entry in *The Films in My Life* (New York: Simon and Schuster, 1978; London: Allen Lane, 1980), 225–29. Truffaut also wrote a brief account of the shooting of the film, "Max Ophüls Tourne *Lola Montès*," published in *Arts* 508 (March 23–29, 1955), 5.

26. Actually, "contradictory" artists Rossellini and Cocteau collaborated on one project, the cinematic adaptation of Cocteau's one-act play, *La Voix humaine*, as part of Rossellini's film *L'Amore* (1948). Rossellini directed both episodes of this two-part film: the Cocteau play was the basis for *Una Voca Humana*; Federico Fellini co-scripted and starred in the other half of the project, *Il Miracolo*. The most detailed and perceptive discussion of this work appears in Peter Brunette's *Roberto Rossellini* (Oxford: Oxford UP, 1987), 87–100.

27. See Jonas Mekas, *Movie Journal* (New York: Macmillan, 1972), 3–4, for a reprint of Mekas's polemic of August 12, 1959, in support of Ophüls's film, entitled "What the Devil Will Do to the Distributor of *Lola Montès* in Hell," which originally appeared in *The Village Voice*.

28. François Truffaut, "Autres films," *Arts* 490 (November 17–23, 1954), 5.

29. François Truffaut, "Autres films," *Arts* 495 (December 22–28, 1954), 5.

30. François Truffaut, "Notes sur d'autres films," *Cahiers du Cinéma* 5.29 (December 1953), 59, signed "R.L."

31. Raymond Fielding's *The March of Time, 1935–1951* (Oxford: Oxford UP, 1978) is unquestionably the standard reference on this series of films.

32. See *The Naked City: A Screenplay* by Albert Maltz and Malvin Wald, edited by Matthew J. Bruccoli (Carbondale: Southern Illinois UP, 1979).

33. Maltz and Wald, *The Naked City*, 3.

34. See Katz, *Film Encyclopedia*, 307.

35. François Truffaut, "Jules Dassin et le *Rififi*," *Arts* 494 (December 15–21, 1954), 5. Truffaut's first review of the finished film appeared in *Arts* 512 (April 20–26, 1955), 5, and is reprinted in *The Films in My Life*. Truffaut also wrote a second notice on the film, "Du *Rififi* à la compétence," which appeared in *Arts* 516 (May 18–24, 1955), 5.

36. François Truffaut, "La Double Crise du cinéma," *Arts* 592 (November 7–13, 1956), 4, signed "Robert Lachenay."

37. François Truffaut, "La Tour des ambitieux," *Arts* 482 (September 22–28, 1954), 3.

38. Edwin T. Arnold and Eugene L. Miller, *The Films and Career of Robert Aldrich* (Knoxville: The U of Tennessee P, 1986), 53.

39. Arnold and Miller, *Films and Career of Robert Aldrich*, 54.

40. Arnold and Miller, *Films and Career of Robert Aldrich*, 54.

41. François Truffaut, "Rencontre avec Robert Aldrich," *Cahiers du Cinéma*

11.64 (November 1956), 8; as quoted in Arnold and Miller, *Films and Career of Robert Aldrich*, 54.

42. François Truffaut, "Feuilles d'automne," *Arts* 594 (November 21–27, 1956), 3.

43. François Truffaut, "Ouragan sur le Caine," *Arts* 484 (October 6–12, 1954), 3.

44. François Truffaut, "Le Prix de la peur," *Arts* 577 (July 18–24, 1956), 5.

45. François Truffaut, "Autres films," *Arts* 495 (December 22–28, 1954), 5.

46. François Truffaut, "Ne me quitte jamais," *Cahiers du Cinéma* 6.35 (May 1954), 56–57, signed "R.L."

47. François Truffaut, "Autres films," *Arts* 490 (November 17–23, 1954), 5.

48. François Truffaut, "En 1956, cinq grands films, sept bons films," *Arts* 598 (December 19–25, 1956), 3.

49. Interview with Anne de Gaspieri, *Le Quotidien de Paris*, May 2, 1975, as quoted in Rabourdin, 214.

Articles by François Truffaut in This Volume

"Prisonnière du désert," *Arts* 581 (August 22–28, 1956), 3.

"Notes sur d'autres films," *Cahiers du Cinéma* 5.29 (December, 1953), 59, signed "R.L."

"Les Dessous du Niagara," *Cahiers du Cinéma* 5.28 (November 1953), 60–61, signed "Robert Lachenay."

"Présence de Marilyn Monroe," *Arts* 582 (August 29–September 4, 1956), 3, signed "R.L."

"Les Extrêmes me touchent," *Cahiers du Cinéma* 4.21 (March 1953), 61–65.

"De A jusqu'à Z," *Cahiers du Cinéma* 4.24 (June 1953), 53–55.

"Girls in the Night," *Cahiers du Cinéma* 6.32 (February 1954), 51–52, signed "R.L."

"Dead Line," *Cahiers du Cinéma* 4.23 (May 1953), 63.

"Petit lexique des formats nouveaux," *Arts* 487 (October 27–November 2, 1954), 3, signed "F.T."

"En avoir plein la vue," *Cahiers du Cinéma* 5.25 (July 1953), 22–23.

"Man in the Dark," *Cahiers du Cinéma* 5.25 (July 1953), 59.

"Cinerama Holiday," *Arts* 603 (January 23–29, 1957), 3.

"La Chasse au gang (City Is Dark)," *Cahiers du Cinéma* 7.38 (August–September 1954), 55, signed "R.L."

"The Mummy's Hand," *Cahiers du Cinéma* 5.25 (July 1953), 59.

"Notes sur d'autres films," *Cahiers du Cinéma* 5.26 (August–September 1953), 59. Signed "F. de M." . . . "François de Monferrand."

"Le Quatrième Homme," *Cahiers du Cinéma* 5.25 (July 1953), 58.

"Autres films," *Arts* 486 (October 20–26, 1954), 3.

"Autres films," *Arts* 491 (November 24–30, 1954), 5.

"Terre année zéro," *Cahiers du Cinéma* 5.25 (July 1953), 55–56.

"La Cinquième Victime," *Arts* 581 (August 22–28, 1956), 3.

"La Charge des Tuniques bleues," *Arts* 581 (August 22–28, 1956), 3.

"Autres films," *Arts* 485 (October 13–19, 1954), 3.

"Petit Journal intime du cinéma," *Cahiers du Cinéma* 7.37 (July 1954), 34–38.

"L'Affaire de Trinidad," *Cahiers du Cinéma* 4.22 (April 1953), 57–58.

"Autres films," *Arts* 484 (October 6–12, 1954), 3.

"Drôle de meurtre," *Cahiers du Cinéma* 7.37 (July 1954), 63; signed "R.L."

"Les Frontières de la vie," *Cahiers du Cinéma* 7.38 (August–September 1954), 54, signed "R.L."

"La Fille de l'Ambassadeur," *Arts* 581 (August 22–28, 1956), 3.

"La Peau d'Un Autre," *Arts* 576 (July 11–17, 1956), 5.

"Un Homme Traqué," *Arts* 576 (July 11–17, 1956), 5.

"Un Pitre au pensionnat," *Arts* 601 (January 9–15, 1957), 3.

"B.B. est victime d'une cabale," *Arts* 597 (December 12–18, 1956), 3.

"Autres films," *Arts* 493 (December 8–14, 1954), 5.

"Le Monstre," *Arts* 615 (April 17–23, 1957), 3.

"La Revue des revues," *Cahiers du Cinéma* 4.24 (Junc 1953), 58.

"Giant," *Arts* 611 (March 20–26, 1957), 3.

"Une Femme diabolique," *Arts* 577 (July 18–24, 1956), 5.

"Autres films," *Arts* 495 (December 22–28, 1954), 5.

"*Lifeboat* d'Alfred Hitchcock," *Arts* 571 (June 6–12, 1956), 5.

"Quelques films récents," *La Parisienne* 33 (May 1956), 114.

"Qui a tué Harry?" *Arts* 560 (March 21–27, 1956), 5.

"John Huston ne sera-ti-il toujours qu'un amateur?" *Arts* 593 (November 14–20, 1956), 3, signed "Robert Lachenay."

"*Animal Crackers*: Reprise d'un classique," *Arts* 465 (May 26–June 1, 1954), 3, unsigned.

"La Comédie américaine," *Arts* 480 (September 8–14, 1954), 3.

"Western et comédie," *Arts* 481 (September 15–21, 1954), 3.

"Autres films," *Arts* 490 (November 17–23, 1954), 5.

"Le Grand Bluff," *Arts* 624 (June 19–25, 1957), 5.

"Écrit dans le ciel," *Arts* 488 (November 3–9, 1954), 3.

"Autres films," *Arts* 494 (December 15–21, 1954), 5.

"Autres films," *Arts* 483 (September 29–October 5, 1954), 3.

"Autres films," *Arts* 489 (November 10–16, 1954), 5.

"Jules Dassin et le *Rififi*," *Arts* 494 (December 15–21, 1954), 5.

"La Double Crise du cinéma," *Arts* 592 (November 7–13, 1956), 4, signed "Robert Lachenay."

"La Tour des amtitieux," *Arts* 482 (September 22–28, 1954), 3.

"Feuilles d'automne," *Arts* 594 (November 21–27, 1956), 3.

"Ouragan sur la Caine," *Arts* 484 (October 6–12, 1954), 3.

"Le Prix de la peur," *Arts* 577 (July 18–24, 1956), 5.

"Ne me quitte jamais," *Cahiers du Cinéma* 6.35 (May 1954), 56–57; signed "R.L."

"En 1956, cinq grands films, sept bons films," *Arts* 598 (December 19–25, 1956), 3.

Bibliography

This bibliography lists those sources directly consulted in the creation of this work, as well as additional volumes of related interest. For a more complete bibliography of works on the life and films of François Truffaut as well as writings by Truffaut himself, see Eugene P. Walz, *François Truffaut: A Guide to References and Resources* (Boston: G. K. Hall, 1982).

Abel, Richard. *French Film Theory and Criticism 1907–1930*, Vols. One and Two. Princeton, NJ: Princeton UP, 1988.
———. "On the Threshold of French Film Theory and Criticism, 1915–1919," *Cinema Journal* 25.2 (1985), 12–23.
Allen, Don. *Finally Truffaut*. New York: Beaufort, 1985.
———. *François Truffaut*. London: Secker & Warburg, 1974.
Andrew, Dudley. *André Bazin*. Oxford: Oxford UP, 1978.
Armes, Roy. *French Cinema*. Oxford: Oxford UP, 1985.
Arnold, Edwin T., and Eugene L. Miller. *The Films and Career of Robert Aldrich*. Knoxville: The U of Tennessee P, 1986.
Artaud, Antonin. *The Theater and Its Double*. New York: Grove, 1958.
Ayfre, Amédée, et al. *The Films of Robert Bresson*. New York: Praeger, 1969.
Balio, Tino. *The American Film Industry* (Revised Edition). Madison: The U of Wisconsin P, 1985.
Bazin, André. *French Cinema of the Occupation and Resistance: The Birth of a Critical Esthetic*. Trans. Stanley Hochman. New York: Frederick Ungar, 1981.
———. *What Is Cinema?* Vol. I. Berkeley: U of California P, 1967.
———. *What Is Cinema?* Vol. II. Trans. Hugh Grey. Berkeley: U of California P, 1971.
Bogdanovich, Peter. *Fritz Lang in America*. New York: Praeger, 1967.
Bordwell, David. *Making Meaning: Inference and Rhetoric in the Interpretation of Cinema*. Cambridge, MA: Harvard UP, 1989.
Braudy, Leo, and Morris Dickstein. *Great Film Directors*. Oxford: Oxford UP, 1978.
Bresson, Robert. *Notes on Cinematography*. New York: Urizen, 1985.
Brunette, Peter. *Roberto Rossellini*. Oxford: Oxford UP, 1987.
Cahiers du Cinéma: Table of Contents. 1–50. Paris 1951–1964; rpt. New York: AMS, 1971.
Cahiers du Cinéma: Table of Contents. 51–100. Paris 1951–1964; rpt. New York: AMS, 1971.
Cameron, Ian, and Elizabeth Cameron. *The Heavies*. New York: Praeger, 1967.
Casett, Francesco. "Antonioni and Hitchcock: Two Strategies of Narrative Investment," *Substance* 51 (1986), 69–86.
Catalog of Copyright Entries: Cumulative Series, Motion Pictures 1940–1949. Washington, D.C.: Library of Congress, 1960.
Catalog of Copyright Entries: Cumulative Series, Motion Pictures 1940–1949. Washington, D.C.: Library of Congress, 1953.

169

Cocteau, Jean. *Cocteau on the Film: Conversations with Jean Cocteau*, recorded by André Fraigneau. New York: Dover, 1972.
————. *Jean Cocteau, Past Tense: The Cocteau Diaries*, Vol. 1. San Diego: Harcourt, 1987.
Crisp, C. G. *François Truffaut*. New York: Praeger, 1972.
Dixon, Wheeler W. *The B Directors: A Biographical Directory*. Metuchen: Scarecrow, 1985.
————. "François Truffaut: A Life in Film," *Films in Review* 36.6–7 (1985), 331–36; 36.8–9 (1985), 413–17.
————. "The Camera Vision: Narrativity and Film," *New Orleans Review* 12.2 (1985), 57–61.
————. "Cinema History and the 'B' Tradition," *New Orleans Review* 14.2 (Summer 1987), 65–71.
————. "The Early Film Criticism of François Truffaut," *New Orleans Review* 16.1 (1989), 5–32.
Doane, Mary Ann. *Femmes Fatales: Feminism, Film Theory, Psychoanalysis*. New York: Routledge, 1991.
Eisner, Lotte H. *Fritz Lang*. Oxford: Oxford UP, 1977.
Faulkner, Christopher. *The Social Cinema of Jean Renoir*. Princeton: Princeton UP, 1986.
Fielding, Raymond. *The March of Time, 1935–1951*. Oxford: Oxford UP, 1978.
Fifield, William. "The Art of Fiction XXXIV: Jean Cocteau, An Interview," *The Paris Review* 8.32 (1964), 12–37.
Franchi, R. M., and Marshall Lewis. "Conversations with François Truffaut," *New York Film Bulletin* 3.44 (1962), 16–24.
Gallagher, Tag. *John Ford*. Berkeley: U of California P, 1986.
Gidal, Peter. *Materialist Film*. London: Routledge, 1989.
Graham, Peter. *The New Wave*. New York: Doubleday, 1968.
————. *A Dictionary of the Cinema*. New York: A. S. Barnes, 1968.
Hardy, Phil. *Samuel Fuller*. New York: Praeger, 1970.
Hillier, Jim, ed. *Cahiers du Cinéma: The 1950s: Neo-Realism, Hollywood, New Wave*. Cambridge, MA: Harvard UP, 1985.
————. *Cahiers du Cinéma: The 1960s; New Wave, New Cinema, Reevaluating Hollywood*. Cambridge, MA: Harvard UP, 1986.
Insdorf, Annette. *François Truffaut*. Boston: Twayne, 1978.
Jacob, Gilles, and Claude de Givray, eds. *François Truffaut: Letters*. Trans. Gilbert Adair. London: Faber and Faber, 1988.
Johnson, Douglas, and Madeleine Johnson. *The Age of Illusion: Art and Politics in France, 1918–1940*. New York: Rizzoli, 1987.
Johnson, William. *Focus on the Science Fiction Film*. Englewood Cliffs: Prentice-Hall, 1972.
Kaplan, E. Ann. *Psychoanalysis & Cinema*. New York: Routledge, 1990.
Katz, Ephraim. *The Film Encyclopedia*. New York: Thomas Y. Crowell, 1979.
Kearns, Audrey, ed. *Motion Picture Production Encyclopedia*. 1948 ed. Hollywood: Hollywood Reporter, 1948.
————. *Motion Picture Production Encyclopedia*. 1950 ed. Hollywood: Hollywood Reporter, 1950.
Klein, Melanie. *Envy and Gratitude and Other Works, 1946–1963*. London: Hogarth Press, 1975.
Kohler, Richard, and Walter Lassaly. "The Big Screens," *Sight and Sound* 24.3 (January/March 1955), 120–26.
Kolker, Robert Philip. *The Altering Eye: Contemporary International Cinema*. Oxford: Oxford UP, 1983.
Kozarski, Richard. *Hollywood Directors 1941–1976*. Oxford: Oxford, 1977.

Lourie, Eugene. *My Work in Films*. San Diego: Harcourt, 1985.
Mancorelles, Louis. "Interview with Truffaut," *Sight and Sound* 31.1 (Winter 1961–62), 35–37.
McCarthy, Tom, and Charles Flynn, eds. *King of the Bs: Working within the Hollywood System: An Anthology of Film History and Criticism*. New York: E. P. Dutton, 1975.
Mekas, Jonas. *Movie Journal*. New York: Macmillan, 1972.
Modleski, Tania. "Film Theory's Detour," *Screen* 23.4 (November/December 1982), 72–79.
Monaco, James. *The Films of François Truffaut*. New York: Zoetrope, 1974.
———. *The New Wave: Truffaut, Godard, Chabrol, Rohmer, Rivette*. Oxford: Oxford UP, 1976.
Narboni, Jean, and Tom Milner. *Godard on Godard: Critical Writings of Jean-Luc Godard*. New York: Viking, 1972.
Naremore, James. *The Magic World of Orson Welles*. Oxford: Oxford UP, 1978.
Negulesco, Jean. *Things I Did and Things I Think I Did*. New York: Simon and Schuster, 1984.
Nichols, Bill. *Movies and Methods*. Berkeley: U of California P, 1976.
Olivier, Laurence. *Laurence Olivier: Confessions of an Actor: An Autobiography*. New York: Simon and Schuster, 1982.
"On Film: Truffaut Interview," *New Yorker* (February 20, 1960), 36–37.
Renoir, Jean. *Renoir on Renoir: Interviews, Essays, and Remarks*. Trans. Carol Volk. Cambridge: Cambridge UP, 1989.
Roud, Richard. *A Passion of Films: Henri Langlois and the Cinémathèque Française*. London: Secker & Warburg, 1983.
———. *Jean-Luc Godard*. Bloomington: Indiana UP, 1967.
Sarris, Andrew. *The American Cinema: Directors and Directions, 1928–1968*. New York: E. P. Dutton, 1968.
Schneider, Steve. *The Art of Warner Bros. Animation*. New York: Henry Holt, 1988.
Siegel, Joel E. *Val Lewton: The Reality of Terror*. New York: Viking, 1973.
Silver, Alain, and Elizabeth Ward, eds. *Film Noir: An Encycolopedic Reference to the American Style*. Woodstock: Overlook, 1988.
Smith, John. *Jean Vigo*. New York: Praeger, 1972.
Spoto, Donald. *The Dark Side of Genius: The Life of Alfred Hitchcock*. Boston: Little, Brown, 1983.
Truffaut, François. *Hitchcock*. New York: Simon and Schuster, 1967.
———. *The Films of My Life*. Trans. Leonard Mayhew. New York: Simon and Schuster, 1978.
———. *Truffaut by Truffaut*. Trans. Robert Erich Wolf. New York: Abrams, 1987.
———. *Letters*. Trans. and ed. Gilbert Adair. London: Faber and Faber, 1989. Originally published as *François Truffaut Correspondance*. Gilles Jacob and Claude de Givray, eds. Rennes: Hatier, 1988.
———, et al. *La Politique des auteurs*. Paris: Editions Champ Libre, 1972.
Wald, Malvin, and Albert Maltz. *The Naked City: A Screenplay*. Matthew J. Bruccoli, ed. Carbondale: Southern Illinois UP, 1979.
Walz, Eugene P. *François Truffaut: A Guide to References and Resources*. Boston: G. K. Hall, 1982.

Index

"About John Ford," 2, 46-47, 48, 157n.9
Acting, 14, 72, 93, 108-109, 112, 114, 118, 120-21, 121, 126, 128, 133, 137-38, 138-39, 140; criticism of, 4, 40, 87, 88, 116, 119-20, 120-21, 129, 147, 149, 150-51
Actors/actresses. See Acting; Directing; Stars
Adam's Rib (1949), 108-109, 110
Admiral Ushakov (1953), 128-29
Affair in Trinidad (1952), 47-58
A films, 8, 20, 40
Aldrich, Robert, 139-42
Alphaville: Une Étrange Aventure de Lemmy, Caution (1965), 113
Ambassador's Daughter, The (1956), 62-63
American cinema, history of, 104-105, 108
American film, 109-10, 118
American Guerrilla in the Philippines (1950), 42-43, 60
American studio system, 26, 41, 87
Animal Crackers (1930), 103-104
Anna Christie (1930), 146
Anti-Americanism, 28, 29, 86
Arnold, Jack, 21-22, 79
Artificiality, 127, 128
Artists and Models (1955), 66-67
Aspect ratio, 23-24
Audiberti, Jacques: Les Jardins et les fleuves, 49, 50
Audiences, 13-14, 17, 49, 70, 73, 135, 137, 153; Alfred Hitchcock and, 93, 95, 96-97, 98; television and, 22-23
Auriol, Jean Georges, 14, 25, 105
Autant-Lara, Claude, 124, 125, 127-28, 151, 152, 155
Auteurism, 5, 99, 115
L'Autocar en folie (1953), 130-31
Autumn Leaves (1956), 139-41
Aux environs d'Aden, 154
Avant-garde, 17, 20, 38, 39

"B. B. Is the Victim of a Plot," 71-75
Bad films, 152, 153
Bardot, Brigitte, 9, 71, 73, 74-75, 76
Barker, Lex, 145
Baroncelli, Jean de, 72
Bazin, André, 1, 4, 5, 25, 48-49, 81
Beaudine, William, 4-5
Beccarie, Michel, 51
Becker, Jacques, 134
Bell Boy, The (1960), 69

Belle Otéro, La (1954), 70-71
B films, 2-3, 16-20, 30-31, 35, 40, 55, 123, 152, 153, 154
Biberman, Abner, 145-46
Bicycle Thief, The (1948), 109
Bidone, Il (1955), 124, 125, 126, 128
Big Knife, The (1955), 139, 140
Birth of a Nation, The (1915), 109
Bob le Flambeur (1955), 115, 154
Body Snatcher, The (1945), 138
Bogart, Humphrey, 143, 144
Bogdanovich, Peter: Fritz Lang in America, 41
Boisrond, Michel, 154
Boissol, Claude, 154
Born to Kill (1947), 13, 15, 61, 137, 138, 139
Bory, Jean-Louis, 84
Breathless (1959), 2
Bresson, Robert, 14, 16, 17, 20, 71, 151, 155; Notes on Cinematography, 30
Brief Encounter (1946), 33, 34
British film, 78-81, 122-23
Brooks, Richard, 22
Brown, Clarence, 146-48
Bruyère, Gaby: Mémoires d'une starlett, 51
Bunuel, Luis, 17, 49, 152, 153
Butler, David, 116-17

Cabanne, Christy, 31-32
Cahiers du Cinéma, 3
Cahiers du Cinéma in English, 1
Caine Mutiny, The (1954), 142, 143-44
Canon, 1, 15, 21
Carbonnaux, Norbert, 54
Carol, Martine, 6
Cartier, Raymond, 28, 29
Casarès, Maria, 14, 15
Cause for Alarm (1951), 121-22
Cayatte, André, 142, 143
Cela s'appelle l'aurore (1956), 152, 153
Censors, 58-59, 70, 71
"Certaine Tendance du cinéma français, Une," 1, 15
Cete sacrée gamine, 154
Charleston (1926), 75, 76
Chauvet, Louis, 72, 74
Chrétien, Henri, 23
Cinema diary, 48-51
CinemaScope, 23-24, 24, 25-27, 71, 72, 75, 117-18, 120, 125, 126, 150

Cinematography, 19, 22, 61, 72, 88, 130, 135, 138, 142, 148; composition, 90, 118, 139; framing, 9, 11, 25-27, 35-36, 86, 93, 126, 127
Cinepanoramic, 24
Cinerama, 24, 28-30, 159n.37
Cinerama Holiday (1956), 28-30
City Is Dark, The (1954), 31
Clair, René, 53
Clément, René, 51
Clifton, Elmer, 17, 20
Club Havana (1946), 114
Cocteau, Jean, 14, 16, 125
Collaboration, 110
Collins, Joan, 122, 123
Color, 72, 75, 98, 99, 113, 120, 125, 126, 144. *See also* Technicolor
Comedy, 65-70, 78, 80, 103-107, 107-108, 108-10
Composition. *See* Cinematography
Condamné à mort s'est échappé, Un (1956), 71, 151, 155
Constantine, Eddie, 113-15
Cooper, Gary, 148, 149, 150-51
Corsaires du Bois de Boulogne, Les, 54
Crawford, Broderick, 126
Crawford, Joan, 14, 15, 87, 88, 140, 141
Critics, 20, 72, 73-75, 76, 81-84
Cronaca di un Amore (1950), 52
Cukor, George, 33-34, 104, 105, 107, 108-109, 110

Dali, Patrice, 113-14
Darvi, Bella, 119-20, 120-21
Dassin, Jules, 131-32, 133-35
Daves, Delmer, 148-49
Deadline (1952), 22
Dean, James, 89-90
Decameron Nights (1953), 122-23
DeMille, Cecil B., 128-29
Desert Fox, The (1951), 58, 59
Desert Rats, The (1953), 58-59, 61
Des gens sans importance, 154
De Sica, Vittorio, 17
Detective films, 37-38
De Toth, André, 28, 31
Detour (1945), 8, 20
Devaivre, Jean, 55
Deval, Jacques, 116
Dial M for Murder (1954), 54-55
Dieterle, William, 34
Dior, Christian, 63
Directing, 37, 98, 114, 118, 120, 129, 141, 142, 143, 148
Distribution, 37, 54, 135, 136
Dmytryk, Edward, 142-44
Doctor in the House (1954), 78, 80
Docudrama, 131-32
"Double Crisis of Cinema, The," 135-37
Doulos, Le (1962), 115

Dreyer, Carl Theodor, 23
Dubost, Paulette, 6
Dubreuilh, Simone, 72, 74
Duck Soup (1933), 104
Duvivier, Julien, 154

East of Eden (1955), 72
Editing, 29, 61
Egalitarianism, 3
Eléna et les hommes (1956), 151, 155
"En avoir plein la vue," 25-27
Enfants Terribles, Les (1950), 115-16, 116, 125
Eroticism, 72-73, 76-77
Et Dieu Créa la femme (1957), 71-77, 151, 152, 155
European film, 109-10
Executive Suite (1954), 137-39
Exhibition, 135, 136

Failure, theme of, 100, 101-102, 103
Failures, 153-54
Family Jewels (1965), 65
Farrow, John, 112-13
Fassbinder, Rainer Werner, 36
Feathered Serpent, The (1948), 3-4
Fellini, Federico, 124, 126, 128
Ferber, Edna, 85
Fernandel, 50, 65
Fetishism, 5-7, 7-8, 9-10, 61, 62
Film noir, 38, 134, 143
Films in My Life, The, 2, 3, 46, 48, 84-85, 158n.12
Fils de Caroline Chérie, 55
Five (1951), 38-40
Flaud, Jacques, 49, 153
Fleischer, Richard, 16-20
Fontaine, Joan, 122, 123
Ford, John, 1-2, 44-48
Forever Female (1954), 124
Form, content and, 28-30, 33
Forty Guns (1957), 119
400 Blows, 135
Framing. *See* Cinematography
François Truffaut: A Guide to References and Resources (Walz), 3, 12, 16, 47, 92
François Truffaut Correspondance, 84
Fregonese, Hugo, 122-23
French Cancan (1955), 50-51, 51
French film, 13, 15, 16, 55, 70, 72, 123, 151-56; distribution of, 54, 135, 136, 137
"From A to Z," 16-20
From Here to Eternity (1953), 144
Fuller, Samuel, 119-21
Fury (1937), 110

Gabor, Zsa Zsa, 133
Gallagher, Tag: *John Ford*, 43
Gance, Abel, 50, 55-56

Gangster films, 107-108, 109, 113-15, 133-34
Garden of Evil (1954), 150-51
Garnett, Tay, 16, 121-22
Garson, Claude, 72
Gassman, Vittorio, 129, 130
Gaulle, Charles de, 83
General Della Rovere (1960), 132
Genre film, 3, 21-22, 41. *See also* Comedy; Detective films; Gangster films; Science fiction; Westerns
Gestural technique, 58
Giant (1956), 84-87, 88-90
Gilda (1946), 57, 129, 130
Girls in the Night (1953), 21-22
Glass Wall, The (1953), 62
Glenn Miller Story, The (1954), 112
Godard, Jean-Luc, 2, 113, 119
Golden Coach, The (1952), 62, 155
Gomes, P. E. Sales, 53
Gordon, Don, 21
Grahame, Gloria, 14, 62, 124
Grand amour de Beethoven, Un (1936), 55-56
Grand Bluff, Le (1957), 113-15
Grand Pavois, Le, 59-60
Granelli, Mireille, 114
Great films, 154-55
Greene, Jaclynne, 21
Guest, Val, 78-81

Haskin, Byron, 121
Hathaway, Henry, 9-10, 11, 58, 150-51
Hawks, Howard, 9-10, 45, 50, 79, 107
Hayward, Susan, 150
Hayworth, Rita, 57-58
Hell and High Water (1954), 119-21
Hepburn, Katharine, 108-109
High and the Mighty, The (1954), 117-19
Hillier, Jim, 1
Hitchcock, 90-91
Hitchcock, Alfred, 2, 14, 16, 18-19, 49, 53-54, 90-91; *Dial M for Murder*, 54-55; *Lifeboat*, 92-95; *Rebecca*, 91-92; *The Trouble with Harry*, 95-99
Holden, William, 34
"Homage to United Artists," 51-52
Hondo (1953), 112-13
Hopper, Jerry, 123-24
Horse Feathers (1932), 104
Hossein, Robert, 124, 126, 128
Houdini (1953), 111-12
Houseman, John, 137, 138
House Un-American Activities Committee (HUAC), 132, 133, 143, 144
Hudson, Rock, 87
Hughes, Howard, 10
Humberstone, Bruce, 16-20, 19n
Hush, Hush Sweet Charlotte (1964), 141

Huston, John, 100-101, 102-103; theme of failure in, 100, 101-102, 103

I Married a Witch (1942), 53
Independent productions, 40, 115, 139-41
Island in the Sky (1953), 117, 118
It Happened One Night (1934), 106
It Should Happen to You (1954), 108, 110
I Vitelloni (1953), 125, 126
I Wouldn't Be in Your Shoes (1948), 37

Jacob, Gilles, 102
Jardins et les fleuves, Les (Audiberti), 49
John Ford (Gallagher), 43
John Ford (Mitry), 47
Jules et Jim (1961), 45

Kanin, Garson, 107, 108-109
Kansas City Confidential (1952), 35-36
Karlson, Phil, 35-36
Katz, Ephraim, 70, 115
Kazan, Elia, 72
Key Largo (1948), 36, 57, 58
King Richard and the Crusaders (1954), 116-17
Kirsanoff, Dimitri, 152, 153
Koster, Henry, 25-27
Kramer, Stanley, 35
Krasna, Norman, 62-63

Labourdette, Elina, 6
Lachenay, Robert, 4, 8, 48
Ladies of the Bois de Boulogne (1945), 6, 13, 15
Lalande, Claude, 54
Landers, Lew, 27-28
Lang, Fritz, 41-43
Langlois, Henry, 52, 83
Last Frontier, The (1955), 43-44
La Strada (1954), 125, 126
Las Vegas Story, The (1952), 34
Lean, David, 33, 34
Leenhardt, Roger, 14, 15-16, 17, 20
Létraz, Jean de, 50
Lewis, Jerry, 65-66, 66-70
Lewton, Val, 2-3
L'Herbier, Marcel, 84
Liberace, 20
Lifeboat (1944), 92-95, 117
Life of Her Own, A (1950), 33-34
Lighting, 9, 61, 130
Little Boy Lost (1953), 60
Lola Montès (1955), 74, 124, 125, 126-28
Long Wait, The (1954), 37-38
Lost Weekend, The (1945), 110
Louis, Pierre, 130-31
Love Happy (1950), 10-11
Lubitsch, Ernst, 105-106
Lure of the Wilderness (1952), 148, 149
Lytess, Natacha, 10

Macbeth (1948), 83
MacDougall, Ranald, 87-88, 90
Maltese Falcon, The (1941), 113, 114
Man Alone, A (1955), 64-65
Man in the Dark (1953), 27-28
Mann, Anthony, 43-44, 112
Man Who Loved Women, The (1977), 7
Marguerite de la Nuit (1956), 124, 125, 127-28, 153
Marshall, George, 111-12
Martin, Dean, 68
Marx brothers, 69-70, 103-104
Mauriac, Claude, 74-75, 76
Meilleure part, La (1956), 153
Melville, Jean-Pierre, 115-16, 125, 154
Mémoires d'une starlett (Bruyère), 51
Mépris, Le (1963), 45
Milland, Ray, 64-65
Miller, David, 10-11, 12-16
Mise-en-scène, 9, 31, 61, 72, 121, 122, 123, 124, 129, 130, 137, 140, 147; criticism of, 5, 29, 39-40, 60, 63, 65, 88, 114, 126, 142, 150; praise of, 4, 32, 33, 37, 130
Misogyny, 66, 67, 69-70, 76-77, 80, 122
Mitry, Jean: *John Ford*, 47
Moby Dick (1956), 101-102
Modleski, Tania, 8, 20
Mogambo (1953), 47
Monogram, 4
Monroe, Marilyn, 5-7, 8-9, 10-12, 44, 52, 71, 74
Moral ambiguity, 93, 95
Mort en ce jardin, La (1956), 152, 153
Mouton a Cinq Pattes, Le (1954), 65-66
Mr. Smith Goes to Washington (1930), 109
Mummy's Hand, The (1940), 31-32
Murphy, Mary, 65
Music, 18, 20, 64, 123, 140
My Forbidden Past (1952), 34

Naked Alibi (1954), 123-24
Naked City (1948), 131-32, 133-35
Naked Jungle (1954), 121
Narrow Margin, The (1952), 16-20
Natural Vision, 24, 25, 27-28, 30
Negativism, 83-90
Négulesco, Jean, 148, 149
Neorealism, 131, 132
Never Let Me Go (1953), 148-49
Niagara (1953), 5-7, 8, 9, 11, 150, 151
Nigh, William, 37
Night and the City (1950), 131, 132, 133, 134
Night at the Opera, A (1935), 103-104
Notes on Cinematography (Bresson), 30
Notorious (1946), 57, 58
Nuit américaine, La (1973), 46
Nuit et brouillard (1956), 151, 154-55
Nutty Professor, The (1963), 70

Objectification, 9-10, 11-12, 31, 32, 58, 71, 74-75, 75-76, 76, 80
Oboler, Arch, 38-40
O'Hara, Maureen, 47
Olivier, Sir Laurence, 12, 83, 158n.25
Ophüls, Max, 124, 125, 126-28
Osso, Adolphe, 51
Our Daily Bread (1934), 110

Pal, George, 112
Panavision, 24
Panic in Year Zero (1962), 64
Pantheon, 1, 43, 46, 71, 90
Pardners (1956), 66-68
Paris-Palace-Hotel, 154
Parrish, Robert, 34-35
Patriarchy, 43, 46, 47, 60, 76-77. *See also* Objectification; Viewer, male
Pays d'où je viens, Le, 153
Pete Kelly's Blues (1955), 63-64
Peters, Jean, 7, 149
Petit Chaperon Rouge, Le (1929), 75, 76, 162n.35
Pinoteau, Jack, 59-60
Plot. *See* Scripts
Plymouth Adventure (1952), 146-48
Pointe courte, La (1956), 151, 155
Pottier, Richard, 70-71
Preminger, Otto, 50
"Presence of Marilyn, The," 9, 10-12
Pretty Maids All in a Row (1971), 76-77
Price of Fear, The (1956), 145-46
Prince and the Showgirl, The (1957), 12, 158n.25
Program pictures. *See* B films
Public Enemy Number One, 133

Quai des Brumes, 109
Quand tu liras cette lettre (1953), 115-16
Quatermass Xperiment, The (1956), 78-81
Queen Bee (1955), 87-88, 90

Racism, 43, 46, 86-87
Radio Cinéma Télévision (Sengissen), 19n
Raging Bull (1980), 69
Rapper, Irving, 124
Ray, Nicholas, 13, 124, 125, 126, 128
Realism, 26-27, 73, 131-32
Rebecca (1940), 91-92
Rebel without a Cause (1955), 124, 125, 126, 128
Remains to Be Seen (1953), 61-62
Remakes, 18, 20, 57-59, 129
Renoir, Jean, 2-3, 14, 91, 151, 155; compared to René Clair, 53; *Eléna et les hommes*, 151, 155; *French Cancan*, 50-51, 51; *Golden Coach*, 62; *Julius Caesar*, 56; *Le Petit Chaperon Rouge*, 75, 76, 162n.35; *Télé-Ciné and*, 81-82
Resnais, Alain, 151, 154-55

Return to Paradise (1953), 148, 149-50
Rhapsody (1954), 129-30
Rififi (1955), 131, 132, 133, 134
River of No Return (1954), 52
Rivette, Jacques, 52
Robe, The (1953), 23, 25-27
Robinson Crusoe (1952), 49
Robson, Mark, 148, 149-50
Rohmer, Eric, 52-53, 161n.16
Roman Holiday (1953), 106
Romm, Mikhail, 128-29
Ronde, La (1950), 127
Room for One More (1952), 32-33
Rosenbaum, Jonathan, 84
Rossellini, Roberto, 51
Ryman, Lucille, 11

Safecracker, The (1958), 65
Sailor Beware (1951), 66, 68-69
Saint-Laurent, Cécil, 6, 55
Salauds vont en enfer, Les (1955), 124, 126, 128
Sarris, Andrew, 43
Saville, Victor, 37-38
Scenario. *See* Scripts
Science fiction, 21, 38-40, 78-81
Scorsese, Martin, 69
Screen formats, 23-24
Scripts, 72, 118, 122, 125, 126-27, 134, 144; criticism of, 113-14, 116, 117, 129, 130, 145, 150
Scriptwriters, 153-54, 154
Scudda Hoo, Scudda Hay (1948), 10
Searchers, The (1956), 1-2, 43, 44-45
Seaton, George, 60
Sengissen, Paule, 19n
Sergeant York (1941), 109
Set-Up, The (1949), 137, 138
Seven Year Itch, The (1955), 12
Sexism, 43, 46, 85. *See also* Fetishism; Objectification
Shane (1953), 86, 112-13
Shane, Maxwell, 62
Sheldon, Sidney, 67
Sherman, Vincent, 57-58
Shoot First (1953), 34-35
Sight and Sound, 23
Silence de la mer, Le (1949), 115
Sirk, Douglas, 17, 20, 36, 87
16mm film, 52-53, 116, 161n.16
South Sea Sinner (1950), 16-20
Spillane, Mickey, 37, 38
Stars, 71, 73-74, 76; collaboration with, 110
Steel Helmet, The (1950), 120
Steinbeck, John, 93, 94
Stereophonic sound, 23-24
Stevens, George, 84-87, 89, 90, 112-13
Stevenson, Robert, 34
Sturges, Preston, 106-107
Sudden Fear (1952), 12-16

Sun Shines Bright, The (1953), 46
Superscope, 24
Symbolism, 86, 89, 93, 94

Tashlin, Frank, 9-10, 107
Taurog, Norman, 32-33, 66-68
Taylor, Elizabeth, 87, 129, 130
Technicolor, 5, 111, 112, 123, 129, 130, 149, 150
Techniscope, 24
Télé-Ciné, 81-83
Television, impact of, 22-23
Temps des assassins, Le, 154
They Live by Night (1949), 13
Thing from Another World, The (1951), 79, 81, 162n.4
Thomas, Ralph, 78
3-D effect, 25, 27-28
Thrillers. *See* Gangster films
Thunder on the Hill (1951), 36
Tirez sur le Pianiste (1960), 45
Touchez pas au Grisbi (1954), 134
Tour de Nesle, La, 50
Toute la ville accuse, 154
Tracy, Spencer, 108-109
Traversée de Paris, La (1956), 151, 152, 155
Trouble with Harry, The (1955), 95-99
Truffaut, François, 1-3, 4-5, 20-21, 36, 83-84, 151, 155-56; *The Films in My Life*, 2, 3, 46, 48, 84-85, 158n.12; *François Truffaut Correspondance*, 84; *Hitchcock*, 90-91; as interviewer, 132, 133-34
Tuna Clipper (1949), 4-5, 8
Turner, Lana, 33, 34
Turning Point, The (1952), 34

Ulmer, Edgar, 8, 114
Ustinov, Peter, 126-27

Vadim, Roger, 71-77, 151, 152, 155
Varda, Agnès, 151, 155
Verdugo, Elena, 4
Verlaine, Paul, 5, 7
Verneuil, Henri, 65-66, 154
Video tap, 69
Vidor, Charles, 129-30
Viewer, male, 9-10, 58. *See also* Objectification; Patriarchy
Vigo, Jean, 53
Vision, 26-27
Voice-over narration, 28, 29, 131

Walker, Hal, 68-69
Walz, Eugene P.: *François Truffaut: A Guide to References and Resources*, 3, 12, 16, 47, 92
Wayne, John, 45, 113, 117, 118
Webb, Jack, 63-64
Week-End (1968), 45
Weis, Don, 61-62, 104, 105, 107

Welles, Orson, 16, 18-19, 35, 64, 83
Wellman, William, 117-19
Westerns, 43-46, 64-65, 107-108, 112-13, 119
Which Way to the Front? (1970), 70
While the City Sleeps (1956), 41
Widmark, Richard, 151
Wilder, Billy, 12
Winters, Roland, 4
Wise, Robert, 13, 58-59, 61, 137-39, 143

Woman on the Beach (1947), 2-3
Women, attitude toward, 5, 47. *See also* Eroticism; Fetishism; Objectification
Written on the Wind (1956), 87

d'Yvoir, Jean, 81-83

Zinnemann, Fred, 144